Building an Import/Export Business

Kenneth D. Weiss

John Wiley & Sons, Inc.

New York • Chichester • Brisbane • Toronto • Singapore

Publisher: Stephen Kippur
Editor: Katherine S. Bolster
Managing Editor: Andrew B. Hoffer
Editing, Design & Production: Publications Development Co.

This publication is designed to provide accurate and authoritative information in regard to the subject matter covered. It is sold with the understanding that the publisher is not engaged in rendering professional advice. If professional advice or other expert assistance is required, the services of a competent professional person should be sought.

Library of Congress Cataloging-in-Publication Data

Weiss, Kenneth D. (Kenneth Duane), 1940–
    Building an import/export business.

    (Wiley small business series)
    Include index.
    1. Commerce. I. Title. II. Title: Import/export
business. III. Series.
HF1008.W43   1987   658.8   86-26560
ISBN 0-471-84259-1
ISBN 0-471-84261-3 (pbk.)

Printed in the United States of America
87 88 10 9 8 7 6 5 4 3 2

Contents

This book is dedicated to Peter Gaffney, whom I have neither seen nor heard from in more than twenty years. In 1965 Peter helped me leave a management trainee position in San Francisco and get on the road to the exciting world of international trade. Peter, I have had many ups and downs since then, but all in all, I've loved it. Wherever you are, thank you.

Acknowledgments

I am grateful to a number of persons for reading chapters of this book and making corrections or additions.

George Haber, of Information Services in Jericho, New York, made useful suggestions for the chapter on choosing target markets and finding customers. Bill Laraque, Manager of the Standard Chartered Bank in Melville, New York, helped enormously, especially with the chapter on import/export credit and payment. Bill Maron, President of Maron International Shipping Corp. in New York City, contributed importantly to the chapter on international shipping and insurance.

The chapter on import/export documentation was ably proofread by Arnold Ceglia, President of Sky-Sea Forwarding Corp. in Valley Stream, New York. For the chapter on customs and other regulatory agencies, which was one of the most difficult, I was greatly helped by Sherry Singer of Soller, Singer & Horn (attorneys at law) in New York City and her associate, Charles Cardile, of C & S Laboratory Consultants, also of New York City. Mr. Cardile made several suggestions regarding the section on the U.S. Food and Drug Administration.

Introduction

Who can go into the import/export business? The answer is easy. I can. You can. *Anyone* can. But how many will stay in the business and be successful? This question is much more difficult to answer. This book is designed to help you to a successful start and ensure you remain successful.

Just what is the import/export business? For purposes of this book, the import/export business is defined as any movement of products across national boundaries. Products are defined in a strictly material sense—commodities such as grain and iron ore, industrial goods such as machinery and equipment, and consumer goods such as transistor radios and clothing. These products may move between countries by any means of transportation—road, rail, water, air—or even carried by people or animals.

Nonmaterial products—construction, advertising, accounting, and the like—are not considered here, nor is "unregistered trade," a euphemism for smuggling and black market activities.

International trade is a business of enormous proportions. In world terms, trade is so massive that statistics actually seem irrelevant. Historically, groups of people have always traded with other groups to obtain goods that were not available locally or were cheaper and better elsewhere, or simply to acquire products that had the cachet of being imported.

In *national* terms, however, statistics are significant to even the smallest importer. This is because the United States has recently been importing far more than it has been exporting. For example, 1986 imports were about $370 billion, $170 billion more than we exported. This flood of foreign products has caused unemployment in the United States' industries such as steel, automobile, apparel, and footwear. It has also resulted in the introduction of more than 300 bills in Congress designed either to restrict imports or to retaliate against countries that make it too hard for us to sell to them. The passage of some of this legislation, which will hurt importers, is a constant possibility.

This fact of life does not mean you should not go into importing. It does mean that, if you import, you should watch events in Washington carefully so as not to be caught off guard by restrictive legislation. This is especially true if you will be importing textiles, apparel, or footwear, or if you plan to buy from countries that run large surpluses in their trade with the United States such as Japan, Taiwan, Singapore, Hong Kong, and Brazil.

To appreciate the scale of international trade, let's examine the volume of trade at a single port, the Port of New York and New Jersey. The 1985 figures show this major port to have handled over 52 million tons of cargo worth approximately $92 billion! These figures include both imports and exports and both ocean and air shipments.

The leading oceanborne cargo exports (by weight) were waste paper, plastic materials, textile waste, and machinery, and the leading markets were Taiwan, Italy, Spain, and Korea. The leading oceanborne imports were hydrocarbons, alcoholic beverages, bananas, and road motor vehicles, and the leading sources were Japan, West Germany, Italy, and Brazil.

The leading air cargo exports (by weight) were office machinery, general machinery, electrical machinery, and printed matter, and the leading markets were the United Kingdom, West Germany, Japan, and France. The leading air cargo imports were clothing, footwear, general machinery, and scientific apparatus, and the leading suppliers were West Germany, Italy, Japan, and the United Kingdom.

In this one example, we see that both the imports and the exports covered a wide spectrum of different goods. There were even imports of items that the United States produces very efficiently, and exports of items that the United States does not produce at all. Opportunities in international trade are virtually unlimited. It is a question of finding the right market for a product, or the right product for a market, and setting up efficient import/export procedures.

The subject of international trade is a large one, and no single book could include everything you need to know to be a successful importer or exporter. My aims in writing *Building an Import/Export Business* are to:

- Touch on the most important aspects of international trade.
- Give you enough information to enable you to decide whether this is a business for you and what steps you should take to get started.
- Tell you what other information and assistance you will need in order to be successful, and where to get it.

In this book you will find a detailed account of what it takes to go into the import/export business and how to set up this kind of commercial operation. There is a discussion of the different factors involved in selecting products, lining up suppliers, choosing markets, and finding customers. These are the most important aspects of the business. If you handle the purchasing and marketing well enough to establish a profitable operation, you will be off to a good start. With the help of this book and the additional resources referenced in it, you will find that you will be able to manage the mechanics of international trade. International credit and payment, international shipping and insurance, and import/export documentation can all be complicated, but with help they can be mastered.

At the back of this book is an annotated list of where you can find the additional information you will need, as well as a discussion of regulatory agencies (especially the U.S. Customs Service) and other helpful material.

In Chapter 1 are two sections that should be very valuable to you. The first is a list of 21 questions to be answered in planning your import/export business. You will probably not be able to answer all of them before you read this book, but these are questions you should keep in mind as you read. The second section describes requirements, skills, and personal traits related to success in importing and exporting. If you review them carefully and match them with your own characteristics and traits, you will have a good idea about whether this business is for you.

1

Importing and Exporting: 21 Essential Questions

Starting a business is a major step requiring nerve and a certain amount of faith. But nerve and faith need to be supplemented by sensible preparation—not just the purchase of desks, chairs, and typewriters, but a rigorous examination of the reasons for wanting to enter this particular field, an evaluation of the personal qualifications to make it a success, and development of a clear understanding of the business activities in which you will participate.

1. Why are you thinking of starting a business? What are your objectives?

Some possible objectives are to make money, to travel, to broaden your knowledge of the world, to acquire business experience, to gain prestige, and to be your own boss. You should decide what your main objectives are and whether an import/export business will help you attain them. Many people think of starting an import/export business because they travel and want to take advantage of products or contacts discovered on their trips. Although this sort of experience is helpful, these travelers usually make the mistake of thinking international trade is a simple venture—just buy it here and sell it there. It is important to understand the full range of complex activities in which you must become involved.

In general, the best reason for starting a business is to earn a living doing something you enjoy. Will you enjoy the main activities in the import/export business, which are purchasing, marketing, domestic and international trade procedures, and administration?

2. What makes you think you will be successful?

Very few people would start businesses if they thought they were going to fail. Entrepreneurs naturally expect success. But what makes you think *you* are likely to achieve it? Do you have some knowledge of international trade or will you make a serious effort to learn? Have you had relevant experience, such as in sales and marketing? Or any business or management experience? Will you have adequate financing?

3. Do you plan to import, export, or both?

Most persons start out by *either* importing *or* exporting, and sometimes go on to develop the other side of the business. Importing is the more common way to start, probably because buying is almost always easier than selling. In importing, the foreign (distant) part of the transaction is the buying, and the selling is done in more familiar surroundings.

4. Do you plan to work as a merchant, agent, broker, or some combination of the three?

Getting involved in the international brokerage business—arranging major deals between two parties, neither of which has a permanent relationship with you, and collecting a commission from one or the other or both is such a difficult business to get into that I have omitted it from this book. That leaves the options of merchant and agent. If you want to spend most of your time selling, and have limited funds, you should be an agent. If you want to perform all the import and export functions, and you have the means to finance the acquisition of goods you will sell, you should work as a merchant. That way you will have more control of your business and have more profit potential.

If you neither like to sell nor have a substantial bank account, you should probably *not* try to start an import and/or export business.

5. When you start, will you be working full time or part time?

If you plan to keep your job and start this business part time, you can afford to work slowly and experiment with different approaches. If you plan to start full time, you will probably have to be making a profit within a few months. If this is the case, you should develop a detailed plan and pay a consultant to discuss it with you and make suggestions. This assumes, of course, that you are willing to accept advice. Every business consultant has clients who want only one thing—for the consultant to tell them how good their business plans are. They are predisposed to ignore criticism and suggestions, even though they are paying for them.

6. Who, if anyone, can help you with the work in the beginning?

This is especially important if you are going to work as a merchant, and if you plan to start the business part time. Remember that there are various functions to perform, and if you drop the ball on any of them it will hurt your business. If you are counting on help from your spouse, as many persons do, try to determine whether he or she has the time, the ability, and the inclination to help you adequately.

One person I know of had a simple plan—he would import children's clothing from the Caribbean and open a small store in which his wife would sell the products. Unfortunately, his wife very quickly tired of waiting on customers, dusting shelves, keeping accounting records, etc., and the business failed. (I do not know what happened to the marriage.)

7. Which type(s) of product(s) do you plan to trade?

This subject is discussed in Chapter 4. You should select products that you understand and enjoy working with and that are available, saleable, transportable, and legal to export or import. These criteria are often conflicting. You may find a delicious ice cream in Sweden, but be unable to sell it in the United States because of transportation costs and quotas. You may have an order from Africa for a well-known brand of staplers, but be unable to obtain them except from a wholesaler who charges a price too high to allow a profit.

8. What will be your sources of supply—countries and/or companies?

If you already have suppliers lined up, you are off to a good start. If not and you are an importer, you will have to go through the process of deciding which countries and which specific companies to buy from or represent. If you are an exporter, you will have to find American firms with products that can be sold abroad. You will need to make sure your suppliers are reliable and, if possible, tie them up with written agreements that give you at least some exclusivity. See Chapter 7 for information about these agreements and the Appendix for examples.

9. What is your target market?

You need to think of who will be the final users of your product, the best channel of distribution to get the product to those persons or organizations, and who you will sell to in that channel of distribution. I once wasted several hours trying to sell natural bath salts to cosmetic manufacturers before learning that cosmetics firms make their bath salts chemically. They leave the natural products to the health food industry.

10. How do you plan to sell to customers in the target market?

This may be the most important question. It relates to the marketing methods discussed in Chapter 6, including using agents, direct mail, etc. Good marketing people can create all the conditions for the sale of a product, but only the sale itself can bring in revenue to keep the business going and growing.

11. What means of international transportation do you plan to use?

As discussed in Chapter 8, you must consider whether to ship by land, air, or sea, whether to use scheduled or other carriers, which specific carrier to give your business, etc. Also, do not forget the options for small shipments provided by air and sea mail and couriers.

12. What will be the shipping terms?

If you are importing, at what point will you take title to the goods you are buying. If you are exporting, at what point will you give title to the foreign buyer? Also who will make arrangements and pay the charges for handling, shipping, insurance, and related functions? The shipping terms discussed in Chapter 8 will help you answer these questions.

13. Which method of international payment do you plan to use?

An import transaction usually has to be worth a few thousand dollars to be profitable. Importers who are not known and established usually have to open letters of credit (LC) to place orders of this size. Do you have the funding required to open an LC, and are you willing to spend the time and money to do it? See Chapter 7 for a discussion of payment terms.

On the export side, you will lose sales if you refuse to sell except on letter of credit or cash in advance. Ideally, you should be willing to take some risks, have the knowledge to analyze the degrees of risk in a transaction, and have enough money to survive a loss and stay in business. One small businessman in Taiwan received an order from the United States for live birds. The Taiwanese exporter invested all of his capital in the products, shipped on Open Account, did not get paid, and was out of business. Do not let this happen to you.

14. Which United States and/or foreign government regulations will concern you?

Whether you are an exporter or an importer, an agent, or a merchant, you should know the applicable laws of the countries on both sides of each transaction. This book describes several types of government regulations and how to find out more about them.

15. What will be your company name and form of organization?

The most important decision here is whether to incorporate, and that is mainly a function of how much profit you will be making and of how likely you are to be sued for illness or injury resulting from the use of your product. With some kinds of merchandise, there is also a danger of being sued for pollution of the environment or for damage to physical property. Forms of organization are discussed at the beginning of Chapter 3.

16. What will you do for an office, office equipment, and supplies?

There are advantages of working in your own home—economy and you do not have to travel to your job. There are also disadvantages, such as unexpected business visitors, distractions when the kids come home from school, and an alarming tendency to run to the refrigerator whenever you get bored with your work.

Equipment is a fairly straightforward matter, although buying wisely takes time and you may end up spending a few thousand dollars. The biggest outlay will probably be for a photocopier, and once you have one you won't know how you ever got along without it. Chapter 3 gives more insights into both offices and equipment.

17. What will be your postal and telex addresses?

I suggest using your place of business as your postal address rather than a post office box, if at all possible. It saves time and trouble. It does not matter much which of several options you use to obtain a telex address, but you should definitely have one. See Chapter 3 for details.

18. Which phone number will you use, and how will the phone be answered?

You should have a business phone, on a separate line, answered in a businesslike way, and equipped with a good quality answering machine. This will give you a listing and allow you to buy advertising in the yellow pages.

19. Who will be your bank, insurance company, accountant, lawyer, customs broker, and/or international freight forwarder?

You may not need all these in the beginning, but you will need at least a bank and a broker or forwarder. Both should be chosen mainly on the basis of their experience with transactions similar to the ones you are planning. Their functions are described in depth in chapters 7–10.

20. Where will you get professional guidance as your business develops?

Chapter 11 discusses the kinds of help and information you may need, and where to obtain them.

21. How much will you invest? How much will you earn?

These two questions should be answered by developing pro-forma (forecasted) balance sheets and profit and loss statements. If the amount of investment is greater than the funds you have available, you will have to consider how to raise the additional capital. Some possible sources are supplier credit, bank loans, friends, and relatives.

ARE YOU RIGHT FOR THE BUSINESS?

Studies show that most new businesses fail within a year or two. Of every hundred businesses formed, there may be

20 or so that are marginally successful and only one or two that are highly successful. Of course, nearly every entrepreneur hopes and expects to be the one to make it big. Although there is no magic answer that will ensure success, it certainly helps to be as sure as you can that you and the business you plan to enter are a good match. Here are some of the required attributes to become a successful importer/exporter.

Business Skills

Import/export is a business, and any kind of business acumen, education, or experience will be helpful. Two of the major causes of business failures are inadequate planning and insufficient management ability.

Salesmanship

Import/export is fundamentally a marketing and selling business. Many people do not realize that they cannot make money importing or exporting unless they can sell their products. Even if you sell indirectly through commission agents, you will have to find the agents, sell them on carrying your lines and continually seek ways to help them to do a better job for you.

One of my favorite stories is of two performing artists who asked me to see them one evening. They were recommended by a mutual friend. They had just returned from a trip to Greece, and their dining room was entirely filled with samples of Greek goods. They had perhaps 20 lines of products, with three or four samples of each line. I looked at all the items and selected those that, based on my knowledge of the marketplace, would be the best sellers, the second best, etc. Then we talked about the market segmentation and target markets for some of the items. Finally we came to the question of how the items were actually going to be sold. My two hosts revealed they had no intention of selling anything to anybody. They thought that I, or someone else, would just pack up their samples and go out to sell while they happily sat back and counted their earnings. I had to break the news that if they had something really new and very exciting they might find someone to sell for them on straight commission; but I did not think they had anything that new or exciting. These gentlemen decided not to go into the import business.

Persistence

The import/export business is not like a fast-food franchise for which you can pay a company a large sum of money to find the location, build the restaurant, put in equipment, train you, do the initial promotion and hand you the key, after which you may start making a profit as of lunch time on the first day. If a person starts an import/export business without a base of suppliers and customers, it usually takes about six months to do any business at all, and about two years before the profits are great enough to support a family, and that assumes that the business in question is successful.

To start this kind of business, you should commit yourself to it for the long term. It is not usually a road to immediate profits.

Interest in and Knowledge of International Economics and Politics

Importing or exporting, even on a small scale, carries with it both opportunities and risks, and the more you know about the world, the better able you will be to take advantage of the opportunities and to reduce the risks. For example, suppose you are exporting electronic security equipment and read about a dramatic increase in crime in some

European country. With that information, you can make a special sales effort in a place where you now know the market should be positively receptive.

On the other hand, suppose you are importing goods by sea from Botswana and they must be routed through South Africa. Civil unrest in South Africa could result in blocked roads or a longshoreman's strike, and if you do not know of it you may find yourself waiting for your shipment, not knowing why it does not arrive.

Suppose you are importing from South Korea, and the Korean won is devalued against the dollar. This means your Korean exporter is receiving more won for every dollar you send him. Since you are probably paying in dollars, the devaluation will not affect you directly. However, if you understand the situation you may be able to negotiate a better price the next time you make a purchase.

On the other hand, you could be importing from Switzerland when the Swiss Franc is revalued against the dollar. If your agreement is in dollars you will not be hurt, but your exporter will be receiving fewer francs for every dollar you pay him. He may react by skimping on labor, using cheaper raw materials, or shipping your orders only after he has taken care of the more profitable ones.

As an importer or exporter, you will regularly need to read newspapers and magazines with worldwide coverage.

Language Ability

You can import and export successfully without knowing a foreign language, but language abilities would allow you to communicate more easily and increase your range of business contacts. The ability to speak the language of your business contacts can sometimes help even when your communications are in English. For example, it is not uncommon in international trade to receive a letter or telex message from overseas that uses English, but is unintelligible. If you know how sentences are structured in the language of the writer, you can sometimes rearrange the words to better understand their meaning.

I was once asked by a graphic arts company in Colombia to find them information on "A very International Company" in the United States. It took at least a week before a flash of insight enabled me to decipher this name. The Colombian writer had simply inserted one space too many. He was looking for *Avery* International.

Cultural Empathy

Sooner than you think, involvement in international trade will result in your meeting foreign buyers or sellers face to face. In these meetings, it can be very helpful if you have some feeling for the culture of these associates or at least are willing to tolerate and respect people who think and act differently from the way you do. For example, it may bother you if people speak to you without looking at you, but this is done out of respect in some countries. It may appear rude for people to belch loudly after eating, but this may be done deliberately to show that the meal was satisfying.

You may need to be careful of your own words and actions. You should not sit with the sole of your shoe facing a Korean; if you do, you are symbolically stepping on him. You should try not to turn the conversation to business too quickly when dealing with someone from Latin America or the Middle East; a person from either area would not want to do business before establishing a degree of personal rapport.

There are some very good books on the subject of culture, notably a paperback called *Do's and Taboos Around the World,* published by John Wiley & Sons, New York, New York.

Writing and Speaking

Since you will probably be dealing with people who are not fluent in English, you will need the ability to communicate in a simple, easily understandable way without using the slang that mystifies our language for foreigners. If you tell someone from overseas that a difficult transaction "drove you up the wall" or a certain supplier was a "pain in the neck," that person may make a literal translation of your expressions into his or her own language and become quite confused.

Attention to Detail

Finally, a successful international trader must be able to pay considerable attention to detail. You will be dealing with people or companies that are far away, whom you may not know, and your meeting of minds will be expressed on paper. All documents must be prepared and read with great care.

For example, suppose you are exporting and expect to be paid by a letter of credit. If the letter of credit says you are to ship from the port of San Francisco, and you ship from the port of Oakland, this careless violation of a term or condition of the letter of credit could lead to a dispute or necessitate obtaining a waiver of the "discrepancy."

I once received an order from Haiti for rolls of paper for calculators and adding machines. Like most products, this kind of paper has a number of specifications. There is the roll diameter, the roll width, the core diameter, the length of paper on the roll, the type of paper, the color, the number of plies, and so on. We were an exporting company; we did not make paper rolls, so we had to order them from a manufacturer. We had the manufacturer deliver to the pier for shipment to Haiti, and the goods arrived in Port-au-Prince. Everything was fine except that someone had typed a $3/8$ instead of a $5/8$ for one of the specifications. The paper was in the warehouse in Haiti, and no one could use it.

Of course it was the secretary who made the mistake (it is always the secretary, right?), but it didn't really matter who made the mistake. The secretary's work should have been checked as a matter of routine. As a consequence we suffered a loss because someone did not pay enough attention to detail. If you are outgoing and aggressive, but have no patience with detail, you will either have to force yourself to do something you are not good at, get a partner, or hire an employee who can fill in where you are weak.

CAPITAL REQUIREMENTS AND PROFIT POTENTIAL

The import/export industry is not one that requires a high capital investment. There are documented cases of people who have started their businesses with less than $200 and have been successful. If you have that little, however, you have to move very slowly and avoid taking any risks.

You can start your business as an agent for a very small sum of money because you do not have to pay for merchandise or international transportation. Unfortunately, you will have to compete with everyone else who is trying to start as an agent. I personally would not try to start in this business as a merchant with less than three or four thousand dollars of expendable capital, and I would feel better if I had 10 or 20 thousand.

Now that I have started out on the low side and built up your investment, let me give you the high side. About two years ago, a friend decided to start a new business. She was working for a major importing company, and, like most of us, wanted to be her own boss and make her own decisions. She had made a business plan and wanted to talk about how much money she would need to make the plan work the way she wanted it to. After some discussion, we concluded that to do what she had in mind in the time period she proposed, she would need 100 thousand dollars. Fortunately, this woman had a backer who was willing to put this sum of money at her disposal. In little more than a year, beginning with solid experience, a workable business plan, and enough capital, she built the business to the point that she was travelling often to the Far East, importing three different lines of merchandise, selling throughout the United States, exhibiting in major trade shows, and even re-exporting some goods to the Caribbean islands.

Books on small business and entrepreneurship give suggestions about how to raise capital to start a business. These include using personal savings, mortgaging your home, borrowing from banks and credit unions, borrowing from relatives, and approaching venture capitalists. In Chapter 7, there is a discussion of sources of short-term money to finance export production and sales.

SOME FINANCIAL EXAMPLES

There really are no *typical* income and expense figures in this business. Everyone's experience is different, but people who are thinking about starting in business need to have some concrete figures as a yardstick. Therefore I have created two small business situations:

Import Merchant

Planned sales for month	$ 20,000
Less cost of merchandise (60%)	− 12,000
	8,000
Less sales commissions, (15%)	− 3,000
	5,000
Less operating expenses (10%)	− 2,000
Profit before tax and owner's salary (15%)	$ 3,000

Export Agent

Planned sales for month	$100,000
Times average commission (14%)	× .14
	14,000
Less foreign agent's commission (6%)	− 6,000
	8,000
Less operating expenses (3%)	− 3,000
Profit before tax and owner's salary (5%)	$ 5,000

The first businessperson is an importer and the second an exporter. I have arbitrarily made the importer a merchant, who buys merchandise overseas, imports it, takes title, takes possession, and then sells and collects the money. The exporter is an agent who sells products overseas for some American manufacturers who are the agent's principals and who is paid a commission on what is sold.

The importer plans on sales of about $20,000 a month. You can think of this as the wholesale value. The total cost of the merchandise landed, duty paid, and delivered to the importer's home or warehouse is expected to be about $12,000, or 60 percent of sales. This will leave a gross profit of $8000. This company is assumed to be using commission agents in various parts of the United States to sell directly to retailers. The agents are paid 15 percent commissions on sales. This figure would be high for some industries. It is probably about average for a new giftware product. After commissions, the importer is left with $5000.

Operating expenses are not large, just $2000. The importer is using a small rented office or perhaps his own home. Most of the expenses are for office supplies, telephone, telex, some travel, and perhaps a part-time secretary.

This leaves a profit before taxes of $3000, or 15 percent of sales, a small return, but enough to begin with as the importer works to reduce costs, increase revenue, or build volume.

One thing people do when they are thinking of starting businesses is consider how much profit they would need to make it worthwhile. Suppose you are now working in a reasonably stable job, 40 hours a week, and are not terribly unhappy. You can try to figure out how much money you would need to earn in order to justify the effort and risk of leaving your job, investing in a business, working 12 or 14 hours a day, and loving every minute of it (at least at first). Of course, the figures will be less if you are thinking of starting part time. Then put your required income figure on the bottom line and add your estimated operating expenses to compute the amount you will need after selling costs ($3000 + $2000 = $5000).

Next (for the import merchant), figure the approximate percentage of sales that will be paid for merchandise and for selling costs (in this case, 60% + 15% = 75%). Subtract the 75 percent from 100 percent and divide the amount required after commission by the result ($5000/ .25 = $20,000). That gives you the amount of sales required to produce your bottom-line figure of $3000. Then try to determine whether there is any way you can sell the required amount. If not you will need to work out a different business plan.

$$\frac{\text{amount required after commissions (100)}}{100 - \text{percentage of sales going for costs}} = \frac{\$5,000(100)}{100 - (60 + 15)} = \frac{\$5,000(100)}{25} = \$20,000$$

The export agent is performing many fewer functions than a merchant and must sell more in order to end up with the same amount of income. In this example, the agent plans on sales of $100,000 per month. You can think of this as the amount the foreign importers pay to the agent's principals.

This agent has negotiated commissions with the principals that average 14 percent of sales. For large-volume products the commission may be lower, and in many cases it is higher. Fourteen percent times $100,000 (.14 × $100,000) gives the agent an income of $14,000 a month. He has to have a way of selling overseas and is using his own commission agents in foreign markets. He is paying them 6 percent on their sales, which means that they are getting nearly half of what he himself receives.

This export agent has slightly higher travel expenses than the import merchant, and somewhat more profit before tax, but he is moving five times as much merchandise. He has to sell more than a merchant, to make the same profit, because he is performing fewer functions and taking less risk.

These examples give some insights into the kind of financial considerations inherent in the import/export business.

2

How to Start

IMPORTING

Let's suppose that you have answered the 21 questions in Chapter 1 and are ready to start importing. How do you begin?

- Make your business a reality. Pick and register a name, open a bank account, get a telephone and a telex address, and have stationery printed.
- Find products to import. You can identify many in a free publication, *Gifts & Housewares Accessories*, from Gifts & Housewares Accessories Association, P.O. Box 34-23, Taipei, Taiwan, R.O.C.
- Select the products that seem to be good bets and write to the advertisers. Just say you are interested in importing their products and would like catalogs and prices.
- When the information comes, choose the products that interest you most and send for samples. You can order samples by registered letter and enclose international money orders as payment.
- When the samples arrive, identify prospective buyers and pay calls on them. Obtain their detailed opinions of the products, as discussed in a later chapter.

- If the buyers are interested, contact U.S. Customs. Find out the duty on the product, how it has to be labeled, and whether there are any other government organizations with whom you should speak.

- If the product has to be modified, order new samples with the necessary changes. Show them to buyers and attempt to obtain small trial orders.

- Order your trial shipment by air freight, freight collect, insured. You can ask for sight draft terms (see Chapter 7), but you may be required to take a chance and send an international money order in advance.

- Determine transportation and insurance costs, add profit and sales commissions, check on prices of similar items, and set your selling prices. You may want to prepare a catalog and a price list.

- If your trial shipment sells easily, you can move on to larger orders, sea freight, other terms of payment, and more sophisticated marketing techniques. You are in business!

To work out your costs, you will have to assume a quantity of goods you think you can sell and a method of transportation and obtain reasonably accurate figures. I will show you how to do this in the context of the following example.

Example: Importing

Suppose you read in a Taiwan trade publication of a battery-operated "World Clock." You write for a catalog and price list and are impressed with the supplier's response. You show the catalog to several people, being careful not to show the supplier's name or address to any potential competitor. The reaction is favorable, and you decide to order a sample of each of four models. This is done with a letter and an international money order (available from most banks) for the value of the samples plus the approximate cost of shipping by air mail.

While the samples are en route you check with U.S. Customs. You find that the clock's movement has tariff number 720.02 and the duty from your supplier country is $0.32 each. The battery in the movement has tariff number 682.95, and the duty is 6.1 percent. The rest of the clock has tariff number 720.34, and the duty is 8.6 percent. This means commercial invoices should show the value of each of the three components for the purpose of calculating duty.

You also learn from customs that both the case and the movement should be marked with the country of origin, die sunk, etched, or in indelible ink. The clock should be marked on both the front and the back. If the clocks are individually boxed, each box should be marked with the country of origin by printing or a paper sticker.

Then you think about the target market and the channel of distribution. You decide that the best use for a world time clock is on desks, and the best potential end-user will be business persons with international interests. You consider trying to reach this market by mail order through airline flight magazines, but decide first to take the cheaper approach of contacting stores. You decide to start with gift shops, especially those in airports and major hotels.

Your samples arrive by air mail about two weeks after you requested them. They are delivered with your mail, and no customs duty is charged. They look good and work well, although the boxes are less than beautiful, and the instructions have insufficient detail.

You know that potential buyers will ask about price. You decide to try to find out what buyers will pay before giving any figures. If pressed, you plan simply to double the country of origin price of US$ 6.50 per piece (for what you think will be the best selling model) and quote an *approximate* U.S. wholesale price of $13 per unit. Judging from the quick receipt of samples, you feel confident you can deliver an order within 30 days if you use air freight and within 60 days if you use sea freight.

From the Yellow Pages you pick out the largest hotels in your city, call them to get the phone numbers of their gift shops, and call those shops. You learn that most of the shops, including those at the airport, are owned by four companies and that buying is done centrally. You get the names and phone numbers of those companies from the shops, call them, and ask to speak with the buyers who are responsible for clocks.

You describe your clocks to the buyers and find three of them interested. However, they do not want to see you or the product. They want catalogs and prices. You convince one buyer to give you an appointment and tell the others you will get back to them when you have the catalogs printed. You keep the one appointment, and also walk into several gift shops with your samples and show them to the salespeople. You doubt they will place orders, but they may have good ideas you can use.

During your research you learn that there are similar clocks on the market but at a higher price. You also see that your clocks are acceptable, except that they do not have the proper country of origin marking as explained to you by Customs. One discouraging finding, however, is that the appropriate retail price is in the range of $19 to $21. You were hoping it would be closer to $26.

You decide to broaden your research by talking with personnel of independent (not chain) gift shops, and you soon learn that if you just go in you can either see the buyers or find out when and where to contact them. Although no one begs you for immediate delivery of the clocks, two buyers tell you that when you have stock they will take small orders (a dozen in one place and 20 clocks in another). On the strength of these promises, you decide to place a sample order.

You know that the clocks are packed 60 to a carton. You write the supplier and say you would like to place a trial order for two cartons of clocks at $5.50 each, by air freight, freight collect. You will pay 50 percent cash in advance and 50 percent on 30-day open account. That way each of you will be trusting the other for half the cost of this small order. You explain the U.S. marking and invoicing requirements, and ask if this trial order can be sent immediately.

In your letter, you ask for the supplier's bank and trade references, and at the same time you order a credit report called a World Trader's Data Report (WTDR) from the U.S. Department of Commerce. You do not ask about a long-term written agreement because you want to get started right away. You believe this is a fad product that will be on and off the market in about 18 months.

A few days later the supplier calls you by telephone at 9:00 AM your time. This is a good sign because you know it is well after working hours in Asia. He agrees to all your terms except the price, saying that on such a small order he cannot go below $6.50. You agree and tell him to pack the clocks and to await your order and part payment. You ask about the bank and trade references, and he promises to send them by telex.

The same day you buy an international money order for $390.00 ($6.50 × 120 ÷ 2) and send it by registered mail with a letter that repeats the terms of your order. (To keep this example simple assume that both cartons of clocks will be the same model at the same price, although you may be requesting various colors.) While waiting for the order, you make additional contacts with potential buyers. You also locate a customs broker and sign a Power of Attorney so he can clear shipments consigned to you.

Ten days later you receive a phone call from Jumping

Air Freight. Your clocks are in. Since this is not a well-known airline you make sure to get the exact address and telephone number, as well as your airwaybill number. Then you phone your broker and ask him to clear the merchandise. To save money, you tell the broker to hold the goods for you at his warehouse.

The next day the broker calls. He has the clocks. You go to pick them up. The two cartons are in good shape and are accompanied by documents, including the exporter's invoice for the remaining $390. The broker says he will bill you for his services, customs duties, and air freight. He will expect you to pay immediately.

You check the clocks. They are as good as the samples received before, but they are not marked exactly as you requested. You put the supplier's invoice in the "Bills to Pay" file and deliver the clocks to your two customers, taking care in each store to open one clock, start it, set the time, and put it on display. You ask for payment. One customer hands you cash, and the other insists that you bill him on 30-day terms.

The supplier's telex with bank and trade references never comes, but the WTDR from the Department of Commerce looks very good. The broker's bill comes in as follows:

Air Freight	$252 (34 kilograms @ $7.41)
Insurance	— (shipment sent uninsured)
Collect charges	22 (to Jumping Freight for collect service)
Brokerage fee	75 (for routine air clearance)
Duty deposit	79 (subject to liquidation within one year)
Bond to customs	30 (for $1,000 of coverage)
Surface freight	20 (to your broker's warehouse)
Total Due	$478

You figure the cost of the clocks at $780 for merchandise, $478 for transportation charges, and $20 for miscellaneous costs such as buying and sending the international money orders. That makes a total of $1278, or about $10.65 per clock. You know this will come down if you can order in larger quantities, but to make even a little money on this trial order you must keep your price at a minimum of $13. You will probably offer a 2 percent discount for prompt payment, and in the future you may also offer a quantity discount.

The clocks sell well enough in small stores at about $22, especially in the store that displays them near the cash register, and you manage to get a small order from a gift shop in a major hotel. As you expected, sales there are excellent. You decide to market through manufacturer's representatives, and place an advertisement for representatives in *Gift and Decorative Accessories* magazine. The cost is only $18, and you receive several replies. You spend $600 to produce 2500 copies of a full color catalog page that your representatives can show their customers. You ask the manufacturer to name you as his exclusive distributor for the entire United States. He refuses, but agrees not to ship to anyone else in this country for 90 days if he receives your order immediately for at least 1,000 pieces.

You agree, and order 17 boxes (1020 pieces) of clocks at $6.00 each, by sea freight, delivered to your port, with shipment within 35 days and payment by sight draft (see Chapter 7). The supplier accepts your order.

When you go to pay the sight draft for this shipment, it shows the following:

Merchandise	$6120 (1020 × 6.00)
Port charges, etc.	84 (There are *always* miscellaneous charges.)
Sea freight	571
Insurance	47 (on $7500 Value)
Total	$6822

Bank charges are $40, raising the total to $6862. Your broker's bill, including miscellaneous charges, his fee, duty, the bond (explained in Chapter 10), and cartage to your warehouse, comes to $1168. That makes the total cost $8030 ($6868 + 1168) or $7.87 per unit ($8030 ÷ 1020). Your cost has gone down by $2.78 per clock, or 26 percent. You can now sell to the stores for $11.00, pay your representatives a 15 percent commission, and have $9.35 remaining [$11 × (1 − .15) = $9.35]. That gives you a margin of 15.8 percent (($9.35 − 7.87) ÷ 9.35)—not great but it will get you by until you find a way to improve it. Your potential profit on this order is (1020 clocks times $1.48 each) $1510. That assumes that your customers are paying domestic freight charges and that you have no credit losses or other extraordinary expenses.

Now you are in business. If all goes well you can obtain bank financing, hire an assistant, add another line of products, and build up your distribution system.

EXPORTING

Let us suppose that you want to start exporting and to develop a marketing plan. You are not sure whether you want to work as a merchant or an agent.

- Make your business a reality. Pick and register a name, open a bank account, get a telephone and telex address, and have stationery printed.

- Look at a publication that includes specific export opportunities. A good one is *Trade Channel,* a newspaper published in Holland and represented in the United States by American Business Communications of Tarrytown, New York (phone number 914-631-1802). Select advertisements for products you know something about from countries you think you would like to deal with.

- Telex or write potential customers to introduce your firm and ask for more information about their needs. You want them to make at least some commitment before you go to the trouble of contacting suppliers and developing quotations. Wait for replies.

- Go to the *Thomas Register of American Manufacturers* for information on firms that make the products you are interested in. Call or write half a dozen for each product. Ask if their lines are available for export to the country your inquiry is from. If so, request catalogs and price lists, and ask whether they prefer to work with you as an agent or as a merchant.

- Analyze the catalogs and prices and decide which manufacturers' products to quote on if there are no complications. Ask each manufacturer for a letter to protect your commission and markup, and for the weight and dimensions of a box on each item.

- Contact your freight forwarder and/or carriers to get forwarding, freight, insurance and miscellaneous charges so you can develop a quotation for the goods delivered to the buyer's port. Add your commission or markup if it isn't included already.

- Send your potential customer a letter and a price quotation along with catalog pages if you think pictures and related information will be useful to him. Include your shipping and payment terms, order lead time, and the number of days for which you will honor your quoted prices. You want to rush the buyer a little, and you cannot ship an order two years from now at today's prices.

- Follow up until you receive either a positive or a negative decision. If you receive the order, make sure there is no risk that you will have to pay for merchandise and not get paid for it. If the payment terms are not secure, delay the shipment until you check the buyer's integrity and financial standing.

- Complete the transaction by shipping or instructing your supplier to ship, and, of course, by receiving your commission or by collecting and paying your supplier.

- Keep in contact to try to obtain repeat orders, and build your business by looking for other products you can sell to the same customer or for other customers to whom you can sell the same product.

Example: Exporting

Suppose you look at *Trade Channel*, as previously suggested, and find that a company in Nigeria wants rolls of paper for accounting machines. You write to the customer to introduce your firm and to ask for more information about the company's needs, including the quantity and the exact specifications of the product. At the same time, you ask for bank and trade references.

The Nigerian importer writes back indicating he needs 40 cartons immediately for a bank that is running out of paper. He sends a small piece of paper from a roll the bank has been using so you can see the type of stock and the width, and he asks you to provide samples and prices.

Since you think the customer is serious, you call the Nigerian consulate to make sure paper can be legally imported by firms in that country. It can be. The consulate is not sure of the exact customs duty, but knows that you must provide a certificate of origin and that the importer will need a "Form M" foreign exchange permit.

You telex the importer about the Form M. You are assured that this will not be a problem, and you get bank and trade references. You immediately contact the customer's bank through your bank and the trade references by letter.

After consulting directories of manufacturers, you find several that make rolls of paper for office machines. You contact half a dozen. Nearly all are willing to work with you but only if you are a merchant; they do not want to involve themselves in shipping to and collecting from a customer in Africa. Three companies quote you prices by phone and agree to send you samples for the customer. The prices quoted are FOB/factory, and the factories are all in different geographical areas.

If you mail the samples to Nigeria it will take about two weeks, and your customer is in a hurry. The cost of sending them by a courier service is about $130. You finally decide to save money and use registered air mail. In the meantime you develop a quotation on 40 cartons by determining inland freight in the United States, ocean freight, and other charges and adding your profit. Each carton is 1.6 cubic feet and weighs 48 pounds. Your estimated charges are as follows:

Merchandise (40 cartons @ $83.75)	$3350
Inland freight	120
Forwarding and miscellaneous charges	180
Ocean freight	880
Marine Insurance	275
Total	$4805

You add banking and other charges of about $150, assuming the payment will be on a letter of credit. You also add a markup, 15 percent of the value of the goods at the U.S. port, or $548 (($3350 + 120 + 180) × .15 = $548). This is a small profit, but you have learned that your markup cannot be very high since it must be shown on the invoice for Nigerian customs purposes. Also, you face low-price competition from suppliers in the United Kingdom. You make a mental note to try for a 5 percent rebate from the supplier.

You send your quotation of $5500 by telex to Nigeria ($4805 + 150 + 548 = 5503), suggesting sea freight and letter of credit terms. To your surprise, you receive a return telex saying your offer is accepted, but for only 28 cartons and by air freight. The customer asks for a pro-forma (preliminary) invoice so he can obtain the Form M and the letter of credit.

You quickly contact your supplier to verify that you can get the smaller quantity at the same price. He agrees. He will not give you the 5 percent rebate, but offers a 3 percent discount if you pay within 30 days of his shipment to you. You calculate your costs exactly and send your pro-forma invoice by telex. The customer replies that the air freight charge is too high, and he suggests a company that can save money by consolidating your shipment with others. This company, Pandair, provides a quotation of $2444, plus $30 for insurance and a $10 processing charge. You send a new pro-forma and receive the order.

The order comes by mail and asks you to ship immediately, but there is an important element missing—the letter of credit, referred to as the LC. You ask about that and are told that it is being opened through the ICON Merchant Bank in Lagos. A few days later you are advised by an American bank that an LC in your favor has been received. You get a copy of it by mail, study it, and find it consistent with your agreement with the customer. You ask the bank about having it confirmed and are assured that it is good and you will have no trouble getting paid if you meet its terms.

At this point you order the merchandise from your supplier, to be delivered to Pandair at Kennedy International Airport. You purchase from the Nigerian consulate a special form entitled "Invoice and Declaration of Value Required for Shipments to Nigeria" and complete it. This becomes your commercial invoice. You also complete and sign Nigerian "Certificate of Value" and "Certificate of Origin" forms, have your signature notarized, and send copies of the invoice to the New York City Chamber of Commerce for "legalization" (certification that it is correct). Finally, you send your invoices, certificates, packing list, Shippers Export Declaration, a letter of instructions, and a check for $2484 to Pandair (having saved money by not using a freight forwarder). You learn later that your merchandise reached the airport on time, marked (by the manufacturer), "Super Hot, Rush, Tailgate Please."

You telex your customer the flight information. When the documents arrive from Pandair you check them, find them all in order, and forward them to the bank that advised you of the LC along with a request for payment. A few days later the merchandise arrives in Lagos, and the money arrives in your account. You pay the supplier in time to take the discount, and the transaction is completed.

Your task now is to build on this success. Ask the customer to place a large order, immediately, by sea freight. Also ask which other products you can supply to him, and consider whether to seek customers in other countries for rolls of paper. If there seems to be a good demand for this product, you should try to work out a written agreement with your supplier. If you are going to spend time and money developing the market for his product you will need some form of exclusivity, or at least a guarantee of continuing (and perhaps preferential) supply. You have established a niche in the export business.

3

Setting Up Your Business

Before you can begin trading you should have a business organization, no matter how small your operation. This chapter deals with what is involved in establishing a business, from choosing a form of organization to saving money on taxes. Although the information applies to setting up almost any kind of small business, it is of special relevance to the business of importing and exporting.

SOLE PROPRIETORSHIP, PARTNERSHIP, CORPORATION, OR S CORPORATION

Which of these forms of organization you choose depends on considerations such as the size of your business, whether you are the only owner or have associates, and your tax position. Look over the descriptions of each type of organization which follow to figure out which best fits your enterprise.

Sole Proprietorship

The sole proprietorship is the simplest organizational form. There is one owner, who usually takes the title of president. He or she can make decisions without consulting anyone.

At income tax time, the sole proprietor figures business expenses and profit or loss on an IRS Schedule C and transfers only the final figure to the 1040 form, thus combining employment income with self-employment income for a relatively simple tax declaration.

Partnership

A partnership is almost as simple as a sole proprietorship. A partnership means that there is more than one owner. Each partner simply declares his or her share of profit or loss on the personal income tax return. In a special type of partnership, called a *limited* partnership, the limited partner is usually not involved in the management of the firm.

This form of organization can be useful in international trade if one partner is well-equipped with purchasing and marketing skills and the other with trade documentation and related skills. Unfortunately partnership businesses often fail quickly when one partner dies or loses interest or when partners disagree with each other. My theory is that the kind of person who is willing to take the risk of starting his or her own business usually wants to make management decisions without interference or the additional time it takes to reach agreement on decisions from partners.

In most of the United States, the process for registering a sole proprietorship or partnership begins with a trip to a commercial stationer for three copies of a form called a *Business Certificate*. Fill out all three (they are very simple), sign them in the presence of a notary public, and send all three copies to the county clerk of the county in which the business will be located. The fee is usually about $35; call the county clerk to ask for the exact amount. You must pay by certified check, cashier's check, or postal money order. You'll get two copies back from the county clerk with an official stamp. You're now in business.

Corporation

A corporation is a more formal way of organizing. It involves registration with a state department of commerce. There are a number of tax advantages to incorporating, such as being able to deduct one's personal life insurance, but there are also accounting requirements and other costs. In general, it is economically better for a business to incorporate when its profit before taxes reaches about $50,000 a year. At that point, the extra savings usually equal the extra cost.

Many importing and exporting firms incorporate at their inception, however, in order for the owners to be protected from product liability. An individual—importer or exporter, agent or merchant—shares in the liability for any harm that may be caused in the distribution of a product. Incorporation limits liability to the assets of the business, unless it can be proved that a person *knew* the product was harmful and incorporated specifically to reduce liability.

I believe an importer of any size should incorporate if he is dealing with a product that is taken internally or applied to the skin or that could cause harm in any way. This includes toys with small pieces that a baby might swallow, clothing that could catch fire, etc. For exporters the problem is somewhat less serious, but it still exists. There are cases, especially in Western Europe, where consumers and industrial users have sued American exporters in the United States.

Incorporating to limit liability is somewhat less important if you, or your foreign business partner, carry product liability insurance. Of course, the more potentially dangerous the product, the more expensive is this kind of insurance coverage. In some cases, your foreign business partners may carry liability insurance that will protect you.

In most states, incorporation costs about $250 if you do the work yourself and about $800 if you use a lawyer. A good bookstore usually carries books about how to incorporate in specific states, with all the necessary forms included as appendices.

You can save time and money by incorporating in one of the handful of states—such as Delaware—where the procedure is particularly quick and inexpensive. The drawback is that you then have to register your business as a *foreign corporation* in the state in which it is actually located. For a very small business, the cost and trouble of double registration make it better simply to register in one's home state.

S Corporation

The S Corporation is no less expensive to form than a regular corporation, but has different tax implications. An S Corporation is a special form authorized by Subchapter S of the United States Internal Revenue Code. It gives protection from liability but still permits the owner of a business to pay taxes as an individual.

It may be worth consulting a certified public accountant (about $40 per hour) or an attorney (approximately $120 to $180 per hour in the New York area) to determine the best way for your specific firm to be organized. An experienced attorney can also advise you on whether to invest in product liability insurance. As with most professionals, lawyers are often highly specific in their areas of expertise. Be certain the lawyer you consult has experience in helping set up new businesses.

SELECTING YOUR TRADE NAME

In the United States, an individual who imports or exports in his own name does not need to register with any government organization. Most companies that deal with products, however, think it wise to select a *trade name* and try to make it known. If you do business under any name other than your own, the trade name must be registered. Registration insures that the owner of a business can be located if, for example, one of its products causes harm to someone.

It is wise to pick a short, easy-to-remember name. Be sure it doesn't have a vulgar or uncomplimentary meaning in the language of any country with which you plan to do business. The most famous example of such a blunder is the Chevrolet Nova, which was introduced in Venezuela before anyone realized that "no va" in Spanish means "doesn't go." The Nova didn't.

For a sole proprietorship or partnership, it is usually enough to check local telephone directories for similar names. A name can be registered if there is not already a similar company with a similar name operating in the same county. For a corporation, one should have a search done to make sure the name selected is unique in the state of registration. If your corporation is doing business nationally or internationally, it may be wise to research the name at these levels.

OPENING A BANK ACCOUNT FOR YOUR BUSINESS

To open a bank account for a sole proprietorship or partnership, present one copy of the executed Business Certificate and a check for the initial deposit. For a corporation, you will need a corporate resolution specifying who may open an account. In some states, you may have to take the actual Articles of Incorporation and/or the corporate seal.

You should open your business account with a first class, international bank. Even a small import or export transaction will be using letters of credit or other specialized international payment instruments. Savings banks cannot handle this kind of transaction, and local commercial banks usually don't have the expertise to do it. You should look for a bank that has a letter of credit department with a staff of at least five persons.

I was once contacted by officials of a small bank in the New York area, who said that two of their clients were starting in international trade and these bankers needed to have me teach them the basics of importing and exporting so they could serve their clients! You don't want a banker who is learning from you; you want one with previous experience, as with the lawyer or accountant you choose.

ESTABLISHING YOUR OFFICE

A small import or export business does not take much space, and many persons save money and travel time by working in their own homes. I have a friend, for example, who has an office—three desks—in his basement. And from this unprepossessing base, functioning as an export agent, he has sold millions of dollars worth of heavy construction machinery such as cranes and bulldozers.

There can be disadvantages to working in your home. A client of mine decided to begin importing from Taiwan. This man worked out of a small home shared with his wife, three children, and a large dog. He ordered a trial shipment. Two weeks after it arrived, he received a telephone call from a shopping center in his suburban town. The Taiwanese exporter had traveled to the United States, with no advance notice, and wanted to meet that day with my client in his office.

A few years ago another friend who was beginning an export merchant business planned to buy products from American manufacturers and sell them abroad. When he attempted to buy on credit, suppliers asked for his Dun and Bradstreet rating. My friend telephoned Dun and Bradstreet, who sent him a form to be completed. A few weeks later, when he was enjoying a leisurely breakfast in his pajamas, there was a knock on the door. It was a Dun and Bradstreet employee who had come to verify the information on the form.

There are additional drawbacks to working out of your home besides being caught *en deshabille* by a zealous credit investigator.

- Most residential areas have laws that restrict the use of one's home for business purposes. Usually there is supposed to be no stock of merchandise, no business visitors, and not more than one employee.
- If you plan to sell directly to consumers in the United States and would like to accept major credit cards, you will probably have to open an office away from your home.
- Homeowner's and tenant's insurance usually do not cover business equipment, supplies, merchandise, or liability. You may want a rider on your insurance policy to protect equipment such as typewriters and computers.

If you do not want to work from your own home, you may be able to save money by renting space from a business that has more than is needed or by locating a company that rents space complete with basic equipment and office services. An import/export business does not need a prime location, unless the office is going to be used as a showroom.

Office Equipment

You don't need a lot of fancy equipment in an import/export business. Desks and chairs, filing cabinets, and a good typewriter are the basics. A photocopier helps also because international trade requires numerous documents. There will be many occasions when you'll want to make a copy or two.

A small postage meter is also useful because international postage uses so many different denominations of stamps. A simple meter can be rented from Pitney-Bowes or Singer for around $20 a month. When the post office has set the machine with the amount of postage you wish to purchase, you can put any amount on a letter or package. While you're at the post office, ask for a booklet or chart that gives the current international postage rates.

I also suggest a separate telephone for your business. Limit the number of people who may answer it and be sure it's answered in a businesslike way; keep the children away from it during office hours. It should be hooked up to a telephone answering machine, which is much cheaper than an answering service and, I think, better. Buy the kind of machine that lets you call in from anywhere and get your messages. I once called my answering machine from a fishing trip in the middle of the north woods in Minnesota—I got my messages, returned two calls, and went right back to catching the big ones.

Mailing Address

Communication is a very important part of the import/export business. If you have a formal office, you'll probably get your mail there. If you're working out of your home you may want to keep its address a secret, either to avoid unwelcome visitors or to keep from giving away the fact that you are working from a private home.

You can use a post office box if there are any available in your area, but that has disadvantages. You will have to go to the post office every day to pick up your mail, and in some countries only very small fly-by-night operations use post office boxes. It could hurt your reputation. You may be able to get around this by simply not using "P.O." or "Post Office." Your address could be something like "687 Fenwick Station." Check with the post office before printing stationery to make sure you'll get your mail.

There are also companies in most cities that offer mail box services. These usually have prestigious addresses, such as "100 Broadway." For a fee, these companies will receive your mail and either forward it to you or hold it for you to pick up. Still another alternative is simply to find a friend who has an office and will let you use his or her address.

Cable Address

The cable, or international telegram, was an important way of sending international messages for many years. Now it is less so. I suggest not getting a cable address. It will cost you about $50 a year and, if anyone wants to send you a cable, he can always send it to your postal address. Likewise, if you should want to send a cable to anyone, you can do it from your telephone without needing your own cable address.

Telex Number

A huge volume of international communications is now sent by telex. If you're going to be an importer or exporter, you must have a way to send and receive telex messages.

Telex is a system of electronic communication that is both faster and cheaper than telegrams. Also there is an *answer back* system by which you know immediately that your message is received. (When you send a cable or a letter you don't know if your message was received until you get a reply.) There's even an *open line* system that lets you actually converse by telex. You receive a message (it is typed out on the telex machine in your own location), and you type in your reply, your correspondent answers, etc.

An advantage to telex over the telephone is that it gives you a written record of all communications. If you're working with companies in the Far East, there's no time during our business day that they are working, and vice-versa. It's easy to send a telex before you stop working in the afternoon, and a reply will be waiting when you go to work the next morning. An exporter I knew had an office, but he had his telex machine in his bedroom at home. He worked mostly with customers in the Middle East, and their working hours, translated to New York time, were from 3:00 until 9:00 P.M., Saturday through Wednesday. If my friend wanted to be able to receive his messages and answer instantly, he was better off with the machine at home.

There are three ways to obtain telex. The low commitment way is to use a telex service. These are companies, found in most large cities, that have the equipment to send and receive telex messages for you. An example is the Aegis Telex Service in New York City. A businessperson who wants to send a message through Executive simply phones them and reads the message. The service transmits it and bills $4.00, plus the transmission charge, usually between about $2.00 and $5.00 depending on the length of the message and the country of destination. When a message comes in, Executive phones its customer, reads the message, and then sends a copy in the mail. The charge is a flat $4.00.

It's a good idea to choose a telex service that you can phone inexpensively. Also, you *may* want to look for one that has service in the evenings and on weekends. By the way, some telex services now offer fax also. It is more expensive, but transmits an exact reproduction of your document.

The medium commitment way to have access to telex is to purchase a personal computer with a modem, printer, and telecommunications software. Then you can send and receive messages through a Western Union Service called "Easylink," an MCI service called "MCI Mail," or other systems. With these, it costs you only the transmission charge to send a message and nothing to receive one (except a local telephone call).

Once you learn to use the personal computer, you'll also be able to get U.S. export statistics, ocean freight rates, credit information on American firms, and other useful information. This is all available now from electronic data bases. With the prices of equipment coming down continually, you can probably buy everything you'll need for under $1000.

The high commitment method of corresponding by telex involves buying or renting a telex machine. You can purchase a machine now (made in Japan, of course) for about $1100, or you can rent one for about $50 a month. Companies that have their own telex machines usually hook them up to special telephone lines, called *dedicated* lines, so whenever a message comes in, the telex machine will automatically print it. If you don't want to invest in a dedicated phone line, the telex carriers have *mailbox* systems. As with the personal computer, you can connect to your mailbox whenever you wish to check for telex messages.

Telephone

I've already argued in favor of a separate telephone with an answering machine. You'll probably want to put this phone on a separate line and get a business listing in your local phone directories. For a reasonable extra charge, you can place five words of advertising in the yellow pages, be listed in the yellow pages in nearby cities, or get other services such as call forwarding.

If you plan to make many long distance calls, you should investigate the long-distance carriers. At this writing, MCI has service to more foreign countries than any carrier except AT&T.

If you plan to import and sell directly to final consumers in the United States, you may want to have your own 800 telephone number. Cheaper, but not quite as good, is the 800 number service. These are like answering services that your customers can call for free from anywhere in the continental United States. You can then call the service to get your messages. The telephone numbers of two such services are 800-235-6646 and 800-237-8400.

Your Company Logo

If you don't want to have a custom logo you can order stationery and related supplies inexpensively by mail. One very good supplier is Stationery House in Rockville, Maryland (phone 800-638-3033).

Remember, though, you aren't IBM or General Motors. Most of the people you do business with will never have heard of you. Their first impression of you will be from the quality of your correspondence. Therefore I think it's worth the money to have a local artist design a logo for your business. I suggest not using a plane, a ship, or a globe, because these are much too common and will mark you as an amateur.

For stationery in small quantities with custom logos, as well as envelopes and business cards, the instant printers are usually the cheapest and fastest. Ask for lightweight paper if you think you'll be doing a lot of international correspondence, because postage to most of the world costs 44¢ per half ounce. Your return address should include the letters, "USA." Remember, this is not the only country in the world. The letterhead should also include your telex number, which you will have with any of the three systems just discussed.

You may not want to put much information on your stationery about the kind of business you're in. That way you can still use it if your business takes off in unexpected directions. The same holds true for your business cards.

Business Forms

For importing, you will not need any business forms that can't be purchased in commercial stationery stores. To save money at first, you can buy stock forms and type in your company name and address. Down the road you may want to invest in imprinted forms.

Exporters, however, often need specialized forms such as the Canadian Customs Invoice or the Nigeria Certificate of Origin. These can be obtained from the consulates of your market countries or from UNZ and Company in Jersey City, New Jersey (800-631-3098). UNZ will send you a free book, the *Sourcebook,* which lists and shows copies of the various forms the company sells.

ACCOUNTING

In this business, like any other, you should keep accurate and timely financial records. It's important to know, for example, which product lines or which representatives are giving you the most profit.

In the beginning you probably will not need an accountant. You can go to a stationery store and buy a recordkeeping system. One of these is the *Dome Monthly*

Record. This is a very simple system that lets you do all your accounting in about an hour a month, if your business is small. (The Dome system has no place for Accounts Receivable or Accounts Payable, but you can keep track of these elsewhere.) This kind of system puts you on a *cash* basis. That means you recognize income only when you actually receive the money and recognize expenses only when you actually pay out the money. This can be an advantage if you have a *merchant* business and are working in such a way that you have to pay for merchandise before you are paid for it. On a cash basis, you will show somewhat less profit at any given time. Less profit on the books on December 31 can reduce your taxes.

If your business is incorporated, your state law may require you to abandon the cash method and use the *accrual* method of recording income and expenses.

If you decide to use the services of an accountant, try to find one who has had experience with import and/or export businesses. He or she will know the laws better and may be able to save you money on taxes. Accountants charge about $40 per hour and up, depending on their locations and the demand for their services.

TAXATION

In import/export, as with any other business, business income is taxable, and business expenses are tax deductible. The latter includes the cost of travel, at home and abroad, for business purposes. Expenses of your spouse can also be deducted if he or she is active in the business. Under current rules, a trip abroad should be less than eight days or, if it is longer, at least 75 percent of the time must be spent on business in order for you to deduct the entire air fare. If you take, say, a two-week trips to Paris and only half the time is spent on business, you can deduct only half the air fare and half the on-ground expenses (plus transportation to business meetings).

I have a good friend who imports giftware from Europe and the Orient. He takes a buying trip every winter to the country of his choice and a selling trip every summer to a resort area in the United States. He keeps detailed records of all his business meetings and is able to deduct nearly all his expenses. Since his wife is active in the business, her travel expenses are deductible as well.

You can also deduct expenses for an office at home on a square foot basis. For example, if 15 percent of your residence is used for an office you can deduct 15 percent of your rent. If you own your home, you can deduct 15 percent of the cost of renting an equivalent place. It's also permissible to take off the same percentage of your electricity, heating oil, and other utilities.

If you deduct for an office at home, the space can be used only for business purposes. If you sell your house and avoid capital gains tax by buying a more expensive house within a year, you will still be liable for taxes on the part that was used as an office. Also, I've often been told that deducting for an office at home increases your chances of an audit by the IRS. If you have any reason to be concerned about an audit, you may decide to forego this deduction.

In a form of business which lets you pay taxes as an individual, you can deduct a business loss from your income for three consecutive years. After that you must show a profit before you can again deduct losses (no deduction for the office at home if you operate at a loss). You will need to read the IRS rules on this or use an accountant to be certain your deductions are legal.

With a regular corporation, you will be subjected to double taxation. You will pay tax on corporate profits, and then pay personal income tax on any money that you receive as dividends. An accountant can help you find legal ways of minimizing taxes.

Some cities tax home-offices, and/or levy an "Unincorporated Business Tax." This means that even sole proprietorships are subject to double taxation—as a firm and then as an individual. The rates are not high but, with a new business, every penny is important.

If you plan to hire employees, you'll have to contact the U.S. Internal Revenue Service for an "Employee Identification Number." This is free, and you can obtain it by mail. You will, however, be thrown into the jungle of payroll taxes and tax deductions. I suggest trying to do without formal employees for as long as possible.

If you plan to buy merchandise for resale in any state that has a retail sales tax, you'll need to contact your state tax department for a sales tax number. For a sole proprietorship, this will probably be your social security number. A sales tax number is vital for an export merchant.

4

Imports: Selecting Products And Suppliers

One of the most important ingredients for a successful import/export business is a good product. Another is the marketing of that product—something discussed in Chapter 6. Knowing how to locate and test product ideas, how to find and evaluate suppliers, and some of the terms and conditions that are often written into agreements between exporters and their agents or distributors are key issues that are discussed in this chapter. There is also a list of names and addresses of some publications you may want to subscribe to for more information.

GETTING PRODUCT IDEAS

People who travel to foreign countries often see products they think will sell easily back home. They return with a few samples, show them to potential buyers, and perhaps move on to develop profitable businesses. A lady in one of my seminars visited Guatemala and bought some native crafts in the Antigua marketplace. She showed them to buyers in several stores and found a great deal of interest.

Two buyers even placed small orders. The lady immediately saw the potential of starting an import business and returned to Guatemala to purchase merchandise and find a reliable supplier for her future orders.

Another excellent way to find products to import is to subscribe to trade publications. One of the best is *Trade Channel*. This monthly newspaper is published in two editions, one for developed and one for developing countries. It is dedicated almost entirely to advertisements, from all over the world, of products that are available to import. There are also a number of specific trade opportunities. For example, a company in Guatemala wants ". . . to import paraffin wax, refined, 'fe6X ash light, caustic soda solid, flakes and beads, glucose," and a company in Great Britain wants to export "1. drinks, snacks & food vending machines, 2. marine engines, 3. hospital, catering, industrial, domestic weighing machines, 4. electric motors."

People who are especially interested in importing from Europe can subscribe to one or more of the *Made in Europe* series. These excellent magazines are devoted to single product categories and published at varying intervals:

- *General Merchandise*, monthly;
- *Technical Equipment* and *Furniture and Interiors*, semi-monthly;
- *Food and Drink* and *Construction Equipment and Machinery*, quarterly;
- *Medical Equipment*, annually.

All can be obtained from *Made in Europe* in Brooklyn, New York, phone 718-383-8100.

There is a similar set of publications for Asian products. These are called *Asian Sources* and are available by subscription from Woodright Enterprises in Chicago, Illinois (312-256-7105). Headquartered in Hong Kong, this publishing company has separate monthly magazines for

Electronics, Electronic Components, Computer Products, Time-pieces, Hardware, Gifts and Home Products, Toys and Sporting Goods, and *Fashion Accessories.* Besides advertisements there are useful articles about specific kinds of products.

Sometimes people decide on a country first and look for products from it. U.S. international trade statistics show what products are being imported from the country in question. These statistics are published by the U.S. Department of Commerce and are available in major libraries as well as in field offices of the Commerce Department's International Trade Administration (see Appendix B).

A potential importer can also contact the relevant countries' trade promotion offices in the United States for information about products to import. Most countries have trade offices in selected American cities. They are especially clustered in New York. Their addresses change often; the most current listing is usually in the telephone yellow pages (in Manhattan the *Business to Business* edition, under the heading, *Governments—Foreign Representatives*). A total of 116 countries are included in the current listing, although not all of them have specialized trade offices.

Foreign countries' export promotion offices can often guide a potential importer to helpful publications from their countries. For example, *Trade Winds* is one of many excellent magazines from Taiwan. The address is P.O. Box 7-179, Taipei, Taiwan, and an airmail subscription costs $50 a year. Taiwan is an excellent first country for trading because it has many experienced exporters who will accept small orders from new importers.

There are several other publications from which you can get ideas of products to import. One of these is the *International Intertrade Index,* published in Newark, New Jersey (201-686-2382). This monthly magazine is inexpensive and contains ideas on low-priced and novelty items from all over the world.

Still another source of import product ideas is trade exhibits. Nearly every kind of product is categorized in some industry, and every industry has exhibits. One example is the American International Toy Fair, usually held in New York in February of each year. In major industries, like shoes and giftware, there are regional shows held in market cities such as San Francisco, Los Angeles, Dallas, Chicago, Boston, New York, and Atlanta.

In each city, the local chamber of commerce or convention and visitors bureau can tell you about the local show schedule. Major shows are listed in a book called *Exhibits Guide*, which you'll find in major libraries, and shows for each industry are written up in trade publications. You can identify (and subscribe to) the publications in any trade by visiting their stands at the shows, by asking people in the trade what they read, or from a book found in most libraries called the *Encyclopedia of Business Information Sources*. This book will also tell you about the trade associations in each industry, but the same publisher, Gale, has a much better book for this purpose, the *Encyclopedia of Associations*.

GETTING SAMPLE PRODUCTS FOR TESTING

When you've chosen several potential products that you might want to import, you'll want to obtain samples and test them in the market. Write or telex some of the firms that supply those products in the foreign country and get catalogs and prices from them.

With that information in hand, you can choose three or four different products (unless you're looking at very large and/or expensive items) and send for samples of these. Take the lowest price quoted (no matter for what quantity) and add the approximate cost of insured air mail. From a commercial bank, buy an International

Money Order for that amount. Write to the supplier saying you are considering importing his product and would like a sample, enclose the money order, and send the letter by *registered* air mail. (You often can get free samples of inexpensive items, but by sending payment you save time.) Occasionally the exporter won't reply, and your money will be lost, but that must be considered part of the cost of starting an import business.

TESTING PRODUCT IDEAS

When the samples arrive you will need to evaluate them yourself and get the opinions of people in the retail area. This is a crucial process for several reasons. The buyers simply might not be interested in your product. The price may be too high. The product will probably need changes to meet American consumer preferences or legal requirements. *Most foreign products have to be modified to make them "right" for the U.S. market.*

First try to determine the uses of your product and who will be the consumers (actual users) and the customers (buyers). Often the two are different people. Try to determine which kinds of business firms the potential customers would buy from. Identify several and show the product to them (in most cases you will have to make appointments). Ask them what they think of it, whether they would recommend any changes, whether they would be likely to buy it from an importer (or from a foreign exporter through you as agent), and if so how often they would order and in which season, how much they would order at a time, and of course how much they would pay. This question of price is critical, and you may have trouble getting an honest reply. If results are not satisfactory when you ask, "How much would you pay for this?" try asking the estimated selling price and percent mark-up, how much they are now paying for similar products, or what price you would have to meet in order for them to buy from you.

You will soon find that each person with whom you speak gives you opinions and ideas, but the opinions are conflicting. This is because each buyer has his individual preferences as well as his unique group of customers. You will have to analyze the various replies to draw conclusions about the viability of your product idea, modifications required, the target market, the channel of distribution, and the pricing structure.

Suppose, for example, you are offered some very nice rag dolls, made in Colombia. They represent storybook characters, such as Little Red Riding Hood. They are actually several dolls in one—turn Red Riding Hood upside down and she becomes the grandmother; flip over the bonnet and Grandmother becomes the big bad wolf. You may decide that the main customers for these dolls are not children, or even parents who buy things for their children, but grandmothers and others who purchase gifts for girls. That would make the product a gift item, not a toy. You might decide the product would sell best in high quality gift shops. You would then need to identify several such stores, make appointments to see the buyers, and show them the dolls. You would be asked questions about the doll clothing (what it's made of and whether it's flame resistant), the buttons (are they toxic and how many pounds of pressure will they withstand before being pulled off?), and the dolls themselves (what are they stuffed with and are they hand sewn?). You might be told that the labeling is inadequate, that the dolls are too big (or too little), that they are too expensive (or too cheap), that the clothing styles should be more modern, the cheeks rosier, the hair more curly, etc. After several interviews you will have a good idea whether the dolls will sell, how they should be modified and packaged, to what market they should be targeted, how they should be distributed, and what prices they would bring at the wholesale and retail levels.

FINDING FOREIGN SUPPLIERS

Although in the process of selecting products to import you will probably find a number of foreign suppliers, you want to do more research to find the foreign companies that can best serve you.

Look in Directories

In addition to finding suppliers in trade exhibits and through magazine advertisements, there are a number of United States and foreign business directories you can consult. Directories are available in the trade promotion offices and consulates of many countries and in major public and private libraries. A superb series of directories, *Kompass*, which you will find in major libraries, includes virtually all ranking firms in a number of important countries, and there are other directories that cover firms in certain regions. A good example is *Latin/American Import Export Directory* (400 pages), which is available free except for postage and handling from the Latin American Trade Council, P.O. Box 12–1007, San Jose, Costa Rica.

Perhaps even more useful is a computerized list of foreign firms maintained by the U.S. Department of Commerce. You have access to this list through field offices of the International Trade Administration and some libraries. They will enter your requirements into a computer terminal and get a printout of firms that you may want to contact. You can specify such criteria as the country, type of business activity, products handled, and even company size for each listing you want to receive. There is a modest charge for this service.

Advertising

You can place your own advertisements in publications such as *Trade Channel* to locate foreign suppliers. If you want to target your messages better, you can advertise directly in foreign trade journals. Good libraries have directories that can give you information about major trade publications in all countries.

Contact Service Firms and Trade Promotion Offices

Other sources of potential foreign suppliers are international banks and transportation companies and various countries' export promotion organizations. Banks and airlines have always helped their clients make trade contacts, and some banks have set up formal procedures for doing this.

The services provided by trade promotion organizations vary enormously in their effectiveness. One of the best is the China External Trade Development Council, 201 Tunhwa North Road, Taipei 105, Taiwan. If you write this organization about a specific product, your request will be publicized to the Taiwan exporting community, and product literature will begin arriving in your mailbox.

You can get the home addresses of these foreign trade promotion agencies from their branch offices in the United States or from a book found in major libraries, *Croner's Reference Book for World Traders*. The administrative organizations of major ports usually publish booklets that list, among other things, the foreign trade promotion organizations that have offices in their areas.

Traveling

Perhaps the most enjoyable way to find foreign suppliers is to travel. If language is not a barrier, you can actually speak with officials of the trade promotion organization in their own country, and with the ministry of commerce, local chambers of commerce, the American chamber of commerce, and other organizations. Often you can make appointments with potential suppliers and visit them immediately.

SELECTING FOREIGN SUPPLIERS

Once you have made contact with one or several suppliers, you will have to choose the ones with whom you wish to do business. There are a number of ways to evaluate suppliers. The first is simply to analyze the firm's correspondence. Do they answer your inquiries promptly and accurately? Does their letterhead show a telex address? Is the stationery of good quality? You must try *not* to judge a foreign firm by the quality of the English used in its correspondence. A foreign executive may be top-notch, except for his English, but may write to you in English to save you the trouble of finding a translator.

A second guideline involves assessing the way your foreign suppliers respond to your requests, especially for product modifications. A good friend of mine was trying to establish herself as an import agent for wooden toys from a Central American country. She asked for product modifications and found it took several months to receive a new sample with a slightly different design or a different color. In frustration, she decided not to do business with the supplier.

A third useful technique is to obtain credit information on potential foreign suppliers. This will be discussed in detail in Chapter 6.

Finally, a visit to your potential supplier is not a bad idea. Even though it costs time and money, it may save you from a major catastrophe like having the Christmas tree ornaments you have already sold to Macy's reach the United States on December 26. It is probably better to make appointments in advance, although that will give your potential suppliers time to clean their factories and perhaps hire extra temporary personnel. One West African firm rented an entire suite of offices, complete with equipment and personnel, in preparation for the visit of a new European customer.

When you get to the exporter's place of business, speak with some of the key personnel, ask if you can see some recent financial reports and look at the production equipment. There's an east Asian country, noted for economic progress and the extreme optimism of its people, where export managers virtually never turn down an order. You want 10,000 men's shirts a month? The factory may have only three sewing machines, of which two are broken (I'm exaggerating a little), but they think that *somehow* they'll be able to deliver the goods. Make sure your supplier has the capability of fulfilling his obligations to you.

In most cases, you will want to import from manufacturers rather than from export trading companies. This is both to save money and to have direct contact with the producers of your goods. You can usually tell the difference by the company name and the catalogs it sends you. If the catalog pages have stickers with your exporter's name and address placed over some other name and address, your exporter is not the manufacturer.

You may want to make an exception to this rule if your orders will be too small for a manufacturer to handle, if you plan to order small quantities of several different items, if you are buying from a country such as Japan, in which exporting is normally done by trading companies, or if you will be dealing in handmade products. Since most producers of handcrafts are too small and unsophisticated to do their own exporting, you will need an intermediary to help you. Ecuador, for example, has both private and public handcrafts dealers who export. You should contact both. The private dealers usually have higher profit margins, but the government dealers are usually less efficient. Also, the government handcrafts marketing companies are set up to help the local craftspersons sell their merchandise. They try to pay the producers fair prices, a noble social goal that raises your cost.

As in domestic business deals, you'll be better off choosing suppliers with whom you feel comfortable. Sometimes the chemistry is right, even by mail, and sometimes it is so totally wrong that it is impossible to establish a business relationship based on understanding and trust.

5

Exports: What Comes First, The Product or the Market?

According to marketing theory, you first ascertain a consumer want or need and then create a product to fill it. In exporting, it's more common to start from the product end—to select a product or group of products and begin to identify possible markets.

STARTING WITH THE PRODUCT

If you take the route of selecting products and then looking for potential customers, you should choose products with which you are familiar and that foreign businesses and governments may want to, and be able to, import. A new product, or one that the United States makes better or cheaper than the importing country can, is a good bet. Import control regulations, an important consideration, are generally less strict for consumer necessities and industrial goods than for consumer luxuries.

To which foreign countries, if any, is the product you are interested in being imported? Check international trade statistics, described earlier in this book, or contact the product specialist at the U.S. Department of Commerce in Washington, D.C. Their names and phone numbers change often, but your local office of the Commerce Department should have a current listing. Many trade associations also have international specialists or officers who know something about export activity and potential.

You will want to build a line of related products, from one to ten manufacturers, in order to make larger sales to the same customers. Later chapters tell you how to identify, contact, and reach agreements with your new suppliers.

Product Modification

In most cases, American products face the same kinds of obstacles abroad that foreign products face here. They often fail to meet consumer preferences or legal requirements, but American manufacturers are reluctant to make product modifications unless you can persuade them that the time and expense are justified by potential export profits.

Details of specifications such as electrical characteristics for each country are in the Dun and Bradstreet *Exporters Encyclopedia*, or you can get them from the U.S. Department of Commerce (USDC) *country* specialists in Washington, D.C. Your local USDC office can give you the current names and telephone numbers. For foreign legal requirements, such as product health and safety laws, see these same sources plus consular officers of the countries in which you are interested.

Products such as pharmaceuticals must usually be tested by foreign government laboratories even though they satisfy all American requirements. This is true even in the least developed countries where medical laboratories may be inadequate. Several countries require instructions and information on packages to be written in the local language, and many prohibit the sale of mechanical and electrical products unless spare parts and service facilities are available locally.

Even simple products, such as cigarettes and toothpaste, may have to be modified to suit foreign consumers. For example, packages may have to be made smaller or colored differently. There are entire books that describe blunders, mostly lack of adaptation, made by large American firms in introducing products for sale in foreign countries.

Testing Product Ideas

An inexpensive way to test a product is to solicit the opinions of several people in the USA who are natives of the potential market countries. This won't tell you for sure that a product will sell abroad, but it may reveal characteristics that should be changed. Sometimes there is no need to change the product itself, but only its name or package or what is said about it. Refrigerators can be (and are) sold in Alaska (to keep food from freezing in the winter) and snowplows in the Middle East (to clear away sand).

When you have selected a product, identified the countries where you may be able to sell it, checked it for conformity with the laws of those countries, and tested it with nationals from those countries, there is little more that can be done in the United States. You will then have to expose the product to foreign markets by going yourself, by hiring a foreign market research firm, or by locating foreign agents and distributors and sending them samples. You may be able to find representatives abroad who will get a lot of valuable information for you with your only cost being samples. In the process you may make actual sales, which of course is the most valid test of all.

STARTING WITH THE MARKET

Suppose, on the other hand, you decide to start with foreign demand and locate suppliers. From *Trade Channel* and other publications, or by placing advertisements in foreign journals such as *The Straits Times* (a newspaper of Singapore and Malaysia), you can identify specific needs of foreign importers. Another way to find needs is to subscribe to publications of the U.S. Agency for International Development, United Nations Development Program, World Bank, and the regional development banks. Their newsletters list products that are needed overseas, the purchase of which is financed by international grants or loans.

For example, a recent *A.I.D. Procurement Information Bulletin* (free from the Office of Business Relations, Agency for International Development, Department of State, Washington, D.C. 20523) informed readers that the government of Guatemala intended to purchase 750 chalkboards and 800 easels. It gave the address to contact for more information, which in this instance was free. You should know, however, that the red tape involved in sales financed by international organizations is long and intricate. You may even have to provide a "standby letter of credit"—a document that allows the foreign importer to take money from you by simply declaring that you haven't performed adequately under the contract.

When you have information about an item needed abroad, and think you can be the supplier, you should first contact the importer. Tell the importer you have his request, are preparing your quotation, and ask any questions that will give you useful information. This simple step also tells the foreign importer that you exist so he won't be completely unfamiliar with you and your company's name.

Lining Up Suppliers

Next you must identify potential suppliers of the product or products in question. There are many directories of manufacturers in the United States, the most comprehensive of which is the *Thomas Register of American Manufacturers* (available in nearly every library). In this series of books you can find companies that are able to supply the needed item(s) with their locations, telephone numbers, and approximate sizes. You should contact four or five for each product.

If there is plenty of time, you can contact these firms by mail, but often there will be an early bid deadline and you will have to use the telephone. You may want to get an 800 number directory or call 800 information (1-800-555-1212), because many large firms now have unpublicized 800 numbers. By letter or by phone, your story will be essentially the same: "I'm with an exporting company located in _____ . I have an inquiry for (chalkboards) from (Guatemala). Are you interested in having me quote on your products?" Of course you don't say who the customer is, because the manufacturing firm may then contact the customer directly.

If your communication is by letter it should be addressed to "Export Sales Manager." If by phone you will need to speak with someone in the Export Sales Department or, if there is none, the Sales or Marketing Department. If the person is interested in having you quote on his products, you should ask for two copies of the company's catalog and export price list. Many firms have established export prices that are lower than domestic selling prices for several reasons, including hard competition in world markets. You should also discuss whether you will work as a merchant or an agent in your relationship with each manufacturer. Some firms will not let you work as a merchant because they will want to arrange for the international shipping. That way they can be sure you won't buy the product for one country and then sell it to a country in which the firm is already represented, or even sell it in the United States to the detriment of the firm's established distributors. Also, if the transaction is quite large, you may have to work as an agent to avoid paying for the merchandise or international freight.

Some manufacturers will not be interested in exporting. They may be willing to cooperate if you plan to work as a merchant and take care of the export details, but not if they have those responsibilities, which will be theirs if you are just an agent. Other firms will not let you quote on their products at all, or will give you only certain products or specify only certain countries you can export to. For example, Lee and Levis are already represented in most of the world. Your quotations on their products may be limited to Chad, Afghanistan, and a few other countries in which it is very hard to sell American goods. In some cases, you may have to deal with a producer's exclusive export agent or even with a wholesaler.

The manufacturer's export prices may already have your commission or profit margin built in. If not, you will have to add it on. In some cases, you can increase your earnings by getting export prices with built-in commissions or margins and then charging your customers a bit extra. In effect, you will be paid double. The manufacturer's prices may be "FOB factory" or they may include transportation to a port or airport. In either case you will probably have to add all costs to the destination in order to deliver a quotation that will let the importer compare his cost from you with his cost from other suppliers around the world. Finally, you will need to send your price quotation and catalog pages to the importer, along with a letter explaining the benefits of buying from you.

Protecting Your Interest

If the foreign importer is a private company, it may try to contact your supplier directly to eliminate your commission or profit. You can try to protect yourself against this by sending only photocopies of catalog pages with the manufacturer's identification removed, but it is better to have a written agreement with the manufacturer. He should promise that if his (chalkboards) are sold to your customer in (Guatemala) within a specified number of days, you will be compensated. This kind of written agreement from an honest firm will give you a high degree of protection.

I was once with a small company in the Boston area that acted as an import merchant for books from Africa and an export agent for American books and school supplies. We received an inquiry from a company in Haiti about desks for schools. After contacting a number of potential suppliers, we chose to quote on products of a company named Adirondack Chair. This manufacturer agreed to pay us an agent's commission. We sent catalogs and prices and, after only a few phone calls and letters, the Haitian importer wrote an order to Adirondack Chair and mailed it to us. Of course we forwarded it immediately and followed up by phone to make sure it was acceptable to the manufacturer. The goods were delivered, the importer paid, and the manufacturer promptly remitted our commission. What we do not know is whether the manufacturer made any subsequent sales to the same customer. Since there was no agreement that we be paid commissions on subsequent sales, neither principal had an obligation to tell us of any that might have occurred.

6

Choosing Target Markets
And Finding Customers

This chapter is a mini-course in marketing, especially for small-scale importers and exporters. It explores ways of getting into domestic and foreign markets on a limited budget. It also attacks the myth that anyone can get rich in a hurry selling imported products by mail order.

WHY SOMEONE WOULD BUY FROM YOU

In today's world nearly every industry is in a *buyer's market.* Buyers in U.S. department stores already have access to all the products they need, and they receive dozens of new offers every week. Why then would they buy from you? I once visited, in Tegucigalpa, Honduras, a successful selling agent for imported products. His in-box was piled high with letters from would-be suppliers in many countries, and half of them had not even been opened. This agent already had all the product lines he could handle. Why, then, would he represent you in his country?

The answer to both questions is the same—to make more money. You need to be able to offer the domestic or foreign buyer a good product that he can't get from anyone else (remember the concept of exclusivity) or to offer him a better product, a lower price, longer credit, or superior service. Lacking all of these, you need to give a superb sales talk, or find a good friend who is also a buyer. Finally, you must be able to do an excellent job of marketing.

As an example of a successful import situation, a good friend of mine was one of the first Americans to bring cloisonné artware from mainland China when trade was resumed in the early 1970s. He practically had a U.S. monopoly on these beautiful products, and of course he was able to sell them at a substantial markup.

A company in Long Island, New York does a good business exporting replicas of European statues *to Europe!* One reason for this small firm's success may be that it never occurred to Europeans to sell replicas of their own statuary, and the American firm was clever enough to see the opportunity. A second reason is their close attention to distribution. The company worked hard to select top-notch distributors and to support their selling activities.

A successful importation may be of an idea rather than a whole product. Small animals made of clay have been available in Mexico for many years. They cost almost nothing and are attractive curios; wet the animal, fill it with water, coat it with seeds, put it in a sunny window, and the little creature sprouts a fine green coat. A few years ago, someone in the United States made up a package of the clay animal, a packet of seeds, and printed instructions. He christened the animal "Chia Pet," placed it in mass-merchandise stores, and advertised it. Chia Pet sold well at retail for about $11.00, an excellent example of how an imaginative marketing approach can be profitable for a product that has been available for a long time but whose potential had not been discovered.

Many efforts end in failure. A person I know well began to work as a U.S. selling agent for towels from Turkey.

First he had trouble getting the manufacturer to produce according to American specifications, and second he was not able to offer buyers anything better than what they were already receiving. He finally abandoned the project.

I don't recommend that you try to bribe buyers, but you should know that you may be competing against vendors who do. In mid-1985 there was a major story in the press about large bribes being paid by foreign exporters to American department store buyers. One of the foreign exporters "blew the whistle" because he thought the bribery had become excessive. It's generally considered all right to offer buyers small gifts on important occasions or do small favors for them.

MARKETING IMPORTS AS AN AGENT

If you decide to work as a selling agent for foreign products, you'll need to find buyers who are willing and able to handle the actual importing. That means you can contact anyone who imports. Here are some examples, some favorable and some not so favorable, of how the process works.

There is a respectable trade in Egyptian paintings on papyrus. Dr. Rageb's Papyrus Institute in Cairo has an agent in the midwest who is responsible for the United States. Since Dr. Rageb's papyrus paintings are the very best, this agent can contact stores that sell high quality antiques and artworks. The number of such stores is not large, and they can be identified from trade sources or from yellow pages phone directories. In this case, the agent does not have to be concerned about who is the final consumer. Also, since this kind of product is usually transported by air mail, any art dealer or museum gift shop should be able to perform the import function.

Two clients of mine decided to become import agents for a new kind of industrial floor sweeper made in northern

Europe. This is a product that can not be imported economically in small quantities. To be practical, several should be brought in at a time, and each one costs thousands of dollars. My clients knew they should contact industrial distributors or end-users that could pay for, sell, or use several machines. Since they weren't likely to make sales without showing the actual product, they imported a sample themselves. They then found an industrial equipment distributor to demonstrate the unit to potential users. As of this writing they have made some sales, but have found that large orders will be hard to get until they become known in the industry.

Recently a friend of mine in New Jersey wanted to become a selling agent for frozen shrimp from Brazil and Ecuador. He discovered quickly that the importers of shrimp knew all the South American suppliers, and did not need an agent to help them.

Locating Importers

If you are working as an agent, the best approach is often to identify American companies that are manufacturing or importing products similar to yours and might add yours to their lines. Locating importers is somewhat more difficult than locating manufacturers (as detailed in Chapter 4).

The Journal of Commerce *Directory of U.S. Importers* is the best nationwide listing available, but it includes primarily companies whose main activity is importing. It does not include many firms that are mainly retailers or manufacturers but also import. Your local library may have other directories of importers, or an industrial directory with designations to show companies that import.

In some libraries you can find the *Import Bulletin,* a weekly publication of the *Journal of Commerce* that shows individual shipments with, in most cases, the name and location of the importer. Besides being hard to find, the

Import Bulletin has two serious drawbacks: It is difficult to use and it covers only major sea and land ports. It does not cover minor ports or any airports. You can also buy a computer printout from the *Journal of Commerce* that shows imports of only your product, but the minimum cost is about $1200.

Some specialized industry directories give the names of importing companies. In the food industry, there is a very good one, the *Thomas Grocery Register*, that identifies manufacturers, wholesalers, importers, and brokers of nearly every product sold in supermarkets. You may, however, have to actually contact companies to find out whether they import.

I once assisted a company in South America that manufactured clothing for dolls. No directories showed U.S. importers of doll clothing, but I found that nearly every U.S. doll manufacturer was importing clothing, mostly from the Far East, and the manufacturers were easy to identify. I had no difficulty making appointments with manufacturers, showing them samples, and explaining that if they imported from South America they could save money on customs duties and forget about "jet lag" during and after their buying trips. Several manufacturers gave me samples of products they were then buying from Asia so that the South American firm could examine them and prepare price quotations.

As an import agent you should obtain orders and forward them to your principal overseas. The principal should ship, receive payment, and send your commission. Except in rare instances you should not work as an agent without having a written supply agreement.

Agenting for Industrial Products

The best definition of an industrial product is anything that is sold to an organization rather than to an individual.

If you buy pencils to use in your home, they are consumer goods. If you buy the same pencils to use in your office or factory, they are industrial goods.

Importers of industrial products usually sell direct to industrial users or to industrial distributors or wholesalers, including mail wholesalers. Following are some examples of importing industrial products.

A young Nigerian imported *unfinished* bootjacks (almost anything unfinished is an industrial product) to the United States and needed to sell them. At my suggestion, he traveled to Texas and "kicked around" in footwear shops until he had seen a number of bootjacks and copied the names and locations of their manufacturers. He then contacted the manufacturers and sold the bootjacks. There was a major problem, however. He imported his stock without first looking into the U.S. resale price, and he took a loss on the transactions.

I also worked briefly with a woman who wanted to import cut sapphires from Thailand. Semi-precious stones are like bulk commodities in that it's hard to use product differentiation to command a higher price. Comparable qualities fetch comparable amounts of money. Since this importer did not want to go to the trouble and expense of establishing a showroom, getting listed in directories, and selling directly to jewelry manufacturers, she had either to sell to gemstone wholesalers or find a unique distribution channel, such as one of the companies that retails stones by direct mail. She chose to contact wholesalers. Since most wholesalers in this trade are themselves importers, she could sell only by having a direct supplier who could send her small quantities by air mail at the lowest possible cost.

I once worked for a Jordanian exporter of very good quality mineral bath salts who wanted to sell in the U.S. market. I discovered that this simple industrial product was quickly converted into a consumer good. There were only a handful of importers, and they packaged the product themselves and distributed it to health food stores. They also sold the salts in bulk to other companies that were doing their own packaging and distributing through various means, including mail order catalogs and "holistic" health fairs.

The preceding examples are for industrial products that can be imported on a small scale. If you intend to work on a larger scale, such as importing buses from Brazil, you will need professional help to work out the financing and other aspects of your business plan.

IMPORTING FOR STOCK

As an import merchant you need to be careful about importing goods to stock for subsequent sale. A large portion of what you import should already have been sold. An individual visiting in South America became enchanted with some handcarved wooden doors. He just *knew* they would be easy to sell, and he imported $5000 worth. The last I heard his garage was filled with handcarved wooden doors, and his car had little chance of getting in from the cold.

MARKETING IMPORTS THROUGH MAIL ORDER

The Mellinger company in California has done very well helping people go into the business of importing and selling by mail order. I've never seen statistics, but my guess is that only a small percentage of Mellinger's customers make substantial profits. I've found that for an inexperienced person to plunge into mail order is even worse than shooting craps at Las Vegas. The odds are against you.

One mail order option is to buy a mailing list from a

company such as Dunhill, prepare your mailing, send it out (two mailings to the same people), and hope for results. However, even the best lists are quickly out of date and both individuals and businesses are now deluged with offers in their mailboxes. Why would someone order from your tiny catalog when the same mail delivery brings expensive full-color catalogs from well known companies? Your chance of covering your costs with just one or a few items is small unless you can find exactly the right list of names and addresses for your particular product.

A second mail order option is for you to advertise in newspapers or magazines (at least three issues of the same publication). You can ask respondents to order immediately, or to contact you for more information. Advertising in general interest publications is unlikely to pay off (although *The Wall Street Journal,* for example, carries ads over and over again for products like fresh fruit that do not seem to be high potential mail order items). But if you have a specialized product and can find a publication aimed at precisely your target market, this kind of marketing will work well. I once met an importer of Scottish bagpipe regalia who told me there was only one magazine that was read by bagpipe enthusiasts in the United States. He advertised in that publication, and his ads paid off.

Once you have designed your advertisement, it will usually cost at least a hundred dollars to have it prepared for printing. An exceptional company that you *must* know about is the Trapkus Art Studio, 5120 11th Avenue C in Moline, Illinois, which produces creative small ads for about $50 each. The only problem with Trapkus is that they're not true to their word—they'll promise your advertisement in two or three weeks, and you'll receive it in *one.*

A third mail order option is to import your product and sell an established mail order company on the idea of including it in their catalog. Save all the catalogs that come to you and try to identify firms selling products similar to yours. Also there are sources, such as the *Facts on File Directory of Mail Order Catalogs*, that will give you names and addresses of mail order companies. Contact the companies you are interested in, by mail or phone, describe your product, and ask if they would consider putting it in their catalog. If the buyer you are speaking with is interested, he or she will probably ask for a sample and prices. (Your sample will not be returned unless you provide a self-addressed label and offer to accept the shipment collect from a parcel service such as UPS, and sometimes even that will not be sufficient.)

Professional mail order firms place a high value on every square inch of every catalog page and are very selective about the products they include. Also, they keep their own inventories to a minimum. They won't want to take a chance on putting an item in a catalog, getting orders for it, and then finding out that you do not have the product. Therefore they will probably insist that you have a substantial inventory in the United States. This means investment on your part, and, of course, risk.

MARKETING IMPORTS THROUGH DEPARTMENT STORES

Suppose you think your product will sell well in the major department stores. First you need to consider which stores sell to the kinds of customers who would want what you have to offer. A client took wool sweaters to a store called Mays, and found they were too high in quality. He then went to Sachs Fifth Avenue and found the same sweaters were too low in quality. He had to identify appropriate stores for his product.

Department store buyers are specialized, professional, and usually hard to contact. Macy's in New York, for example, has different buyers for "Collector Separates," "Clubhouse Separates," "Expression Blouses," "Better Petite Sportswear," "Moderate Petite Sportswear," and more. You can usually at least get a buyer's secretary by calling a store's main office and asking for the buyer for your type of product. You can also find buyers' names and telephone numbers in books such as *Stores of the World*, although these are already partly outdated by the time they're published. More accurate sources are books from The Salesman's Guide Inc., 1140 Broadway, New York, NY 10001. From outside New York, their toll-free number is 800-223-1797. Salesman's Guide publications cover the New York City rag trade (apparel) in great detail, but they also cover apparel and mass merchandise stores nationwide. Other publishers of directories of stores and buyers are Department Store Guide Inc., Merchandiser Publishing Company, and Phelon, Sheldon & Marsar Inc., all in New York City.

Some stores have "open buying days," when vendors can just wait in line, without an appointment, to show their products. This gives you an easy way to get your foot in the door, but you should call before you go because buyers are not always in on their open buying days. When you get in to see a buyer, either on his or her open buying day or by appointment, you should be ready to answer all questions. If a buyer asks you what kind of loom the cloth in a blouse was made on, you must know the answer or come across as unprofessional. The buyer can probably tell just by the look and feel. Also remember that buyers for big stores have worked hard to get to where they are and don't want to risk their reputations by buying from an untried vendor. What if you don't deliver on time or the quality is wrong? To get a department store buyer to cooperate, you must have a very attractive product, a competitive price, and an excellent sales presentation.

MARKETING IMPORTS THROUGH SMALL STORES

You may feel that your product will sell well in boutiques, hardware stores, pharmacies, or other specialty retail outlets. Identify a number of likely stores, call to make appointments with the buyers, and try to get them to place small orders. If you can get orders for perhaps 100 of your products, you may feel safe in bringing in a shipment of two or three hundred. A woman interested in importing high quality wooden furniture from France began by locating a few stores that sold products similar to hers and persuading them each to stock a few pieces. Her goal was to sell enough furniture to fill a forty-foot shipping container.

Often you can just walk into small stores and ask to see the buyers. If a buyer is not present, find out his or her name, hours, whether you need an appointment, and if so how to make one. There are even some stores where you can walk in and, if the buyer likes your product and its price, get a small order on the spot. If you have the merchandise with you the buyer may pay you then, in cash or by check.

In chain operations, the buying is usually done centrally, and you will need to find out where the buyers are located and which one handles your kind of merchandise, and call for an appointment. Most buyers are busy and won't want to see you unless they are quite interested. They usually will ask you to send your catalog and prices. Here you will have a problem. It will cost you at least $500 to have a catalog page made in color. Instead you might choose to have a professional photographer take a good color picture for you. One shot and 25 copies should cost just over a hundred dollars. Have the photograph printed on a full-size sheet of paper, type in the item number and name, and the dimensions and weight if relevant, and you have a catalog page. You can type the price on the same page or put it in your cover letter, or if you have several models, you can prepare a separate list of prices. Your price list could mention your minimum order quantity, any discounts for large orders or prompt payment, and whether delivery charges are included.

If you succeed in placing your product in a few stores, and it moves off the shelves, you will be ready to start selling in earnest. Since you won't physically be able to call on stores over a wide area, you'll need to work either through wholesalers or with manufacturers' representatives. You can find wholesalers in the telephone yellow pages, in some trade directories, or simply by asking retailers of products similar to yours which wholesalers they buy from. Approach them by phone with your product idea. Sales to wholesalers are usually large, but they negotiate hard on price and credit terms and they, not you, will own the retail customers.

Your other option is to sell directly to retail stores through manufacturers' representatives. Many *reps* are listed in the yellow pages, but not by product. Many libraries have directories of manufacturers' representatives, but none is complete. Sometimes you can find them in trade directories or by speaking with retailers, and an easy (though slow) way is to *advertise* for them. Trade magazines have classified pages in which you can advertise inexpensively for representatives. An ad I placed for a client said simply, *"REPS WANTED* for new line of clocks from Taiwan. Contact . . ."* Of course these independent businesspersons need something with which to sell, and you will have to provide them with catalogs and/or product samples. When one of your reps gets an order you will ship to his customer, collect, and send him a commission.

MARKETING IMPORTS THROUGH FLEA MARKETS

In the United States, door-to-door sales are declining, house parties are holding their own, but flea markets are growing like crabgrass (or sunflowers, depending on your point of view). People seem to love the experience of walking from vendor to vendor, bargaining for their purchases, and not being charged sales tax. Flea marketing is now an established industry with its own publications, associations, and wholesalers. To find these wholesalers, try asking flea market dealers who they buy from. Often they'll tell you if they believe you are an importer and not a potential competitor.

You can also get into the flea market channel through at least two magazines. These are *Marketers Forum*, 160 Eileen Way, Syosset, New York 11791 and *National Flea Market Dealer*, 11565 Ridgewood Circle North, Seminole, Florida 33542. In either of these, you can find wholesalers advertising to flea market dealers, and you can place your own advertisements if you want to. This is a very price conscious marketing channel. You may have to settle for a lower price than if you sell through the regular wholesaler-retailer channel.

Often the same wholesalers who sell to flea markets also reach street vendors, house party dealers, and other kinds of nontraditional retailers.

MARKETING EXPORTS

Except for whether or not you handle procedures such as transportation, insurance, documentation, and payment, the job of marketing exports is not much different whether you are acting as an agent or as a merchant. In either case, you have to select and test products, select market countries, find agents and/or importers in each country, and support your agents or promote to the importers. I'm using the word promotion in its broad sense to include advertising, sales promotion, public relations and publicity, and personal selling.

Chapter 4 discussed ways of selecting and testing products and selecting market countries. International marketing textbooks go into other ways of selecting countries, such as using market indicators for each product. If you want to export nurses' caps, look for countries with large and growing numbers of nurses and few or no local cap producers. Of course, this technique isn't foolproof. You may, for example, find a country with many nurses, no local suppliers, and only one small problem—the president's brother is importing your product from his cousin in Europe. The problem could be even simpler: Nurses there may not be required to *wear* caps. These are the realities of international marketing.

There are many good sources of information for market indicators. One of the easiest to use is the *World Development Report*, published each year by the World Bank in Washington, D.C.

Exporting to End-Users

Once you have chosen countries to which your products can legally be imported and in which they seem likely to be competitive in both price and quality, you must decide whether to sell to end-users or to intermediaries and whether or not to use foreign selling agents. There are a few cases of direct exports of American consumer goods. For example, an exporter in New York City sold high quality women's wear directly to consumers in other countries. She could sell only in countries with well-developed postal systems because she depended on the mails to deliver both her promotional literature and her products.

Industrial goods are often exported directly to end users. In the case of popcorn, which is an explosive product in some countries, small poppers for the home go through normal consumer goods channels. Commercial popcorn poppers like those on street corners and in movie theatres are usually exported to foreign importer/distributors or importer/wholesalers. Larger industrial poppers are often sold directly to the companies that will use them.

On a larger scale, a Chinese businessman once asked me to contact American firms that could supply complete plants for producing sanitary napkins. There were very few such firms, and they would not export to anyone except an actual end user. One of these firms had named a small company in New York, a thousand miles from the factory, to act as its exclusive export agent.

If your product is expensive and likely to be exported directly to end users, you can identify these potential customers from foreign industrial directories. You can then contact them by mail and follow up with personal visits. It will usually take several trips to a market to sell directly to end users.

Using Foreign Distributors and Agents

If you plan to sell to foreign import merchants, wholesalers, retailers, or industrial distributors, you must go through the process of identifying and contacting these organizations. To find retailers try the book mentioned earlier, *Stores of the World*. Foreign wholesalers and industrial distributors are harder to identify. You may find directories that will help, and the U.S. Department of Commerce has a very useful computerized file, the *Foreign Traders Index*. A more direct way is to travel to a country and make inquiries of chambers of commerce and of people in the trade.

In many cases, especially if your budget is limited, you'll find it hard to make direct contact with foreign organizations that will agree to import your products. Your solution may be to contract with agents. The job of a foreign selling agent is to locate companies that can import your product, persuade them to do so, get orders, and send them to you. The agent can also tell you of needed product modifications, new market opportunities, or increased competition, can give you credit information on new customers (but *you* must make the credit decisions), and can give you data such as the prices at which your products are being sold and kinds of end users who are buying them. They work for commissions, payable by their principals, which vary greatly but are usually in the range of 5–10 percent of sales.

The U.S. Department of Commerce can help you find foreign representatives through its Agent/Distributor Service. For around $50 per country, U.S. commercial officers will identify and give you information on three potential agents or distributors. You can also find representatives by participating in foreign trade exhibits, by media advertising, or through direct mail.

There are a large number of trade exhibits overseas, and the U.S. Department of Commerce as well as some state and local governments help American exporters participate. Often you don't need to send personnel, only your products, and in a few cases you can simply exhibit your catalogs or other sales literature. Look for specialized, not general, fairs that are open only to the trade. The main disadvantage to exhibiting is its cost in both time and money. Most fairs will cost you at least $1000 for the space and another $1000 for related expenses, not counting shipping your products, product literature, air fare, hotel, exhibit personnel, and miscellaneous expenses.

If you choose to advertise for agents or distributors you can use a variety of international, regional, or local publications, some of which I have already discussed. During the days of rising oil prices, for example, a number of new publications were started in the Middle East. In most cases, the reason wasn't that Arab businessmen needed more reading matter, but that exporting companies needed more places in which to advertise. I remember seeing in *Arab News*, an English-language newspaper published in Saudi Arabia, a display advertisement for electronic components. The address and phone number in the ad were not in Saudi Arabia, but in Singapore.

Unfortunately you may not automatically be able to attract the foreign representatives you would like to have. You must offer them some incentive. Like any other businesspeople, they will be motivated by research results that show substantial sales and profit potential from your products.

Your own main criterion for choosing foreign agents or distributors is how well equipped they are to do the job you need done. If you are exporting electronic products that will need servicing, your distributor must have service facilities and trained personnel. If your product is a line of expensive clothing that will be sold to high-quality department stores, your agent needs good contacts among the buyers of this kind of store.

Choosing the right agent or distributor in the beginning is critical. If you select one who has a poor reputation in his or her own country, your reputation will suffer, and if the representative does not sell your product effectively, you will be wasting time and money. Also, if you pick the wrong agent or distributor, local laws may make it nearly impossible for you to get rid of him. I once heard of an American exporter who traveled to Saudi Arabia and fired his local agent and was detained at the airport on his way home by the accusation that he had violated Saudi law.

Once there is a mutual decision that an agent or distributor will handle your products on a continuing basis, you will want to have a written agreement with him. The information on agreements in Chapter 7 applies to these, except that now *you* will be the supplier. You will need to determine or negotiate your agent's commission or distributor's mark-up and other aspects of your business relationship.

BUILDING YOUR SALES

On the Import Side

Unless you are making very large commodity deals (a business that is extremely hard for a newcomer to get into), your objective should not be to make isolated sales. You will want to develop ongoing business relationships. Your first import sales will probably be small trial orders. This is because buyers aren't likely to give you large orders until they are sure you can deliver as promised. These small orders are to your advantage, even though you may lose money on them. They give you the chance to test your import procedures and make sure they work satisfactorily before investing a large amount of money. You don't want to have a million dollars worth of meat from Spain setting on the docks in Norfolk, Virginia, only to find out it's illegal to import meat from Spain (which is the case). Better try your system with a smaller quantity.

Once you have trial orders and the goods are in stores, you need to follow up. Don't let the members of your distribution channel be walls that separate you from the end user. You should know where your merchandise is, how it is being displayed, how much it is selling for, how it is being promoted, if at all, and who is buying it. You may even want to spend some time in a store that sells your products and *observe* the people who walk by. See whether they notice your product, whether they pick it up, and whether they buy it. You can ask questions to see what the store's customers think of the product, its package, and its price.

Your objective is to find ways to increase sales of the product and increase profits. My friend who imported the cloisonné from China also brought in a few large expensive cloisonné vases that were really museum pieces. She loaned these vases to certain stores, which agreed to insure them and pay transportation both ways, to build traffic and increase sales. Many importers of industrial products voluntarily spend time with their customers to make sure that there is no problem, that everyone is satisfied, and that there are no obstacles to repeat orders. You may decide to help with advertising or hire a public relations firm to generate publicity, which can often sell a product more effectively and less expensively than advertising.

On the Export Side

On the export side, it is important to make sure your foreign representatives *understand your product thoroughly.* Send information, write them, call them, and if possible visit them. At least one company gives three types of training to its foreign distributors—product training, sales training, and business management training.

You should do as much as possible to *motivate* your foreign representatives. If you're an agent, try to get your principal to involve them in price discount offers, sales contests, etc. It's surprising how many American manufacturers work hard to motivate their distributors in the United States and practically forget about the ones they have abroad. If you're an export merchant rather than an agent, motivate your foreign representatives with frequent correspondence, an occasional gift, a visit now and then, and above all, information and ideas that will help them sell. For example, suppose you are exporting security cameras and you read of a sharp increase in bank robberies in Belgium. Your distributor is selling the cameras to parking lot firms but does not realize they will work very well in banks. You can not only tell him, but offer to help him develop a new brochure aimed specifically at banking executives.

One last point is that your foreign representatives will stop selling for you very quickly if they get the idea you are incompetent or are not being fair with them. Try hard to answer all correspondence quickly and make every shipment right, and on time. If you turn down an agent's order because of the customer's poor credit, explain your decision in detail and offer alternatives, such as part payment in advance. If you receive an order from a country in which you have an exclusive agent, make sure he receives his commission. He will probably find out about the order, and he may even have arranged it just to test your honesty.

7

Communications, Credit and Other Concerns

Suppose you ask an exporter in Taiwan for a quotation on his products and he sends you the following telex message:

RCA AUG 10 0343
226078 AEGIS UR

ATTN: KENNETH D. WEISS

RYL 7/29 RE A-6825 AUTO FLOOR MATS, RUBBER WI TEXTILE BACKING, SIZE 26X18 INCH PACKED 36 PCS/ CTN(1.95 CUFT/22KGS) AT FOB US# 4.21/PC BASED MIN QTY 500 PCS OR 3.89/PC IF QTY OVER 1,000 PCS, APPROX SEAFT TO N.Y. #0.23/PC, SHPMT W/IN 45 DAYS AFT L/C RECD.

RGDS, PETER CHEN
68934 AUTOPART

DURATION 111 SECS LISTED 06:50 EST 08/10/86

This is a paraphrase of an actual message, and you must be able to understand it exactly if you are going to do business with Mr. Chen. It seems like a foreign language, but it is not; it is "cabelese," a kind of abbreviated form of

English developed when most international correspondence was by cable, and each word was expensive. It has carried over into telex messages.

This message was sent through RCA on August 10 to my telex address, 226078. AEGIS UR is the answerback code. Translated, the message says:

Regarding your letter of July 29 about model A-6825 automobile floor mats, rubber with textile backing, size 26 x 18 inches, packed 36 pieces to a carton (a carton is 1.95 cubic feet and weighs 22 kilograms) at Free On Board US $4.21 per piece, based on a minimum quantity of 500 pieces, or $3.89 per piece if the quantity is over 1,000 pieces, approximate sea freight to New York is $0.23 per piece and shipment will be made within 45 days after your letter of credit is received.

This telex came from Peter Chen, telex number 68934, answerback AUTOPART. It took 111 seconds to transmit and reached RCA in the United States at 6:50 A.M., August 10.

Go back and read the original telex again and see how much you have learned. The message begins by saying which letter of mine it refers to. It gives the product's model number, description, size, and number of pieces per carton. It gives the size and weight of each carton which might be needed to calculate freight rates, the prices at various quantities, the approximate shipping cost, and the number of days needed to ship. "FOB" is the suggested shipping term, and "L/C" is the suggested payment term. This chapter explains various payment terms, and Chapter 8 deals with the shipping terms.

CREDIT INFORMATION ON SUPPLIERS AND CUSTOMERS

Whether you import or export, as an agent or as a merchant, you are acting as an intermediary. You must be sure that both your suppliers and your customers are legitimate businesses that can and will fulfill their obligations to you. As a merchant you need to devote extra attention to your customers because, if they do not pay, you will be the one who loses. The only time a merchant does not have to do a credit check is when he is selling for cash in advance or for an equally secure means of payment.

Bank Trade References

The least expensive way to check on a firm's credit worthiness is to ask for its bank and trade references. Ask your own bank to check your supplier's or customer's bank reference. You should receive a report that tells you how many years the account has been open, the approximate average balance, the amount of the credit line that is open, and in general terms how satisfactory the account has been to the bank. That is not a great deal of information, but it will help. If you are checking on a foreign business and need information quickly, ask your bank to communicate by telex, the charge for which will be billed to you. Otherwise the bank will use mail, which will take approximately a month.

To check with trade references, design a model letter. For a customer who has given you other suppliers as references, your letter can read something like this:

Dear Sir or Madam:

The company named below has listed you as a credit reference. We will be very grateful if you will answer the questions at the bottom of this page and return this letter in the enclosed self-addressed, stamped envelope. Your prompt attention to this request will help us make an appropriate credit decision. We will be pleased to assist you in the same way if the occasion should ever arise. Thank you very much.

Sincerely,
(your signature)

Name and Address of Applicant: (You will fill this in) _____

_____

_____

Number of years you have sold to this company: _____
Highest recent balance: _____
Current outstanding balance: _____
Terms you extend this company: _____
Payment record: Discounts ( ) 30 days ( ) 60 days ( ) Over 60 ( )
Your rating of account: Excellent ( ) Good ( ) Fair ( ) Poor ( )
Additional comments: _____

_____

Your name: _____ Title: _____ Date: _____

If you are checking on a potential supplier, the letter will be almost the same, but the questions will be something like this:

Number of years you have dealt with this vendor: _____
Please comment on:
—Size of order supplier can fill: _____
—Adherence to shipping schedules: _____
—Accuracy in filling orders: _____
—Any problems experienced: _____
Other comments: _____
Your Name: _____ Title: _____ Date: _____

Nearly all companies will answer this kind of letter if it looks professional and is accompanied by a stamped, self-addressed, return envelope.

Credit Reporting Services

A number of credit reporting services are available to give you information on American suppliers and customers.

Look in the Yellow Pages under "Credit Reporting Agencies." You will find firms that will get you a report on any company or individual for about $40. If you grow and have a need for many credit reports you can use one of the major services, TRW or Dun & Bradstreet. Also, if you are adept at using a personal computer, you can access credit services via some of the computer information companies.

Dun & Bradstreet can also give you information on foreign firms, but the minimum charge is about $120. This fee is for a firm in a friendly, developed country. If you need a report on a firm in the Bhutanese countryside, the charge will be much higher.

There is a U.S. Department of Commerce service that can help you, *World Trader Data Reports.* For about $65 you can buy a report from them on any foreign firm. If there is a current report in Washington on your prospective customer or supplier, you can get it in about two weeks. If there is no current report, the Commerce Department will have one of its foreign representatives prepare one for you, and it will take about two months. The information you get will not be as detailed as in a TRW or D & B report, but it will help you decide whether to deal with the firm in question.

You can also make use of local credit reporting services in most developed countries. You can locate them through foreign chambers of commerce, and you can find these through *Johnson's Worldwide Chamber of Commerce Directory* (in most libraries). In most underdeveloped countries, the credit services are underdeveloped too.

It can be very helpful to visit your potential business partners. If you see your supplier using bald tires on his delivery trucks and patching them with chewing gum, you are in for trouble. If you see your customer using typewriters with worn ribbons, expect the worst.

INTERNATIONAL PAYMENT SYSTEMS AND TERMS

In international trade there are a number of means of payment, each of which has its costs, its advantages, and its risks. The most important are:

- Open account.
- Documents against acceptance.
- Documents against payment.
- Letter of credit.
- Payment in advance.

These means of payment are arrayed in order of *risk*, with open account being the riskiest for the exporter and payment in advance being the riskiest for the importer. Sometimes *consignment* is listed also as a payment term and is placed near the top of the list in terms of risk to the exporter.

Since these payment terms vary with respect to risk, cost, and complexity, and what is best for one party is usually much less desirable for the other, payment terms are negotiated like other aspects of import/export transactions. Unless you understand these methods of payment, you run the risk of simply accepting the one suggested by your foreign suppliers or customers, which is likely to be the one that is the most to their advantage—and the least to yours.

Open Account

International open account transactions are similar to those encountered in domestic U.S. commerce. The exporter ships, and after every shipment or at the end of each month, he sends the importer an invoice. The importer can pay in various ways, such as sending an official check or an international money order. The cost of this method is low, and there is no risk for the importer, but there is no protection for the exporter except that derived from the underlying contract of sale and/or the importer's word and reputation.

Open account is the most widely used method of payment in international trade, but that is because about two thirds of world trade is between affiliated companies: Volkswagen in Germany deals with Volkswagen in the United States, for instance. Since affiliated companies know and trust each other, they have no reason to incur the extra cost for a more secure means of payment.

If you are a small importer, you probably will not get open account terms from a foreign supplier for several years, but you will probably be giving open account to most of your domestic customers. If you are a small exporter, you will often be asked for open account and will have to decide in each case whether to agree. If your customer is Harrods in England, or Nestlé in Switzerland, you are quite safe in agreeing to an open account shipment.

You have to be careful of a little game played by some importers. They start by paying you on secure terms, then switch to open account. They pay promptly. Their orders get a little larger each time and, when you finally ship the big one, the money does not arrive. If you try to collect, it will cost you time and money and you may not be successful.

Documentary Drafts for Collection: Against Acceptance and Against Payment

A draft is an unconditional order in writing, signed by the seller, addressed to a foreign buyer, ordering him to pay the amount of the draft either when it is presented to him or on a specified date in the future.

This system is used almost exclusively in international trade, and you may have heard it referred to by names such as "sight draft," "time draft," "SD/DP," etc.

It works like this: I agree to sell you 100 straw baskets for $900 (expensive baskets), delivered to your door. I ship the baskets to you. I then have my bank (Citibank) prepare a piece of paper that looks something like a bank check. It says, "Pay Citibank $900." Citibank sends this draft to your bank, and the cashier calls you to come in or sends it on to you. You have already received the merchandise, and are an honest person, so you promptly sign the draft and return it to your bank. The cashier takes the money from your account and transfers it to Citibank for my account. Technically, we would not even need a sales agreement. I could just take your name from the telephone directory, send you some merchandise, and have the "draft" sent to your bank. If you signed it, the merchandise would be yours and the money would be mine.

This simple document is called a "draft" or a "bill of exchange." When your bank sends it to you, they are "presenting" it to you. The first time you see it is "first presentation." When you sign the draft and write the word "accepted" across it, you are "accepting it." If you are supposed to pay as soon as the draft is presented to you (as soon as you have sight of it), it is called a "sight draft." If we agree that you do not have to pay immediately, we can make the draft payable any time in the future, usually 30 or 60 days or even up to 180 days or more after sight or after the date of the draft. This is a "time draft" or a "date draft." After the buyer ("drawee" or "signer") accepts it, it becomes a "trade acceptance." The accepting party has the obligation to pay it at maturity.

The risk is all on the exporter for this payment instrument as it has been described so far. You, the importer, can get the merchandise whether you pay or not, and with a time draft you may even be able to sell the merchandise and get paid for it before you have to make payment.

There *is* a way the exporter can control the merchandise so that you cannot obtain it until you accept the draft. This method makes use of a "to order bill of lading." (This document is discussed in more detail in Chapter 9.) When the exporter places the merchandise on a ship or other vehicle for transportation, the ship's captain or his representative signs and gives the exporter a document called a "bill of lading" (an "airwaybill" if it is an air shipment). This document serves, among other things, as title to the merchandise. The person the goods are "consigned" to on the bill of lading can claim them. If the exporter wants you to have the goods without regard to payment, he or she can use a "straight" bill of lading, which means the document shows the goods are consigned directly to you. If the exporter does not want you to have the goods without accepting the draft, it will be a "to order" bill of lading, usually "to order of shipper" (who is the exporter). Using this method, the goods will be delivered to the person designated by the exporter.

Suppose the shipper is in Africa and you are in the United States. The exporter ships the merchandise and delivers a *to order* bill of lading to the bank with other documents, and "endorses" it, either "in blank" or to the bank. The bank sends the documents, including the draft and the bill of lading, to your bank in the United States. When the vessel arrives in port, you receive an "arrival notice" from the carrier. By that time, if all has gone well, your bank has sent you the draft. When you accept the draft and send it back to the bank, the bank endorses the bill of lading to you and gives you the documents. With these, you or your customs broker can claim the goods.

Who bears the risk? If it is a sight draft, both parties do. The seller bears the risk that you will simply refuse to pay or to accept the draft and refuse to claim the goods. While the shipment was en route you may have changed your mind, gone out of business, or gotten a better offer from someone else. The seller can go through legal channels to try to force you to claim the goods, but that will cost time and money and may not be successful. In such a case, the seller must either find another buyer for the goods (in the United States or elsewhere), have them returned, or abandon them. In any case, the exporter is likely to lose money. If the choice is to abandon the goods, they will eventually be sold at a customs auction, and you will probably be there, trying to see how little money you can get them for. At the same time, *you* bear a risk as well. The merchandise may not be the merchandise you ordered, but your money will already have been paid.

When the payment instrument is a *time* draft you have less risk because, if the shipment is not correct, you can instruct your bank not to pay it. The exporter's risk correspondingly is increased (although as a practical matter, it is quite rare for a time draft to be accepted and not paid).

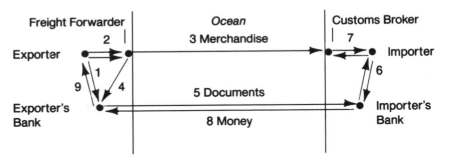

1. *Exporter* fills out form at his bank.
2. Sends goods and documents to freight forwarder.
3. *Freight forwarder* sends merchandise.
4. Sends documents to bank.
5. *Bank* sends them to importer's bank.
6. *Importer* pays or accepts; gets documents.
7. Hands over documents; gets merchandise.
8. Importer's bank transmits funds.
9. Exporter's bank credits his account.

Figure 1. Bill of Exchange Transaction.

MARINE MIDLAND BANK, N.A.
INTERNATIONAL BANKING DEPARTMENT
COLLECTION SECTION
P.O. BOX 2903, CHURCH STREET STATION
NEW YORK, N.Y. 10008

Direct Collection Form

ATTACH THIS COPY TO
SHIPPING DOCUMENTS

(1) Via Airmail To –
MARINE MIDLAND BANK, N.A.
C.P.O. BOX 4369
CHONGRO-KU, SEOUL, KOREA

(2) DATE FEB. 1, 19--

REFER TO
COLLECTION No. DS **4142978**

We enclose the following draft and documents for collection in accordance with the instructions shown below. Please accept this collection FOR ACCOUNT OF MARINE MIDLAND BANK, N.A. as if received directly from them and SEND PAYMENT. ALL REPORTS AND YOUR ACKNOWLEDGEMENT TO MARINE MIDLAND BANK, N.A., INTERNATIONAL BANKING DEPARTMENT, COLLECTION SECTION, P.O. BOX 2903, CHURCH STREET STATION, NEW YORK, N.Y. 10008, MENTIONING THE COLLECTION NO. SHOWN ABOVE. SUBJECT TO UNIFORM RULES FOR THE COLLECTION OF COMMERCIAL PAPER. INTERNATIONAL CHAMBER OF COMMERCE, BROCHURE NO. 322

DRAWERS REFERENCE NUMBER	DATE OF DRAFT	TENOR	AMOUNT
(3) D-123	**(4)** February 1, 19--	**(5)** SIGHT	**(6)** $25,000.00

DRAWER AND ADDRESS **(7)** ABC CO.
000 MAIN ST.
N.Y.C., NY

DRAWEE AND ADDRESS **(8)** XYZ TRADING CO., LTD.
000 KWANCHUL-DONG
CHONGRO-KU, SEOUL, KOREA

(9) BILL OF LADING ORIGINAL DUPLICATE	PARCEL POST RECEIPTS	INSUR CERT'S	INVOICES	CONSULAR INVOICES	PACKING LISTS	WEIGHT CERT'S	CERT'S OF ORIGIN	OTHER DOCUMENTS
3 | 2		1	4	1	1	1	1	NONE

(11) X DELIVER DOCUMENTS AGAINST **(10)** Acceptance [ ] | Payment [X]

(11) X ADVISE BY CABLE   Non Acceptance [X] | Non-Payment [X]

(12) REMIT PROCEEDS BY CABLE   Drawee's Expense [ ] | Our Expense [ ]

(13) X REMIT PROCEEDS BY AIRMAIL

(14) X PROTEST   Non Acceptance [ ] | Non-Payment [X]

(15) DO NOT PROTEST

ALL CHARGES INCLUDING STAMPS, EXCHANGE, TAXES, ETC. FOR DRAWEE'S ACCOUNT PLUS MARINE MIDLAND BANK, N.A. CHARGE OF $30.00 PLUS POSTAGE OF $2.25. TOTAL $32.25.

[X] WAIVE CHARGES IF REFUSED **(20)**

[ ] DO NOT WAIVE CHARGES **(21)**

[X] HOLD FOR ARRIVAL OF MERCHANDISE **(22)**

(16) IF DOLLAR EXCHANGE IS NOT IMMEDIATELY AVAILABLE OR DRAWN AT MATURITY (OR ON PRESENTATION IF DRAWN AT SIGHT) AND IT IS NECESSARY TO PROVISIONALLY ACCEPT LOCAL CURRENCY PENDING AVAILABILITY OF DOLLAR EXCHANGE IT MUST BE DISTINCTLY UNDERSTOOD THAT THE DRAWEE SHALL REMAIN LIABLE FOR ALL EXCHANGE DIFFERENCES. THE DRAFT MUST NOT BE SURRENDERED TO DRAWEES UNTIL FINAL PAYMENT IN U.S. DOLLAR EXCHANGE

(17) ALLOW A DISCOUNT OF   IF PAID

(18) COLLECT INTEREST AT THE RATE OF   % FROM

(19) IN CASE OF NEED REFER TO
AB KOREA CO.
123 KWANCHUL-DONG
CHONGRO-KU, SEOUL, KOREA

OTHER INSTRUCTIONS

WHO IS EMPOWERED BY US: TO ACT FULLY ON OUR BEHALF I.E. AUTHORIZE REDUCTIONS EXTENSIONS FREE DELIVERY WAIVING OF PROTESTS ETC	WHO MAY ASSIST IN OBTAINING ACCEPTANCE OR PAYMENT OF DRAFT AS DRAWN. BUT IS NOT TO ALTER ITS TERMS IN ANY WAY

FROM **(23)** ABC CO.
(DRAWER'S NAME)
Signature
AUTHORIZED SIGNATURE

SEE REVERSE SIDE FOR ADDITIONAL INSTRUCTIONS

(24) $ $25,000.00

(25) Date FEB. 1, 19--   No. **4142978**

(26) ~~DAYS AFTER~~ sight   of this SOLE BILL OF EXCHANGE

pay to the order of MARINE MIDLAND BANK, N.A.

(27) TWENTY-FIVE THOUSAND US DOLLARS

Value received and charge the same to account of

(28) To XYZ TRADING CO., LTD.   **(29)**

000 KWANCHUL-DONG

CHONGRO-KU, SEOUL, KOREA   **(30)** *Signature*
A.B.C. Co.

SOLE BILL OF EXCHANGE

Figure 2. **Documentary Collection.** (Reprinted from *Introduction to International Banking Services,* 1983 Edition, page 13, Published by Marine Midland Bank. Reprinted with permission.) Numbers 1–30 indicate features of the document.

103

In sum, the documentary draft is a simple payment instrument, initiated by the exporter, that goes through banking channels but is not guaranteed by the banks. It can be used for transactions of any size and is often favored for those in the range of about $500 to $2000 between companies that know and trust each other. There is risk for both parties with a sight draft and for the exporter with a time draft. The cost is low, usually about $40 for the exporter and the same for the importer, and normally each party in the deal pays his own charges.

Figures 1 and 2 show the steps involved and the collection instrument.

Letter of Credit

The most talked about payment method in international trade is the "commercial documentary letter of credit." "Commercial" means it is used in a business transaction, and "documentary" means it is payable upon presentation of specified documents. The letter of credit is commonly known as an "LC." It has many variations and can be used in domestic as well as in international trade.

As an illustration, an exporter in Africa sells you 100 baskets and the price is $4000 (obviously they are made of gold-plated straw). Since the seller wants to be sure of receiving payment, you are asked to furnish a letter of credit. In this case *you* must initiate the payment procedure. You go to your bank and *apply* for a letter of credit. The fact that you apply for an LC does not mean you will get it.

You can think of a letter of credit as a letter, written by the importer's bank to the exporter, and communicated to the exporter through banking channels. Your bank is telling the exporter that, upon presentation of specified documents containing specified information, payment is guaranteed. Your bank does not want to take the chance of paying the exporter and later finding it cannot collect from you. When you apply for an LC, your bank will usually look for some way to ensure that you can pay—an account relationship and an average balance that will easily cover the amount of credit, or the fact that you are financially strong and stable enough to let the bank feel confident in extending you credit to cover the amount of your LC (or LCs) outstanding. In some cases, a bank will allow you to pledge assets, such as a certificate of deposit, to guarantee payment on a letter of credit. It is difficult to get a letter of credit for more than you are actually worth. That $100,000 deal is hard to make if your account balance is only $2000 and your credit line is not adequate.

When the importer's bank ("opening" bank) receives a letter of credit, it usually transmits it to its branch or

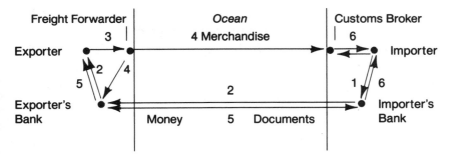

1. *Importer* applies for letter of credit.
2. *Opening bank* sends LC, through correspondent or branch, which advises exporter of receipt of LC.
3. *Exporter* sends goods and documents to freight forwarder.
4. *Freight forwarder* dispatches merchandise and provides documents to the advising bank.
5. *Advising bank* forwards documents to negotiating bank, which checks documents against LC, and authorizes payment if no discrepancies are found. The importer's account is debited.
6. *Importer's bank* gives him the documents with which he can claim the merchandise.

Figure 3.   Letter of Credit Transaction.

the exporter a credit has been received in his or her favor (hence the term "advising" bank). Banks send LCs through branches and correspondents partly to help prevent fraud. Branch and correspondent banks can check signatures on LCs against those they have on file, and there is a coding system that helps identify real LCs, as opposed to those that may be written fraudulently on existing banks or even written on fictitious banks.

Nevertheless, importers can specify their own banks as advising banks. In some cases, importers use their own banks as intermediaries between themselves and the advising banks, but the cost is higher in those instances because three banks are involved.

Nearly all letters of credit are "irrevocable," which means they cannot be changed or canceled without the consent of the beneficiary. This means that, once an importer opens an LC, and the exporter is advised of it the money is going to be paid out if the exporter presents the required documents. If the exporter has any doubt that the opening bank is solvent, and that the country in which the opening bank is located will have "hard" (convertible) currency with which to pay, he can ask to have the LC "confirmed" by the advising bank or even by a different bank in the same or a third country. For example, LCs written in Nigeria to American exporters are often confirmed in the United Kingdom. Confirmation means that, if the opening bank is obligated to pay but for some reason is unable to, the confirming bank *will* pay. This gives the exporter extra security, but of course there is an extra charge involved.

Upon receiving a letter of credit, the exporter must study its terms and conditions carefully to be sure each one of them can be met. For example, if an LC calls for a shipment of 5 boxes, each containing 20 baskets, and the shipping documents show that the actual cargo consisted of 20 boxes, each containing 5 baskets, there will be a

MARINE MIDLAND BANK, N.A.
140 BROADWAY, NEW YORK, N.Y. 10___

IRREVOCABLE DOCUMENTARY LETTER OF CREDIT

PLACE & DATE OF ISSUE	DATE & PLACE OF EXPIRY
NEW YORK, FEB. 1, 19--	KOREA, MAY 1, 19--

APPLICANT:	BENEFICIARY:
A.B.C. Co. 000 Main Street New York City, New York	XYZ Trading Co., Ltd. 000 Kwanchul-Dong Chongro-Ku, Seoul, Korea

M
A
I
L

T
O

ADVISING BANK:	AMOUNT:
Marine Midland Bank, NA C.P.O. Box 4369 Chongro-Ku, Seoul, Korea	TWENTY EIGHT THOUSAND FIVE HUNDRED TWENTY FIVE AND 00/100 U.S. DOLLARS $28,525.00

PARTIAL SHIPMENTS: ALLOWED
TRANSHIPMENTS: ALLOWED
SHIPMENT/DISPATCH TAKEN IN CHARGE
FROM/AT: FOB GLOBAL KOREA NOT LATER
THAN APRIL 15, 19_ _ FOR TRANSPORTATION
TO: N.Y., U.S.A.

CREDIT AVAILABLE WITH:
BY: PAYMENT, AGAINST PRESENTATION OF
THE DOCUMENTS DETAILED HEREIN AND OF
YOUR DRAFT(S) AT SIGHT DRAWN ON MARINE
MIDLAND BANK, N.A., NEW YORK, N.Y.

Commercial invoice in 4 copies.
Customs invoice.
Packing list.
Invoice must carry percentage of stainless steel composition
on stainless flatware and overall length of each item.
On board ocean bill of lading (if more than one original has
been issued all are required) issued to order of MARINE MIDLAND
BANK, N.A. notify DEF Freight Forwarders marked freight collect
and showing letter of credit number.
Insurance covered by buyers.
This refers to our cable of today.

COVERING: 12,500 DOZ. SONNET PATTERN STAINLESS FLATWARE BUYER
         P.O. #13455 DATED OCTOBER 17, 19-- F.O.B.

DOCUMENTS TO BE PRESENTED WITHIN 10 DAYS AFTER THE DATE OF ISSUANCE OF THE SHIPPING
DOCUMENT(S), BUT WITHIN THE VALIDITY OF THE CREDIT.

WE HEREBY ENGAGE WITH YOU THAT ALL DRAFTS DRAWN UNDER AND IN COMPLIANCE WITH THE TERMS
OF THIS CREDIT WILL BE DULY HONORED ON DELIVERY OF DOCUMENTS AS SPECIFIED IF PRESENTED
AT OUR COUNTERS ON OR BEFORE THE EXPIRATION DATE INDICATED ABOVE.

EXCEPT SO FAR AS OTHERWISE EXPRESSLY STATED THIS DOCUMENTARY CREDIT IS SUBJECT TO THE
"UNIFORM CUSTOMS AND PRACTICE FOR DOCUMENTARY CREDITS" (1974 REVISION) INTERNATIONAL
CHAMBER OF COMMERCE (PUBLICATION NO. 290).

Figure 4.   Commercial Letter of Credit. (Reprinted from *Introduction to International Banking Services,* 1983 Edition, page 105, Published by Marine Midland Bank. Reprinted with permission.)

"discrepancy." This may cause payment to be delayed until the discrepancy can be "waived" by the importer or otherwise resolved.

The letter of credit is an extremely flexible method of payment because the importer can ask his bank to make any legal stipulation. If an LC states that an exporter must personally load the baskets on the ship while wearing nothing but green sneakers, payment will not be made unless the luckless exporter presents documentary evidence of having done exactly so.

There are many specialized types of letters of credit—far too many to describe here in any detail. There are some that operate like revolving lines of bank credit, and others that arrange for part payment for part of the goods, or let a trader use his or her customer's credit to guarantee payment, or guarantee that the party who opens the LC will perform as promised. Your bank can advise you on the different varieties and suggest the most appropriate one for your situation.

To summarize, a letter of credit is a formal payment document opened by the importer and communicated through banking channels. The opening bank is the party obligated to pay the exporter. The cost for this service is often a fixed fee plus a percentage, for example, a $60 opening fee plus a payment commission of a least a quarter of one percent, with a minimum commission of about $50 per payment. Since the advising bank charges for its services too, the minimum total cost of a letter of credit is nearly $200. The charge is higher if an LC is not payable at sight, if more than two banks are involved, or if the exporter wants the credit confirmed. Confirmation costs from about a twentieth of a percent to one percent, depending on the amount of risk involved.

If by chance you as an exporter receive a letter of credit and cannot find a bank that will confirm it, the risk is probably very high and you should consider carefully whether the potential gain from the transaction is large enough to justify going ahead.

Many exporters ask for letters of credit for all their sales, but as the importer you do not have to accept the terms that are proposed to you. Come back with a counter offer and negotiate. Better yet, be the first to propose the payment terms and propose terms that benefit you. The other party can, if desired, try to negotiate. Figures 3 and 4 represent, respectively, the steps in a letter of credit transaction and a sample import letter of credit.

Payment in Advance

Under "cash in advance" terms, the buyer prepays the entire shipment or part of it. This term is used more often than you would expect. If you believe the supplier is honest, the simplest method of payment is for you to buy and send an international money order. Of course, you will be bearing all the risk, and there is a chance you will lose your money, but the risk may be justified by the savings of time and cost. If you order an item custom made, like a suit from Hong Kong, you will probably be asked to pay about half the money in advance. The same may hold true where considerable manufacturing expense is involved before a product can be shipped to you.

If you export to developing countries, you will find that many Caribbean and Latin American importers have bank accounts in Miami or New York, and that many African importers have accounts in the United Kingdom, France, or Switzerland. They use these accounts to pay for small import orders without having to apply to their central banks for foreign exchange. An importer in Jamaica who needs a small shipment quickly is likely to send you a dollar check drawn on a Miami bank account. You can get the merchandise and the paperwork ready and, when the check clears, ship.

Consignment

Consignment is not actually a form of payment but a sort of agency arrangement in which the buyer takes possession of the goods but does not take title. Suppose you buy a $1000 dress for a party, wear it once, and then decide you do not want it anymore. You may take it to your nearby used gown shop and leave it there—on consignment. You tell the store owner you want 75 percent of what he sells it for, and no less than $250. If the dress is sold, you get paid, and the storekeeper keeps the 25 percent fee. If it is not sold within a set period of time, you may reclaim it, or the store owner may ask you to take it back. If it somehow gets lost or damaged, you will be paid the $250 minimum.

Consignment in international trade works much the same way. It is often used for U.S. imports of fresh fruits and vegetables, works of art, and a few other products. If I were to import fresh fruit, I would have no way of knowing ahead of time how much of it would arrive damaged or at what price I would be able to sell it. The prices change in the marketplace several times a day. To solve this problem, I might import on consignment, and pay the exporter a predetermined percentage of my actual revenue. If I had to throw away some produce because it could not be sold, I would give the exporter a certificate to that effect. The exporter may have someone checking on me to make sure I was being honest with him, but that of course would be at his expense. Similarly, if I had an art gallery and were willing to display paintings from Mexico, I may not be willing to buy them outright. I may agree to take them on consignment, much like the dress in the first example. If they did not sell in my gallery, I would probably cooperate in moving them to another gallery where the customers may be more interested in Mexican art.

In U.S. export trade, the main use of consignment is to help distributors of heavy machinery and equipment.

If a tractor manufacturer wants to sell in the Dominican Republic, its distributor there will need floor models and demonstrators as well as an inventory of equipment for sale. Part or all of this may be in the Dominican Republic on consignment; if and when it is sold, the distributor will pay the manufacturer.

This method of payment favors the importer. Since the exporter is bearing risk as well as in effect, providing financing, he will usually not offer this payment term unless it is the only way he can sell. There are some exceptions, however. I know of a Brazilian exporter of baler twine who sells to a distributor in the midwestern United States on consignment for the entire haying season. The distributor can sell at a competitive price without being concerned about his cost or profit margin. The system insures that no competitor can take the market by underselling the Brazilians.

SUPPLY AGREEMENTS

If you are dealing with each product on a one-time basis or with products that other traders already handle, there is probably no need for you to have a written supply agreement. If, however, you plan to spend time and money building up a market, there should be a written statement of the terms of your relationship with your supplier.

A young man from Thailand who lived in California was acting as an agent, without a written agreement, for a spice exporter from his country. Apparently he did a very good job, because import brokers who were also handling the product complained to the Thai exporter. The exporter promptly told my friend that he should not call on the spice packers, the part of the market he had done best with, but should confine his efforts to compounders. He already knew from experience that the compounders would not buy from him because he could not offer them more than the brokers, their established suppliers. He was literally put out of business.

By contrast, a neophyte export agent entered into a written agreement to be the exclusive U.S. agent for a new kind of art supply from Japan. She spent an entire year contacting art supply dealers, wholesalers, importers, and manufacturers before making her first sale. That sale was to a manufacturer of similar products who already had a distribution network and could easily place the new product in stores all across the country. Right after the first shipment was made, this woman learned later, the U.S. importer contacted the Japanese exporter and proposed that the agent be cut out of the arrangement. It is probable that her services were no longer needed, but she had a signed agreement and the exporter decided to honor it. Her commissions were safe for the term of the existing contract.

Supply agreements may be very brief or very long. Your supplier may have a standard agreement form that is acceptable to you, or you can try to write one yourself using the sample agreements in this book or in books on international commercial law. You may want to buy a copy of *Commercial Agency: A Guide to Drawing up Contracts,* from the ICC Publishing Corporation in New York City. If, however, the stakes involved are high, financially or in other respects, you should seriously consider using an attorney. Be sure the lawyer has actual experience with the kind of situation into which you are getting. The situation is likely to be one of the following:

- As a U.S. selling agent for a foreign exporter.
- As a U.S. importer/distributor for a foreign exporter.
- As an export selling agent for an American manufacturer.
- As an export merchant for an American manufacturer.

Here are some topics to include:

The Products.   An agreement may read that you can handle all the products of your principal, or it may limit you by naming only specific products.

Competing Products.   Some suppliers will try to restrict you from handling products that will compete with theirs. Other suppliers want you to carry as many items as possible in order to maximize the value of your services to your customers.

Sales Targets.   Your supplier will often try to set specific sales targets, usually minimum order quantities, and frequency of orders. Your failure to meet a target may be grounds for cancelling the agreement. An obvious reason for the supplier to insist on sales targets is to prevent you from gaining control of the products through an exclusive agreement and neglecting to sell them actively. Why would you do this? Suppose, for example, you were the only exporter of Bayer aspirin. Would it not be ideal to become the exclusive exporter of all other brands of aspirin and do nothing with them? You and your Bayer would have the market all to yourselves.

The Territory.   On the import side, you may be authorized to sell in the entire country or only part of it. If you sell outside your assigned territory you are breaking the agreement, and the supplier may have the option to cancel it; if you are an agent, orders from customers outside your territory may simply not be honored.

On the export side, you may be authorized to sell in, or given exclusivity for, only certain countries or groups of countries. If a U.S. manufacturer has his own sales offices in Western Europe, but no distribution in Africa, he probably will give you the latter but not the former.

Prices, Mark-Up, Commissions.   If you are an agent, the principal usually sets the price at which you must sell. The agreement specifies the percentage commission you earn and when you will be paid. Commissions usually are in the 5–15 percent range, the higher range reserved for products that are hard to sell and for which individual sales are small. Payment is usually for each sale, or monthly, for sales for which your principal has collected.

If you are a merchant you usually will set the selling price, and the supplier may want to limit your markup. This is because you can make as much money with a low volume and high mark-up as you can with a high volume and low mark-up, but, assuming what you pay remains the same, there is more profit for the supplier in high volume.

Payment Terms.   If you are a merchant the agreement probably stipulates when you will pay—something like "net amount in sixty days." If you are an agent, the agreement may stipulate the payment terms the principal will extend to importers.

Shipping Terms.   For both merchants and agents, the agreement often states the shipping and related tasks for which the supplier is responsible.

Level of Effort.   The principal may want to insert a clause giving a minimum number of man-hours or sales calls that you must devote to the product. More often a vague term like "best effort" is used, but if the supplier wants to cancel the contract and finds no other grounds, you can be accused of not putting forth your best effort.

Promotion.   There often is a clause about the level of promotional or advertising expenditures and who will pay for it. This could include furnishing a certain amount of free units of the product for promotions.

Warranties and Services. In an agreement between a Nigerian producer of phonograph records and an importer in Atlanta, the manufacturer was required to ship 20 percent more records than the importer ordered. Half of these were for distribution to disc jockeys and promotional purposes; the other half were to cover expected breakage and defective records. Nearly any product can sometimes be defective, and many kinds of products require service or repair. Your agreement should state how these problems will be handled.

Priority of Orders. As an export merchant or agent, you would like your orders to take priority over your supplier's domestic orders. Otherwise you may not be able to guarantee delivery dates to your foreign customers.

Lead Times. You may want your principal to agree to ship within a certain number of days after receiving an order from you. You may also want a guarantee of a minimum lead time for price increases. Otherwise you may find you cannot fill an order at the stated price because your supplier has increased the price you must pay.

Reporting. Your principal may want a clause in the agreement that requires you to submit reports of sales activity and actual sales, on a periodic basis. This will mean extra work for you, but may help by encouraging you to keep accurate and complete records.

Patent and Trademark. This is a complex area that involves international laws for the protection of intellectual property. If you are dealing with a patentable product or process, the foreign manufacturer may ask you to obtain patent protection in the United States. This will usually be done in the supplier's name and at his or her expense. You may also be asked to be on the lookout for patent violations and to report them to the supplier.

The registration of trademarks and brand names may be even more complex. Under U.S. common law, the first person or company to sell a product in interstate commerce becomes the owner of its trademark. After establishing common law ownership of a trademark, it is common to register it with the Commissioner of Patents and Trademarks, Washington, D.C. 20231, to obtain code law protection. A trademark can be registered either in the U.S. importer or selling agent's name or in the foreign supplier's name (and if you are an exclusive importer the supplier can assign the trademark to you). Having a trademark in your name or assigned to you gives you considerable control of the product.

Trademarks and brand names can also be registered with the U.S. Customs Service. Customs will try to stop imports of counterfeit goods, like fake Apple computers. The law is currently in flux with regard to enforcement of exclusive distribution agreements. The governor of California recently refused to sign a bill that would have prevented imports to that state of trademarked goods by companies that were not authorized by the manufacturer to import them. You may have read of certain products, such as cameras, which are warranteed by retailers because the manufacturer's warranty does not cover them. These are usually authentic Nikons, Canons, etc., that have been purchased in free port areas, like Colon in Panama, and brought into the United States by companies other than the authorized distributors. They are called "grey market" goods.

As an export merchant or agent you may be asked to help your U.S. supplier obtain and maintain patent and/or trademark registration in market countries. This complex procedure is explained in the book, *Foreign Business Practices,* available from U.S. government bookstores or from the Superintendent of Documents, U.S. Government Printing Office, Washington, D.C. 20402. This is, however, an area in which you will need expert legal assistance.

Relabeling, Repackaging.   A manufacturer will sometimes want to make sure you do not relabel or repackage the merchandise to disguise its origin by placing your own label on the product. In other cases, this may be quite acceptable. I once worked with a West African producer of an instant cocoa drink. The most economical procedure for this producer was to ship the powder in bulk and allow the U.S. importer to do the packaging. This meant the importer would own and control the brand name and trademark.

Legal Agent.   Most supply agreements have simple statements that the intermediary is not a legal agent of the supplier. That is, you cannot enter into commitments that he will be legally obligated to fulfill.

Assignment.   There usually is a statement that you cannot assign the agreement to anyone without the supplier's approval. Without this clause you could assign your agency to someone who may be unable to do the job that the principal wants done.

Duration and Termination.   There usually is a statement that sets forth the term of the contract, whether it will be automatically renewed if neither party disagrees, and what each party must do to cancel the agreement. Normally the initial term should be for at least two years. You do not want to work hard for twelve months and have your principal cancel the agreement just when orders are about to start pouring in.

Disputes.   Finally, there usually is a clause relating to the settlement of disputes. The agreement may state in which country disputes will be settled and which country's laws will apply, but it is more common to specify arbitration. If your contract is with a supplier in the United States, it probably calls for settlement of disputes under the auspices and rules of the American Arbitration Association. If the contract is with a foreign supplier, it may call for settlement under the auspices and rules of the International Chamber of Commerce, based in Paris, France.

Although supplier agreements are useful and even necessary, they cannot take the place of business dealings conducted honestly and in good faith by two parties, each of whom realizes that success in the venture can only be achieved jointly. Throughout the world, business may be fueled by profit, but it is oiled by friendship and trust.

EXPORT CREDIT AND CREDIT INSURANCE

If you export on open account, consignment, time draft, or time letter of credit, you are actually financing the importer's business. Financing can be even more important to foreign buyers than the price of the merchandise. Why would an importer in Argentina buy from you and pay at sight if he can get six months credit from a Japanese supplier, especially if the rate of interest in his country is in double digits per month?

Exporters who provide financing rely most often on company funds or commercial bank loans or credits. For very small exporters, about the only source of help is the U.S. Small Business Administration, which has a limited facility for export credits and loan guarantees. An exporter may sell on a time letter of credit basis and then discount the LC in order to receive the money immediately. For larger export sales, about $10,000 and up, the U.S. Export Import Bank (EXIMBANK) can often provide loan guarantees. Exporters apply to EXIMBANK through their commercial banks. For export shipments of selected agricultural products, the Commodity Credit Corporation in Washington, D.C. has some financing available. Another financing organization, the Private Export Funding Corporation, is only for huge transactions.

If a foreign importer needs time to pay and does not want to go to the trouble and expense of providing a confirmed, irrevocable letter of credit, a U.S. exporter may be able to sell on less secure terms and buy export credit insurance. This kind of coverage is not completely desirable, however. It can make it much easier to obtain financing, but it is expensive, there are long time lags before settlements are made, and coverage is usually for less than the full amount at risk.

The insurance is available through the U.S. government's insurance underwriter, the Foreign Credit Insurance Association (FCIA), which is now effectively a part of EXIMBANK. There are also private companies that write export credit insurance. These usually are approached through brokerage firms, such as Cook & Miller International or Marsh & McLennan, both in New York City.

These matters are also important for importers. Many foreign countries, especially developed countries, have similar export credit and credit insurance facilities. If you want time to pay for a large shipment, and the foreign exporter says it is not possible, you can find out from that country's export promotion office in the United States what kinds of export credit facilities might be available to the exporter. Armed with this information, you may be able to persuade the exporter to turn to one of these sources of credit, and/or credit insurance.

FOREIGN CURRENCY TRANSACTIONS

A very high percentage of international transactions are paid for in currency, rather than goods, and perhaps as much as 90 percent of world currency transactions are in

U.S. dollars. As an American importer, you will rarely be asked to pay any other way. In 1985, however, when President Reagan and four other heads of state agreed to reduce the value of the U.S. dollar, American importers were immediately asked to pay in other currencies, mostly German marks and Swiss francs. If that happens to you, the best thing is to say no. Insist on using your own currency unless you make the payment immediately.

If you must agree to make future payments in a foreign currency, you have the problem of not knowing what the value of that currency will be when your payment is due. If it increases against the dollar, your dollar price will be higher than expected. You can negotiate for a lower price to compensate for your risk, or you can use the foreign exchange forward market. This means buying the right to purchase a specified amount of the foreign currency on the date you will need it at a predetermined rate. This is a form of "hedging." Of course, the more the market expects the currency to rise against the dollar, the more you will have to pay for the right to buy it at a predetermined rate.

On the other hand, U.S. *exporters* are often asked to *take* payment in foreign currencies. In these cases, there are only a few options. You can say no, but may lose the sale. You can agree but increase your price to compensate for the risk. In some cases, you can go along with taking payment in foreign currency but at a rate that gives you the number of dollars you want. This lets the foreign importer pay in his currency, but still gives you the required amount of dollars. Finally, you can hedge by buying the right to *sell* a fixed amount of foreign currency on the date you will receive it, at a predetermined rate.

Many foreign currencies are nearly worthless outside the countries in which they are used. Never agree to take a foreign currency without checking with your bank unless you know the country in question is sound economically and its currency is freely convertible.

COUNTERTRADE

"Countertrade" is the overall name given to transactions that are not paid for entirely in currency. There are several variations—barter, compensation trade, buy-back, counterpurchase, and offset. This kind of trade dates back to the time before money existed, and it has continued to be used by importers in Eastern Europe where there is a perpetual shortage of hard currency. In recent years, when a number of countries have literally run out of money, countertrade has become increasingly important. Colombia and Malaysia have passed laws that regulate international countertrade transactions and, in several countries, it is very hard to sell a U.S. product unless the exporter is willing to take payment partly or entirely in merchandise.

Barter and related transactions should be avoided by small-scale exporters. Even very large American firms have been stuck with cases of wine or dozens of hams that they did not know what to do with. You have either to be able to sell the goods you take in trade, and most small exporters are short on domestic marketing expertise and contacts, or hire a "barter house" or countertrade department of a major bank to find someone who can use what you take in trade and can pay you cash for it. Either way the procedure is likely to be expensive.

If you are determined to make an export sale and the only way you can is through countertrade, be very careful. Remember that there will be two shipments, two customs clearances, two of almost everything. That means twice as many chances for something to go wrong and end up costing you money.

8

International Shipping And Insurance

International shipping, and related functions such as packing and insurance, is critical to successful importing and exporting. If these functions are not handled properly, your goods can arrive too late, in poor condition, or not arrive at all. There is a direct financial aspect, too. The cost of shipping can sometimes be even more than the cost of the products.

SHIPPING TERMS

Around every activity there develops a unique language, a special jargon or list of terms, the use of which saves time and trouble and prevents confusion. Import-export is no exception. There is a set of standard *shipping terms* to specify who makes the arrangements for each step in international shipping and who pays the charges. Most important, these terms indicate where the transfer of title takes place. Who has title determines who bears the risk for loss or damage to the cargo at each point in its voyage.

Historically there have been two sets of definitions, the American Standard Foreign Trade Definitions, revised in 1941, and the INCOTERMS (International Commercial Terms), revised in 1980. Although the INCOTERMS are now by far more common, the other system is still in use. Since there are several differences between the two sets of definitions, an importer and an exporter should agree not only on the shipping term, but also on which set of definitions they are using: for example, "c.i.f. according to INCOTERMS."

There are fourteen INCOTERMS in an order that follows the shipment from the point nearest the exporter to the point nearest the importer:

1. Ex Works
2. Free Carrier (Named Point)
3. FOR/FOT
4. FOB Airport
5. FAS
6. FOB
7. C&F
8. CIF
9. Freight or Carriage Paid To . . .
10. Freight or Carriage or Insurance Paid To . . .
11. Ex Ship
12. Ex Quay
13. Delivered at Frontier
14. Delivered Duty Paid

Ex works means that the exporter need only place the goods on the loading dock outside the door of the factory or warehouse. The importer/buyer is obligated to make all arrangements, pay all costs, and bear all risks from that point.

At the other extreme, *Delivered Duty Paid* usually means that the exporter/seller must make the arrangements, pay all costs, and bear all risks until the goods are delivered to the buyer's warehouse or other premises. As you can imagine, very few importers want to buy Ex Works and very few exporters want to sell Delivered Duty Paid. Therefore, terms more toward the middle are the most common.

In fact the great majority of international shipments are made under just five terms: FOB Airport, FAS, FOB, C&F, and CIF. For land shipments, such as between the United States and Mexico, "Delivered at Frontier" is very common, and the advent of multimodal transportation has generated considerable use of the term, "Free Carrier (Named Point)." There is an excellent book, *Guide to INCOTERMS*, (ICC Publishing Corporation, 1212 Avenue of the Americas, New York, NY 10036) that lists the responsibilities of the importer and of the exporter under each term and gives case studies that can help you understand which term to use in each situation.

Here are brief definitions of these most common terms: The initials *FOB* stand for *Free on Board*, and a shipment can be FOB anywhere. If I were to sell to you under the term, FOB Donkey, Hollywood and Vine, my responsibility would be to place the goods on a donkey at that location. The goods would be considered "free" to you at that point, because I would have paid all costs *before* that point. *FOB Airport* means that the exporter must deliver the goods to an airport and place them in the custody of an air carrier. When the goods reach an air carrier, they are considered to be "on board" a plane and the title passes to the importer. With this term, the *ex*porter will often decide which airline to use, but the *im*porter will be paying the freight charges.

FAS means *Free Alongside Ship*. If I ship to you in the United States, *FAS Rotterdam*, I am obligated to place the merchandise at a point where it is ready to be loaded on a vessel at that Dutch port. If a box falls off the truck on its way there, I will not have fulfilled my obligation and I will, therefore, be responsible.

Since goods can technically be Free on Board any kind of conveyance, anywhere, FOB is a confusing term. When using it under the INCOTERM definitions, a specific point should always be named. If you say simply *FOB Rotterdam* it is assumed that you mean *FOB Vessel, Port of Rotterdam.* With this term, the seller must actually place the goods on board the ship, *on board* being defined as over the ship's rail. At that point, title to the goods passes from seller to buyer. The difference between FAS and FOB can be substantial. Although the physical distance between the locations in these two terms is minimal, there may be freight forwarding charges, export taxes (in a few countries), loading charges (if the shipment is very large or heavy), and other costs occurring after *alongside ship* and before *on board.* With FOB the exporter will choose the carrier, although the importer will often participate in the decision.

C&F means *Cost and Freight.* The exporter is obligated to pay the ocean freight costs, but does not provide insurance. This means the importer bears the risk of loss or damage to the goods from the time they are on board the ship. The importer should and normally will protect himself against these risks by buying insurance.

CIF (Cost, Insurance, Freight) implies that the exporter carries the process one step further by buying and paying for marine insurance. Technically the importer buys the freight and insurance *from the exporter,* along with the goods. Thus, if the cargo is lost or damaged, the buyer must file an insurance claim.

In addition to the five terms above, in Europe where trucks are the major means of transportation in international trade, the term *Delivered at Frontier* is used widely. In North America, the phrase is used primarily at the Mexican border. Where the United States imports, the Mexican exporter must place the goods on the U.S. side of the bridge but does not have to clear them through U.S. customs. The importer's work begins in the customs yard in Laredo, El Paso, or the other border crossings.

Free Carrier (Named Point) is becoming an important term because of the growth of multimodal transportation, whereby a carrier, such as U.S. Lines, can pick up a container of cargo (containers are discussed later in this chapter) and move it by road or rail and then by sea. Under this term the exporter's obligation is discharged when he delivers the goods to the carrier, even though they have yet to be moved to a port and loaded onto a vessel.

The illustration on page 129 will help you understand the locations at which the exporter's responsibilities end, and the importer's begin, with some of the shipping terms. Each term is placed at the geographical point to which the exporter must *pay the costs of shipping*. The term shows who makes the arrangements and pays the bills for shipping, insurance, etc., and who has title to the goods (and therefore bears the risk of loss or damage) at each point in their voyage from seller to buyer.

Several factors influence which shipping term to use for an import or export transaction. Usually a beginner knows little of the logistics in the foreign country and therefore wants to make arrangements that reduce his or her risk and involvement. Importers therefore tend to look for *FOR (FREE ON RAILCAR)*, *FOB*, *C&F*, or *CIF* terms. Exporters ideally like to ship *Ex Works*, but usually must sell *FAS*, *FOB*, *C&F*, and *CIF*.

As you gain experience you will probably want to decide which carrier is used in order to minimize the freight charges for the level of service you want. This means using conditions under which you choose the carrier or, if you import C&F or CIF, stipulating the carrier the exporter is to use. Keeping control of the insurance enables you to select the coverage and seek a competitive premium rate.

If your seller has no shipping experience, you may want to use the services of a foreign freight forwarder in the port of lading so you are in complete control of the cargo movement. One former client buys wool sweaters from a small firm in Ireland that has no export experience. The importer, therefore, buys FAS and has a shipping agent in Ireland make all the arrangements for her.

Another importer I know brought frozen food from Western Europe by air. Since most airline terminals in the United States have no freezer space, the importer wanted to pick the airline and the actual flight. He did not want frozen vegetables coming in on a weekend and thawing before he received them. He arranged to import FOB Airport, but to select the airline and reserve the space on specific flights himself. Also, if you buy in small quantities from several sources abroad, you may want to have a foreign freight forwarder consolidate your goods into one shipment and reduce expenses. You should therefore buy FAS.

As a small exporter, ideally you would like to ship FAS but in reality you must give your customers the terms they want or they will look elsewhere. Government, steamship, or airline requirements also frequently dictate terms. Several countries insist that insurance on import shipments must be purchased locally, and some air and steamship lines insist on prepaid freight for export shipments from the United States to countries with weak currencies.

If you export on terms such as CIF, your price quotation must show the cost of shipping and the cost of insurance separately. Under CIF, you will be paying out cash for the transportation and insurance, and it may take some time for you to be reimbursed (which will occur when you are paid for the goods). A good freight forwarder can help you by explaining the ramifications of the various shipping terms with respect to a specific transaction.

Even experienced exporters hesitate to get involved in shipping beyond CIF. For example, I was once asked to

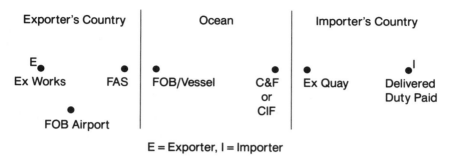

Figure 1.   Principal Shipping Terms.

quote on an export shipment to be sent "Delivered Duty Paid" to an importer in David, Panama. Besides being responsible for Panamanian customs clearance and duty, I would have had to arrange and pay for *inland freight* in the buyer's country. General Motors could do that, but I couldn't. I agreed to ship CIF and not an inch beyond.

INTERNATIONAL CARGO TRANSPORTATION

Modes of Transportation

Except for U.S. shipments to and from Canada and Mexico, where there is a land option, international transportation basically is by sea and air. For large shipments, this means sea freight or air freight; for very small shipments sea mail and air mail are possibilities. In *multimodal* transportation, where the same goods go by different modes (air, sea, road, or rail) at different points in their journey, intermodal carrier issuing *through bills of lading* (TBLs) take charge of the cargo throughout its journey.

Compared with air freight, sea freight is nearly always slower and less expensive. If you do a total *distribution cost analysis*, however, you may find that the total cost of moving a shipment by air is less than the cost of surface

freight. That is because shipping by air often means reduced costs for packing, forwarding, documentation, and
insurance. Since the goods arrive sooner, it is quicker for
the importer to receive them, sell them, and collect for
them; it is not necessary for the importer to keep as much
inventory as when the goods are transported by sea, and
there is less interest to pay on money borrowed to finance
inventory. There is an obvious advantage to air freight
when the shipment is going from one inland city to another because most cities have airports but relatively few
have seaports.

Determination of the best means of shipment requires
a distribution cost analysis. You will have to look at all the
cost elements in the transaction, by air and by sea. For a
really precise comparison, you can try to test a shipment of
the same size by each mode of transport; this will only be
practical, however, if your test shipments are the first two
of many.

Steamship services are either *scheduled, nonscheduled,* or *charter.* Most of the major lines sail on regular
schedules. You can find out about sailing dates from any
of several magazines, including *Brandon's Shipper and Forwarder,* published by a company of the same name, and
Shipping Digest, published by Geyer-McAllister Publications, both in New York City. Also the newspaper of
world trade, *The Journal of Commerce,* carries shipping
schedules. You can save money by buying just the Friday
editions. Nonscheduled lines are often less expensive, but
may be less reliable as well. They usually are represented
by steamship agent firms in major port cities. Figure 2
produces a page from *Shipper and Forwarder* showing the
schedule of vessels departing from South Atlantic and
Gulf ports.

Shipping lines may be classified as *conference lines* or
independents. Many major steamship lines have formed associations or *conferences,* each of which connects specific

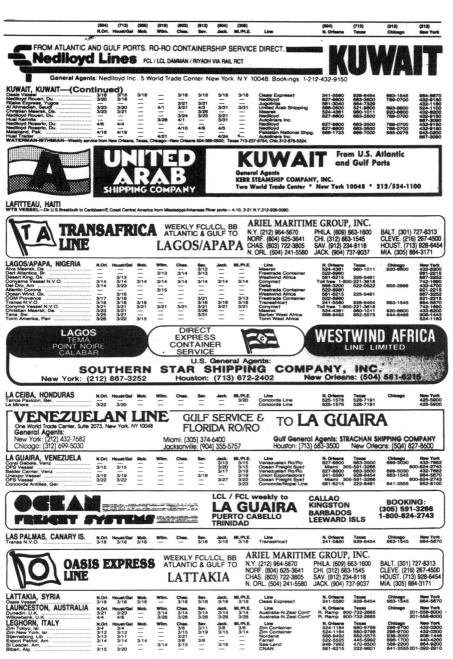

Figure 2. Shipping Schedule. (Reprinted from Brandon's Shipper and Forwarder, March 11, 1985. Copyright 1985 by International Thomson Transport Press.)

131

areas of the world. The conference covering U.S. Atlantic and Gulf to West Africa, and the North Atlantic to Europe, are two examples of such alliances. Lines outside the conferences are independents, with tariffs generally 10–15 percent below the conference's lowest ("contract") rates.

The Shipping Act of 1984 permits conference shipping lines to set rates independently when the members of a conference cannot agree. It also permits service contracts, by which steamship lines can give special rates for a number of large shipments. The effects of this act are scheduled to be reviewed by Congress in 1989.

U.S. exporters can also ship through *Non Vessel-Owning Common Carriers* (NVOCCs) and *Shippers Associations*. These organizations, which are under review since being recognized in the Shipping Act of 1984, can often reduce freight costs by grouping small shipments from different companies. Since these are technically ocean carriers, you should deal with them through a foreign freight forwarder.

Using charter vessels is feasible only for very large quantities, although sometimes a ship charterer or broker will know of a chartered vessel that has extra space and can carry your cargo for a low rate. The more you explore shipping alternatives, the better your chance of finding satisfactory service at reasonable rates.

There is no conference system for airlines, and most air freight is carried on scheduled passenger flights, scheduled all-cargo flights, or charter flights. A monthly publication, *International Air Cargo Guide*, gives schedules for flights that carry cargo.

Mail Shipments

Air or sea mail—even couriers when the goods are very high in value—are often useful for shipping small quantities. A mail shipment must be within the size and weight limits of both countries, and the maximum insurance is small. However, you can save on documentation, freight forwarding, and customs brokerage. Under current U.S. law, you can import a shipment of most products of up to $1000 in value by mail every mail day, and the postal department will do the customs work for you. You will still have to pay the duty if any is charged, but not a penny for customs clearance.

There is room for creativity in every area. For example, one importer developed a catalog of lightweight, low-priced consumer goods from Taiwan. He planned to mail his catalog in the United States and forward the orders to an agent in Taiwan, who would pack each individual order and send it by mail. Each customer could decide whether he wanted the speed of air mail or the cost advantage of sea mail, just as many mail order customers within the United States have the option of Parcel Post or (for an additional charge) private parcel service.

Shipping Rates

What is the most important fact in determining shipping rates? The usual answer "distance" is wrong. It can cost less to bring a large quantity of shirts to Boston from Hong Kong than from an island in the Caribbean. Shipping rates are designed to make money for the carriers, and the expectation of that is based mostly on the amount of traffic, the competition on the route, and the characteristics of the cargo itself. If there is a large traffic in men's shirts between Hong Kong and Boston, several shipping lines will be competing for this traffic since men's shirts are a desirable cargo that is easy to handle; the rates will be low.

Both airlines and steamship lines have rate books, known as *tariffs*, that show the rates for different kinds of cargo between specific areas of the world. Figures 3 and 4

U.S.A.
AREA NO. 3
TAIWAN

CONTAINER GENERAL COMMODITY ARBITRARIES

TABLE E (Continued)

Applicable from Taiwan to points in the U.S.A.

from WEST COAST (XXX) to PHILADELPHIA (PHL)

RATE TYPE	BULK/CONTAINER TYPE	NOTE	MIN. WEIGHT IN KGS.	RATE PER KG./MIN. CHARGE PER CONTAINER	PIVOT WEIGHT IN KGS.	RATE PER KG. OVER PIVOT in NTD
GEN	1	-	1	141600.00	6210	22.80
	2	-	1	73880.00	3241	22.80
	2A	-	1	68000.00	2983	22.80
	2D	-	1	60320.00	2645	22.80
	2H	-	1	90800.00	3982	22.80
	3	-	1	50160.00	2200	22.80
	4	-	1	42680.00	1872	22.80
	5	-	1	42680.00	1872	22.80
	6	-	1	32280.00	1415	22.80
	7	-	1	24160.00	1060	22.80
	8	-	1	18000.00	790	22.80
	8B	-	1	18000.00	790	22.80
	9	-	1	18000.00	790	22.80

from WEST COAST (XXX) to PITTSBURGH (PIT)

RATE TYPE	BULK/CONTAINER TYPE	NOTE	MIN. WEIGHT IN KGS.	RATE PER KG./MIN. CHARGE PER CONTAINER	PIVOT WEIGHT IN KGS.	RATE PER KG. OVER PIVOT in NTD
GEN	1	-	1	129160.00	6210	20.80
	2	-	1	67400.00	3241	20.80
	2A	-	1	62040.00	2983	20.80
	2D	-	1	55000.00	2645	20.80
	2H	-	1	82840.00	3982	20.80
	3	-	1	45760.00	2200	20.80
	4	-	1	38920.00	1872	20.80
	5	-	1	38920.00	1872	20.80
	6	-	1	29440.00	1415	20.80
	7	-	1	22040.00	1060	20.80
	8	-	1	16440.00	790	20.80
	8B	-	1	16440.00	790	20.80
	9	-	1	16440.00	790	20.80

from WEST COAST (XXX) to ST. LOUIS (STL)

RATE TYPE	BULK/CONTAINER TYPE	NOTE	MIN. WEIGHT IN KGS.	RATE PER KG./MIN. CHARGE PER CONTAINER	PIVOT WEIGHT IN KGS.	RATE PER KG. OVER PIVOT in NTD
GEN	1	-	1	119220.00	6210	19.20
	2	-	1	62240.00	3241	19.20
	2A	-	1	57280.00	2983	19.20
	2D	-	1	50800.00	2645	19.20
	2H	-	1	76440.00	3982	19.20
	3	-	1	42240.00	2200	19.20
	4	-	1	35960.00	1872	19.20
	5	-	1	35960.00	1872	19.20
	6	-	1	27160.00	1415	19.20
	7	-	1	20360.00	1060	19.20
	8	-	1	15160.00	790	19.20
	8B	-	1	15160.00	790	19.20
	9	-	1	15160.00	790	19.20

from WEST COAST (XXX) to SYRACUSE (SYR)

RATE TYPE	BULK/CONTAINER TYPE	NOTE	MIN. WEIGHT IN KGS.	RATE PER KG./MIN. CHARGE PER CONTAINER	PIVOT WEIGHT IN KGS.	RATE PER KG. OVER PIVOT in NTD
GEN	1	-	1	141600.00	6210	22.80
	2	-	1	73880.00	3241	22.80
	2A	-	1	68000.00	2983	22.80
	2D	-	1	60320.00	2645	22.80
	2H	-	1	90800.00	3982	22.80
	3	-	1	50160.00	2200	22.80
	4	-	1	42680.00	1872	22.80
	5	-	1	42680.00	1872	22.80
	6	-	1	33280.00	1415	22.80
	7	-	1	24160.00	1060	22.80
	8	-	1	18000.00	790	22.80
	8B	-	1	18000.00	790	22.80
	9	-	1	18000.00	790	22.80

RATE TYPE	BULK CONT TYPE	F N T	MIN WT LB/KG	RATE/MIN CHARGE PER CONTAINER	PIVOT WT LB/KG	RATE OVER PIVOT

TAIWAN

from TAIPEI(TPE) to HONOLULU(HNL)   in KGS NTD

GEN	BULK -		1	370.80	33	-
	BULK -		45	270.80	91	-
	BULK -		100	254.80	221	-
	BULK -		300	188.40	420	-
	BULK -		500	158.40		-

from HOUSTON(HOU) to TAIPEI(TPE)   in LBS USD

GEN	BULK -		1	3.91	75	-
	BULK -		100	2.98	191	-
	BULK -		220	2.60	517	-
	BULK -		660	2.05	999	-
	BULK -		1100	1.86		-

from TAIPEI(TPE) to HOUSTON(HOU)   in KGS NTD

GEN	BULK -		1	426.40	34	-
	BULK -		45	325.60	92	-
	BULK -		100	302.40	233	-
	BULK -		300	235.60	436	-
	BULK -		500	205.60		-

from INDIANAPOLIS(IND) to TAIPEI(TPE)   in LBS USD

GEN	BULK -		1	3.97	75	-
	BULK -		100	3.03	191	-
	BULK -		220	2.65	517	-
	BULK -		660	2.08	999	-
	BULK -		1100	1.89		-
SCR4416 1			1	14451.00	12419	0.95
SCR4417 3			1	8350.00	5984	1.39

from TAIPEI(TPE) to INDIANAPOLIS(IND)   in KGS NTD

GEN	BULK -		1	429.60	34	-
	BULK -		45	329.20	92	-
	BULK -		100	305.60	234	-
	BULK -		300	238.80	438	-
	BULK -		500	209.20		-

from KANSAS CITY(MKC) to TAIPEI(TPE)   in LBS USD

GEN	BULK -		1	3.91	75	-
	BULK -		100	2.98	191	-
	BULK -		220	2.60	517	-
	BULK -		660	2.05	999	-
	BULK -		1100	1.86		-

TAIWAN

from TAIPEI(TPE) to MIAMI/FT. LAUDERDALE(MIA)   in KGS NTD (cont)

SCR9905	8 -		1	107840.00	817	132.00
	8 -		1	108840.00	817	132.00
	9 -		1	107840.00	817	132.00

from MILWAUKEE(MKE) to TAIPEI(TPE)   in LBS USD

GEN	BULK -		1	3.91	75	-
	BULK -		100	2.98	191	-
	BULK -		220	2.60	517	-
	BULK -		660	2.05	999	-
	BULK -		1100	1.86		-

from TAIPEI(TPE) to MILWAUKEE(MKE)   in KGS NTD

GEN	BULK -		1	426.40	34	-
	BULK -		45	325.60	92	-
	BULK -		100	302.40	233	-
	BULK -		300	235.60	436	-
	BULK -		500	205.60		-

from MINNEAPOLIS/ ST. PAUL(MSP) to TAIPEI(TPE)   in LBS USD

GEN	BULK -		1	3.86	75	-
	BULK -		100	2.94	191	-
	BULK -		220	2.57	517	-
	BULK -		660	2.02	999	-
	BULK -		1100	1.84		-

from TAIPEI(TPE) to MINNEAPOLIS/ ST. PAUL(MSP)   in KGS NTD

GEN	BULK -		1	423.60	34	-
	BULK -		45	323.60	92	-
	BULK -		100	300.00	233	-
	BULK -		300	233.20	436	-
	BULK -		500	203.60		-

from NASHVILLE(BNA) to TAIPEI(TPE)   in LBS USD

GEN	BULK -		1	4.01	75	-
	BULK -		100	3.06	191	-
	BULK -		220	2.67	517	-
	BULK -		660	2.10	999	-
	BULK -		1100	1.91		-

from TAIPEI(TPE) to NASHVILLE(BNA)   in KGS NTD

| GEN | BULK - | | 1 | 433.20 | 34 | - |
| | BULK - | | 45 | 330.40 | 92 | - |

TAIWAN

from SAN ANTONIO(SAT) to TAIPEI(TPE)   in LBS USD

GEN	BULK -		1	3.91	75	-
	BULK -		100	2.98	191	-
	BULK -		220	2.60	517	-
	BULK -		660	2.05	999	-
	BULK -		1100	1.86		-

from TAIPEI(TPE) to SAN ANTONIO(SAT)   in KGS NTD

GEN	BULK -		1	426.40	34	-
	BULK -		45	325.60	92	-
	BULK -		100	302.40	233	-
	BULK -		300	235.60	436	-
	BULK -		500	205.60		-

from SAN DIEGO(SAN) to TAIPEI(TPE)   in LBS USD

GEN	BULK -		1	3.65	75	-
	BULK -		100	2.78	191	-
	BULK -		220	2.43	517	-
	BULK -		660	1.91	999	-
	BULK -		1100	1.74		-

from TAIPEI(TPE) to SAN DIEGO(SAN)   in KGS NTD

GEN	BULK -		1	414.00	34	-
	BULK -		45	313.60	92	-
	BULK -		100	290.00	230	-
	BULK -		300	223.20	433	-
	BULK -		500	193.60		-

from SAN JUAN(SJU) to TAIPEI(TPE)   in LBS USD

GEN	BULK -		1	3.73	77	-
	BULK -		100	2.93	194	-
	BULK -		220	2.60	537	-
	BULK -		660	2.12	1014	-
	BULK -		1100	1.96		-

from TAIPEI(TPE) to SAN JUAN(SJU)   in KGS NTD

GEN	BULK -		1	473.20	35	-
	BULK -		45	372.80	93	-
	BULK -		100	349.20	242	-
	BULK -		300	282.40	447	-
	BULK -		500	252.80		-

from TAMPA(TPA) to TAIPEI(TPE)   in LBS USD

| GEN | BULK - | | 1 | 4.13 | 75 | - |
| | BULK - | | 100 | 3.15 | 191 | - |

Figure 3.   Air Tariff.

		ORIG/REV	PAGE
		1st	313
		CANCELS	PAGE
		Original	313
		EFFECTIVE DATE	
		April 15, 1986	
		CORR.	324

ASIA NORTH AMERICA EASTBOUND RATE AGREEMENT (ANERA)

RATE AGREEMENT NO. 202-010776

COMMON RATE TARIFF NO. FMC-16

FROM: PORTS IN KOREA TO: PORTS AND POINTS IN THE UNITED STATES, PUERTO RICO AND U.S. VIRGIN ISLANDS

(AS SPECIFIED IN RULE 1)

(R) SECTION 1—COMMODITY RATES

EXCEPT AS OTHERWISE PROVIDED, RATES APPLY PER TON OF 1,000 KGS. (W) OR 1 CUBIC METRE (M), WHICHEVER PRODUCES THE GREATER REVENUE.

COMMODITY DESCRIPTION AND PACKAGING	RB	RATES IN US$				ITEM NO.
		WC	MLB	AG	PRVI	
ELECTRICAL AND ELECTRONIC GOODS AND COMPONENTS AND PARTS, N.O.S.	M	122.00	140.00	140.00	138.00	11300
	W	166.00	201.00	201.00	181.00	
	D20	1720.00	2910.00	2910.00	3660.00	
	D40	2450.00	3885.00	3885.00	5200.00	

FOR APPLICATION OF RATES AND FOR RATES ON CONTAINERS NOT SHOWN, SEE RULE 2 OF BOTH THIS TARIFF AND SECTION 1, FMC NO. 15.

FOR EXPLANATION OF ABBREVIATIONS AND REFERENCE MARKS SEE PAGES 3 THROUGH 5.

ITS (703) 284-7500   ADO/7123/at

AUTHOR'S NOTE ON ABBREVIATIONS:

AG = Atlantic and Gulf	D = Container	FMC = Federal Maritime Cmsn.
M = Measurement	MLB = Mini Land Bridge	NOS = Not Otherwise Specified
PRVI = Puerto Rico and Virgin Islands	W = Weight	WC = West Coast

Figure 4. Ocean Tariff.

137

show sample pages from air and ocean tariff books. These tariffs have specific commodity rates for many products, and in some cases there is more than one possible classification for the same item, each with a different rate. If there is no commodity rate for your product in an air or ocean rate book, it will be charged the *general cargo* rate, which is usually high. If there is no commodity rate for your product, you can also ask for one to be set. For example, a firm in Haiti wanted to ship bars of medicinal soap to New York. Since no one had shipped soap from Haiti to New York in significant quantities before, no steamship line had a specific commodity rate. The exporter requested a form on which to request a specific rate, and the steamship line agreed to set one.

If there is already a rate for your product that seems high, you can apply for a rate reduction. If the steamship company gives you a lower rate, it should do the same for all other shippers of the same product on the same route, but there may not *be* any others competing with you. A carrier's main reason for lowering a rate is, naturally, to increase profit. You have to be able to show that, if the rate is lowered, you will increase shipments to the point where the carrier will make more money.

Both air and ocean carriers rate a product for their pricing on what is called a *W/M* or *Weight/Measure* basis. Products that are heavy in relation to their size are rated by weight and charged, for example, at so much per pound for an air shipment or at so much per ton for an ocean shipment. But a ton is not always a ton—you need to be sure you know whether the steamship company is using a short ton (2000 pounds); a metric ton (2204 pounds); or a long ton (2240 pounds), in its tariff.

Products that are bulky with respect to their weight are measured, and a formula is used to convert size to weight. The formula results in your being charged for more than the actual weight of the shipment. The formulae are based on 162 cubic inches per pound, by air, and 40 cubic feet per short ton, by ocean.

Many kinds of products can be rated either by weight or by measure. To get the shipping cost you have to provide both the weight and the "cube" (size in cubic feet, for example). The carrier will calculate the freight both ways and charge you whichever is higher.

Each air and steamship line has a minimum bill of lading, which means that a minimum charge is levied on even very small shipments. This varies from line to line. Air tariffs are generally structured so that the rate is reduced as a shipment passes 100 pounds, again at 220, 440, 1000, and 2000 pounds. Suppose the rate for boxing gloves imported from Pakistan is $0.20 per pound for 100 pounds and $0.18 per pound for between 100 and 219 pounds, and your shipment weighs 95 pounds. You can calculate the cost both ways: 95 × $0.20 and 100 × $0.18. If the 100 pound rate turns out to be cheaper you can call your shipment 100 pounds and save money.

MARINE INSURANCE

All international shipments should be insured against loss and damage, and this rule is followed with very few exceptions. A woman who was importing Christmas tree ornaments in small quantities by air, found the insurance rates so high that she decided against getting coverage. When she saw the way her first shipment arrived she was sorry. She is still trying to get by without insurance, however, and is working on getting the exporter to improve the way the fragile goods are packed.

There are various types of limited coverage that major shippers can use to save money on premiums, but most small-scale importers and exporters purchase all risk insurance, which covers *nearly* all risks. It does not cover loss or damage caused by war, so if you are shipping near a war zone (as the area around Iran and Iraq), you will want to pay extra for a *war risk* clause. Nor does all risk insurance cover losses caused by strikes, riots, or civil commotion (SR&CC). If your goods go through South Africa, for example, you need an *SR&CC* clause. All risk insurance does not cover "inherent vice in the cargo," which means something destructive in the goods itself, such as a moth larvae in sweaters or deadly bacteria in the shrimp. You can buy separate coverage for this also.

No standard cargo insurance covers late arrival or rejection by buyers or government agencies. These *are* insurable risks, but not every insurer will cover them and the premiums are high.

You will want to make certain you are insured against *general average*. This means that if the ship is in a bad storm and some heavy cargo is jettisoned, you are responsible for a part of its value, even though your own goods may come through unscathed. Your all risks policy should cover this.

Who buys insurance on a shipment is determined by the terms under which it is shipped. If you are importing C&F, *you* have to buy it. In many cases, however, the party who buys the insurance is not the one who will have to file a claim if there is loss or damage. Suppose you are *exporting*, C&F, on Open Account, and the shipment is lost. Technically, the foreign importer should pay you, but he or she may decide not to pay before being paid by the insurance company. In this case you must hope that the importer has a good policy, but you may become involved in the claim.

Suppose you are importing CIF under a letter of credit, your cargo is lost, and you find out the insurance is inadequate. You have a major problem.

To prevent this kind of problem, you can import C&F (get insurance yourself), give the exporter detailed instructions on what kind of coverage to buy and for how much (and specify on your letter of credit that he must provide an insurance certificate), or purchase *contingent* insurance. That is a kind of policy that will cover an insured loss if the primary insurer does not pay. It costs roughly half as much as the primary insurance.

As a general rule, small-scale importers and exporters buy insurance supplied by freight forwarders under their blanket policies, or directly from airlines, while medium-size shippers buy from insurance brokers. Large importers and exporters usually have "open" policies that automatically cover all the shipments of their *normal* merchandise which they make in their *normal* trading areas. They report each shipment to the insurer, but do not have to buy a separate policy for each.

In order to earn foreign exchange, about 40 countries require purchase of insurance on import shipments and sometimes on export shipments from local insurance companies. Venezuela is one example. Since, American exporters are reluctant to buy Venezuelan insurance, they usually elect to ship C&F.

The cost of insurance coverage varies enormously, but a rough approximation is 1 percent of the value of the cargo. It is customary to make the insured value CIF plus 10 percent. That means you are insuring the cost of the merchandise, the freight, the insurance premium itself, and 10 percent more. The extra amount is to pay for the time, trouble, lost profit, and perhaps lost customers that can result if a shipment does not arrive or arrives in poor condition.

A successful businessman traveled to China and ordered $5000 worth of hand-carved wooden furniture for his first importing venture. But he did not tell the Chinese exporter to insure for CIF plus 10 percent, and the exporter insured for a much smaller amount. The shipment arrived with $1800 worth of damage and the insurance in force paid only about a third. My friend, who was importing under a letter of credit, could have avoided this loss by having the opening bank write into the LC the condition: The exporter is to be paid only with the presentation of a certificate showing all-risk insurance, warehouse to warehouse, for the CIF value plus 10 percent.

The term *warehouse to warehouse* needs explanation. It means simply that the goods are covered from the exporter's warehouse to the importer's warehouse, provided there are no long, unexpected delays in the importing country and public transportation is used. This is obviously more complete coverage than warehouse to port, port to warehouse, or port to port.

If there is loss or damage on a shipment, the appropriate party (who this is depends on the shipping term) must file a claim with the underwriter. This requires presenting the bill of lading, the insurance certificate, and a survey report with an invoice showing the amount of damage or loss. If the insurance company agrees that it has an obligation to pay, it usually makes payment from about one to six months later.

To summarize, make sure your small shipment is covered by marine insurance, all risk, warehouse to warehouse, for the CIF value plus 10 percent and that the insurance underwriter is a strong, reliable company.

Incidentally, the word *underwriter* (now in general insurance use) originated in the days when ships' captains visited Lloyd's Coffeehouse in London to find wealthy people who would share the risks of a voyage. A ship's captain would write down details of the voyage, including kinds and values of the cargo he was carrying, and would sign the document. Someone would *write under* the captain's signature the amount of risk he would accept, and how much he would charge for accepting it. He was the *lead underwriter.* Other men, who agreed with the lead underwriter's opinion of the riskiness of the voyage, would *write under* his name the portion of the risk they chose to accept. These men were called underwriters, and their coffeehouse group grew into the famous worldwide insurance firm, Lloyds of London.

EXPORT PACKING

This is an insignificant sounding function that can have a very significant effect on your success. If packing is inadequate to protect the goods, your risks of loss and damage will be greatly increased and, if packing is grossly inadequate, the insurance company will cite that as justification for nonpayment of a claim. If you go to the other extreme, and *overpack*, the packing will be more expensive and will add bulk and weight, making transportation more expensive.

If you load individual boxes into a ship or plane your shipment is said to be *break-bulk*. This is the way all shipments used to go, but times have changed. Many years ago, shippers learned they could reduce handling costs and pilferage by strapping several boxes together to make one unit. This is called *unitized* cargo. Since units tended to be too heavy for cargo handlers to lift, the shippers began to put wooden platforms with small legs under them so they could be lifted by forklift trucks. This is known as *palletized* cargo. All of these can be called *LCL* (Less than Car Load) cargo.

The real revolution came with *containerization*. A shipping container is a large box that can be packed with cargo and sealed in such a way that it is nearly impossible to get into without breaking the seal. The seals' numbers are recorded to prevent a thief from breaking a lock and a seal, doing his dirty work, and then putting on a new lock and seal. Thus a container protects cargo against both loss and damage. (This assumes that the container is "sound," that is, has no places where water can get in, and is properly packed so that cargo cannot bounce around inside.)

There are several sizes of both oceangoing and air freight containers. The most common for ocean freight is 8 feet wide, 8 1/2 feet high, and 40 feet long. One of these holds an enormous amount of cargo (about 2,374 cubic feet of 42,000 pounds) and is the safest, most economical way to pack. This means large shippers that can fill containers have an advantage over smaller firms.

If your shipments are small, they will probably go break-bulk. This is not a serious problem for air shipments. The stresses and strains are not much greater in international air freight than in normal domestic freight. By sea, however, there are special hazards that make proper packing a *must*. Boxes can get dropped, thrown around, or crushed by other cargo. Logic tells us that heavier boxes should be loaded on the bottom and lighter ones on the top, but most steamships call at several ports. What goes in first, or what will come out last, usually ends up on the bottom. That means there may be a bulldozer resting on top of your pingpong balls. There are also risks of water and salt damage, and even sweat from condensation. Believe it or not, cargo inside a waterproof box and still get wet. If the box is packed under hot, humid conditions, and the ship passes through cold weather, moisture in the air inside the box can condense and get the cargo wet. That is why we used to see, in old war movies, shipments of firearms coated with grease and wrapped in waxed paper. Now firms can shrink-wrap cargo and/or add materials to the package that absorb the moisture.

All this means that importers and exporters must pay close attention to the way their cargo is packed. If you are an importer, look over the first few shipments carefully and tell the exporter if the packing seems inadequate or excessive. Even if there is no damage this time, there could be next time.

Some kinds of packing materials may get you in trouble with U.S. regulatory authorities. An importer who wanted to bring wooden bowls packed in straw from Grenada into the United States was prohibited from doing so by the U.S. Animal and Plant Health Inspection Service. Straw can harbor insect pests that are destructive to U.S. agriculture, and its use as a packing material is banned.

If you are in the export field but do not manufacture what you export, you will be dealing with products made by other firms. American manufacturers who have not exported before usually know nothing about export packing, and you may have to tell them how to pack for shipment by sea. You can get guidance from marine insurance companies such as Insurance of North America, headquartered in Philadelphia. If the exporter will not do the job the way it needs to be done, you will have to have the goods delivered to a specialized export packing company. These organizations usually have excellent service, but of course you or your customer will have to pay the charges.

MARKING

Companies that prepare boxes for export should know how to mark them properly. If your shipper does not know, you will have to help him learn. Shipping boxes are usually marked, "Made in (country of origin of merchandise)." They usually bear the gross weight, net weight, and outside dimensions, often in both metric and English systems. If there is more than one box in a shipment, each one is numbered. Very often a box bears the exporter's name and the importer's (or his agent's) name, address, and order number. In the case of cargo that is especially subject to pilferage, however, such as expensive cameras or watches, the customer should use *blind marks*. These are symbols used to identify the box without telling a thief what may be inside. Pilferers sometimes thwart the system by looking for boxes with blind marks, or by noting the marks used on a box that breaks or is opened by Customs and that contains very valuable cargo. Blind marks should be changed often.

Cautionary markings are often placed on boxes as well, sometimes in more than one language: "Handle with Care," "Glass," "Use No Hooks," "This Side Up," "Fragile," "Keep in Cool Place," "Keep Dry," and "Open Here." These can be stenciled on the package or just written on with an indelible marker.

Since cargo handlers in many ports cannot read any language, there are international symbols that can be used on shipping crates. A little penguin means "Keep frozen," an umbrella with raindrops above it means "Keep dry," etc. You can find pictures of all these in the book, *Ports of the World*, available free from CIGNA (a major insurance company), P.O. Box 7728, Philadelphia, Pennsylvania 19101.

There is an even more extensive set of symbols used for marking boxes containing hazardous materials. If you plan to deal in any product that is explosive, flammable, spontaneously combustible, water reactive, oxidizing, poisonous, radioactive, or corrosive you need to be sure your packing and marking are as required by the U.S. Department of Transportation, Coast Guard, and/or Civil Aeronautics Board. The captain of a vessel is the final authority with respect to carrying hazardous materials. If he thinks the shipment is unsafe, he can reject it, even though it may be in compliance with all regulations. Also port authorities are concerned about hazardous materials, and some ports prohibit loading or unloading the most dangerous kinds.

FREIGHT FORWARDERS AND CUSTOMS BROKERS

Forwarders and brokers are your agents in the ports of lading and unlading. In the United States, there are four different types of firms, three of which need licenses from regulatory agencies. They are:

- Air freight forwarder (not licensed)
- Foreign freight forwarder
- Customhouse broker
- Domestic freight forwarder

In practice most firms that hold one of the licenses hold two or all three. That way they can serve as your handling and clearing agents for both imports and exports.

Foreign Freight Forwarders

Air and ocean freight forwarders serve exporters by giving them freight rates to help them develop CIF quotations, booking space on vessels or aircraft, taking charge of cargo at a port or airport, arranging for packing, preparing export documents, making sure the cargo is on the vessel, collecting or assembling the documents, and transmitting them to the exporter or to his bank.

For this work a forwarder is paid a commission by the carrier, which for sea freight can range from about 1.25 percent to 10 percent. It is illegal for a forwarder to kick back any commission money to the shipper. The forwarder also receives a fee from the exporter. Forwarder's fees are not regulated and vary with several factors, but are usually around $125 for sea freight. With air freight the forwarder's fees are usually around $50 per shipment and the commissions about 5 percent. It is, however, legal for air forwarders to charge you, the shipper, whatever rate they can and want to. For example, an airline could quote a price of $2000 for a specific shipment and pay the forwarder 10 percent of that as a commission. The forwarder could in effect reduce his or her commission by charging you only $1900. Thus it would actually be cheaper for you to use a forwarder than to work directly with the airline.

Freight forwarders are listed in the yellow pages, port handbooks, and some trade magazines. You will want to pick one who has an office near the port(s) or airport(s) you will be shipping from, who has experience with the kind(s) of cargo you will be shipping and with the destination(s) you will be shipping to, and who has friendly competent personnel and a good financial standing. The financial aspect is the most important. If a forwarder makes a shipment for you and you pay for it, and the forwarder's company goes broke before paying the carrier, you may have to pay again.

Many forwarders pick up freight at inland points of origin, and several can save you money through their roles as freight consolidators or nonvessel-operating common carriers (NVOCCs).

Although most forwarders are competent and honest, you must remember that the more you pay for freight, the more your forwarder will earn from commissions. You should check on forwarders from time to time by getting rate quotations directly from airlines or steamship lines. Simply call a line's cargo department and ask for an *outbound rates clerk*. Give the details of your shipment, and the clerk will give you a rate. An importer can check on rates the same way by speaking with an *inbound rates clerk*.

Brokers and Domestic Forwarders

In the United States, a licensed U.S. customhouse broker is your agent for clearing goods through Customs. His job is to locate your goods, fill out a form called an *entry* (there are different types, as we shall see in Chapter 10), and arrange for a customs inspector to clear your goods. In most cases, the broker pays the customs duty for the importer and bills for it. Brokers have two weeks to pay Customs and, of course, like to be paid by importers within the same time period.

A brokerage fee for a routine clearance is about $75, but these fees are unregulated and vary considerably. If there are other agencies that need to clear your product, such as the U.S. Food and Drug Administration, the broker will arrange for this. The bill to you will include cartage to the FDA, the FDA fee, cartage back to Customs, and an extra broker's fee (usually $20 to $40 total). If there are problems with documents, such as a missing or incomplete commercial invoice, the broker can usually resolve them. Of course, this again costs you extra.

Finally, when you import merchandise, you have to know that when the goods are cleared for entry into the United States, you pay only the *estimated* duty. The inspectors at airports and ports cannot be experts in every type of product, and they usually accept the classification your broker puts on the entry form and charge duty accordingly. The Customs Service then has one year for a product specialist to review the entry and determine whether you were charged the correct amount of duty. The specialist can request *redelivery* of a sample if desired, and in some cases will have a sample that was originally retained by the inspector. If the specialist finds you were charged too much duty, you will receive a refund. If you were charged too little, you will receive a notice of money due and then an invoice.

Customs is afraid an importer will bring in a shipment, be charged too little, and disappear or go out of business before being assessed extra duty. To reduce this risk, rules stipulate that, with few exceptions, each shipment valued at more than $1000 must be covered by a *bond* for the full value of the cargo plus the estimated duty. (At this writing each shipment of any size or worth of textile products must be covered by such a bond.) You can go to a bonding company yourself and purchase either a *single-entry bond* (to cover just one shipment) or a term bond (to cover all your shipments for a year), but bonding companies protect themselves by checking your income and financial position. If you use a broker to take care of customs clearance, he or she will get the bond for you. That will cost you as much, or more, but will be an easier process because bonding companies usually accept the word of a broker that an importer is honest and financially sound.

If there is a small problem with your entry such as a missing document, the same bond will guarantee Customs that the document will be submitted within 120 days (within 60 days for the FORM A, Certificate of Origin).

In most ports there are many licensed brokers. You should select one who will tell you clearly and honestly what the brokerage fees are and what they cover. If you have special requirements, such as rush shipments or highly perishable cargo, look for a brokerage firm that can guarantee the kind of service you need. I once had an urgent shipment of product samples land at Kennedy Airport on a Saturday with everything mixed up. The shipment was consigned to the wrong party, it contained quota goods and even a prohibited item, and there were *no* documents. My brokerage firm sent its number one broker, a lady about five feet tall with a voice like a tiger, and believe it or not the goods were out of customs and in Philadelphia by 6:00 P.M. on Sunday.

There is nothing in U.S. law that says you *have* to use a customs broker, and in fact you can do the brokerage yourself if your shipment is by air *and* its value in the country of origin is less than $1000, *and* you are sure there will be no complications such as missing documents, *and* you live or work near the airport. If any of these conditions is not met, I suggest you use a broker.

Once your goods are cleared through Customs, you can pick them up, but a better choice is to have the broker get them loaded on a truck and delivered to your door. The broker will then be performing the role of *domestic* freight forwarder. Some broker/forwarders have their own trucks for delivery; more often they use the services of private trucking companies. In either case, you will be billed for forwarding, trucking, and perhaps insurance if the policy in force does not cover through to your warehouse.

9

The Importance of Proper Documents

People in international trade talk a great deal about documentation. It's a procedural matter that is required on every shipment. It's also a no-win matter. No one gets praised for having perfect documents, but international traders can have serious problems because of imperfect documents.

Altogether there are about 120 documents used in international trade, and a single shipment can have as many as 70. Luckily, most shipments have far fewer than 70 documents, and many of those are never seen by the importer or the exporter. They are created and used by service firms and government agencies.

The characteristics of a shipment determine the complexity of the documentation. A shipment of toothpicks from the United States to Germany, by air freight, open account, does not require much attention to documents. A shipment of automatic rifles from the United States to El Salvador, by sea freight on a letter of credit, on the other hand, requires so many documents you will need a good reading light and a new pair of glasses.

The four kinds of international trade documents are:

- Commercial documents
- Banking documents
- Transportation and insurance documents
- Government formalities documents

In general, the purposes of all of them are to facilitate, control, and keep track of international cargo movements. Figure 1 is a list of 32 different documents, classified according to these four categories. Following is a discussion of the most important ones and samples of some of them.

COMMERCIAL DOCUMENTS

The first step in an international transaction is an exchange of correspondence between a buyer and a seller. This often leads to the importer sending a *request for quotation*, for which there is no universal form. It can be any written statement of the product and its price, usually with a shipping term, a payment term, and other information. Figure 2 is a standard quotation from an exporter in Taiwan. The exporter can send this exact document to any importer who inquires about the products.

Pro-Forma Invoice

The *pro-forma invoice* is a more formal document. It is used when an importer wants the exporter to put in writing the exact cost of a specific order of merchandise with a specific shipping term, such as ex quay or FAS. An importer can open a letter of credit based on a pro-forma invoice, and in many countries an importer needs this document to apply for an import permit or a foreign exchange authorization.

A pro-forma invoice is like a regular commercial invoice, but with the words "pro-forma" written at the top.

Commercial Documents
  Terms and conditions of sale
  Contract, or purchase order and acknowledgement
  Pro-forma invoice and commercial invoice

Banking Documents
  Letter of credit application, LC, advice of LC
  Bank draft(s)

Transportation Documents
  Packing list
  Delivery instructions to domestic carrier
  Inland bill of lading
  Dock receipt
  Insurance request, insurance certificate
  Shipper's letter of instructions
  Ocean bill of lading or airwaybill
  Booking request
  Freight bill
  Brokerage payment
  Forwarder's invoice
  Arrival notice
  Carrier's certificate and release order
  Delivery order
  Freight release

Government Control Documents
  Import license, foreign exchange authorization
  Export license application, validated license
  Certificate of origin
  Inspection report (SGS, FDA, etc.)
  Consular invoice
  Shipper's export declaration
  Manifest (carrier to Customs)
  Special customs invoice
  Customs entry

Figure 1.   International Trade Documents.

The words mean: "This isn't really an invoice, and you don't have to pay it, but this is what the actual invoice will look like."

There is another type of pro-forma invoice which you must not confuse with the type just discussed. If you import merchandise, and the foreign seller does not send

OK INTERNATIONAL LTD.

TLX: 22781 OKFRANK
CABLE: "OKFRANK" TAIPEI
TEL: (02) 3931857, 3938504

ALL LETTER PLEASE MAIL TO:
P.O. BOX 5-222 TAIPEI
TAIWAN, REP. OF CHINA

2FL., NO. 38, NINGPO W. ST.
TAIPEI, TAIWAN, R. O. C.
台北市寧波西街 38 號 2 樓

QUOTATION   No. KQ-07/412

Messrs. TREICO

Date: July 23, 1935

Dear Sirs,

In compliance with your esteemed inquiry HAIR ORNAMENT
We are Pleased to quote you as follows:

Time of Shipment: 30 days after receipt of your L/C.

Terms of Payment: By irrevocable & confirmed L/C at sight in our favor.

Item No.	Unit Price/US Dollar FOB/DZ	Item No.	Unit Price/US Dollar FOB/DZ	Item No.	Unit Price/US Dollar FOB/DZ
JUMBO-LACE		B-033	USD 1.25	N-007	USD 4.29
A-1	USD1.39	B-050	0.89	N-014	10.01
A-2	1.25	B-051	0.89	N-023	10.01
A-3	1.00			N-024	10.01
		BRACELET		N-025	5.00
BROOCH		C-001	USD 2.07	N-026	4.29
B-001	USD0.95	C-002	2.07	N-028	5.00
B-002	0.95	C-003	2.07	N-033	3.57
B-003	0.95	C-004	4.11	N-035	7.15
B-004	0.95	C-005	0.71	N-036	5.00
B-007	0.95	C-006	0.78	N-039	10.01
B-008	0.95	C-007	3.57	N-040	5.72
B-010	0.95	C-008	6.43	N-041	5.72
B-015	0.71			N-042	7.86
B-016	0.71	**EARRINGS**		N-044	7.15
B-017	1.07	E-266	USD 1.96	N-045	3.21
B-018	0.89	E-268	1.78	N-089	6.79
B-019	0.89			N-090	5.72
B-020	0.89	**HAIR-BAND**		N-091	5.72
B-021	0.89	H-018A	USD 11.79	N-092	14.65
B-022	0.71	H-019A	10.00	N-093	15.37
B-023	0.71	H-020A	11.79	N-094	15.01
B-024	0.89			N-095	14.65
B-028	1.07	**NECK-LACE**		N-096	15.01
B-029	1.78	N-002	USD 4.64		
B-031	1.43	N-003	7.15	**SUPER-ROLLER**	
B-032	1.25	N-006	5.36	S-001	USD 1.25

Figure 2.   Quotation.

an invoice, Customs will ask you to make one. They will probably call the one that you (or your broker) provide them with a pro-forma invoice.

Order and Acceptance

If the importer is satisfied with the quotation or pro-forma invoice and wants to go ahead with the transaction, he or she will place an order. There is no universal form for this, although established companies often use standard purchase order forms for international as well as domestic transactions. An order can be a written statement as simple as "We hereby order as per your pro-forma invoice 627," but it usually includes more details, for example, "We order 100 dozen Model R FILEMFAST bicycle pumps, CIF New York, to be shipped by ocean no later than June 1, 1986, with payment by irrevocable letter of credit." An order can include other conditions such as documents that should be provided, or even what should be said on the documents. For example, the exporter is sometimes asked to provide a *Certificate of Origin* (discussed later in this chapter), and in some cases to show on the invoice the values of different components of a product.

The exporter should respond with a simple statement such as, "We accept your purchase order no. 291/86, dated May 2, 1986." In international trade, an order and an unconditional acceptance make a contract that *theoretically* can be enforced by either of the contracting parties.

In many cases, importers order informally, even by telephone, and ask their suppliers to provide formal confirmations of their orders. When an importer receives an order confirmation, signs it and sends it back to the exporter, there is a kind of international contract.

Figure 3a and b are two examples, the first of a formal international purchase order and the second of an order confirmation.

```
TREICO
93 Willets Drive
Syosset, NY 11791          BANK: Citibank N.A.
USA                             Syosset, New York

                          P.O. DATE: Jan. 8, 1986
TO: Exportadors Uribe
    77 Calle Inventada     P.O. NO.: 3/86
    Rogelio, Panama
                          SHIP TO: TREICO
                                   93 Willets Drive
                                   Syosset, NY, USA
```

NO.	MODEL	DESCRIPTION	UNIT	TOTAL PRICE
10	S33	Cartons each containing 4 dozen Panama hats	$146.00	US$1,460.00
5	S29	Cartons each containing 4 dozen Panama hats	120.00	600.00
		TOTAL F.O.B. COLON, PANAMA Ocean Freight		US$2,060.00 421.15
		TOTAL C&F NEW YORK		US$2,481.15

```
MARKS:  TREICO      | 3/86 |
        Syosset, NY

PAYMENT: SD/DP

SHIPMENT:  By sea, C&F New York

INSURANCE:  TREICO will cover




        _____
             PURCHASING DEPT.
```

Figure 3a. International Purchase Order.

158

(SELLER)
CORPORATION

TAIPEI, TAIWAN, P O C

| Original for Seller |

SALES CONFIRMATION

P. O. BOX   TAIPEI, TAIWAN.
CABLE:
TELEX:
TEL:

Date: FEB.20, 1986

Ref. No: SC-861013

Referring to   (BUYER)   LTD, U.S.A.

(Please indicate the above
number in the covering L/C)

we confirm the following sale to you on the terms and conditions set forth hereunder and on the reverse hereof:

Item No.	Description	Quantity	Unit Price	Amount
			FOB TAIWAN NET	
	P.O. 239			
4505	5 LBS/PR WRIST/ANKLE 6PCS/CTN/0.56'/15KGS	576PCS	US$2.02	US$1,163.52
4502	2 LBS/PR WRIST/ANKLE 12PCS/CTN/0.57'/12.5KGS	456PCS	US$1.47	US$670.32
5016	16LBS DUMBBELL WTS. 4PCS/CTN/0.26'/24.5KGS	24PCS	US$7.10	US$170.40
	TOTAL...........................	...1,056PCS vvvvvvvvv		US$2,004.24 vvvvvvvvvvv

SAY TOTAL IN U.S. DOLLARS TWO THOUSAND FOUR AND CENTS TWENTY FOUR ONLY.

PAYMENT : By Irrevocable and Confirmed Letter of Credit available against drafts drawn at sight in favor of Seller or transferable

SHIPMENT : MAR. 17, 1986

DESTINATION: NEW YORK

VALIDITY : 30 DAYS SUBJECT TO UPDATE

REMARKS : IND. CO.

SHIPPING MARK
(BUYER)
NEW YORK
C/NO.
MADE IN TAIWAN
R.O.C.

SIDE MARK
STYLE NO:
Q'TY:
ORDER NO: 239
N.W.:
G.W.:
MEA'T:

Agreed and accepted by:

Buyer:

_____
(Buyer's signature)

(SELLER)   CORPORATION

_____
(Seller's signature)

DIRECTOR OF BUSINESS DIVISION

Figure 3b. Order Confirmation (Sales Confirmation). (Reprinted with permission of Jonquil International, Ltd.)

Commercial Invoice

The commercial invoice is the most important document used in international trade. It is often called a *bill*. It says, in effect, "For this transaction you owe me this amount of money." Even if the importer has opened a letter of credit, the exporter will usually not be paid until he presents a commercial invoice (along with other documents) to the bank. The invoice also serves as a record of the essential details of a transaction and, perhaps most important, it provides Customs in the importing country with a statement of the value of the goods. Since most customs duties are based on value, the prices on the invoice are very important.

Each country has its own requirements for commercial invoices on imports, and some countries even have special forms on which invoices must be presented. The United States used to require a "Special Customs Invoice," but that has been discontinued. Exporters can obtain special invoice forms from the consulates of the countries they are shipping to, or from UNZ & Company, in Jersey City, NJ.

For shipments to the United States, the commercial invoice must show the following information:

- Port of entry of the merchandise
- Names of the seller and buyer, or shipper and receiver (usually addresses are shown as well)
- Invoice date
- Country from which the shipment is made
- A detailed description of the merchandise including the name and quality of each item, marks used in domestic trade in the country of origin, and marks and numbers on the export packing
- The quantity of each item (some products are quantified by the number of pieces, others by weight, others by volume)

- The purchase price of each item, in the currency actually used for the transaction (If the shipment is on consignment and there is no purchase price, the value must be shown.)
- Charges involved in moving the freight from FOB Vessel to where the U.S. Customs inspection takes place may be shown on an attachment to the invoice (which the customs broker can prepare)
- Any rebates or similar incentives the exporter will receive from his government for having made the exportation.

The invoice should be in English, or accompanied by an accurate translation. It should show any significant "assists" the importer gave the foreign producer, such as dies or manufacturing equipment.

A more detailed description of invoicing requirements is in the book, *Importing into the United States*, published by the U.S. Customs Service and available from the Superintendent of Documents. Figure 4 shows a computer-generated invoice for an actual export shipment from the United States.

BANKING DOCUMENTS

Of the four types of documents, those involved in payment are the fewest in number. Cash in advance and open account shipments do not require complicated banking documents. With bill of exchange shipments, there is only one, which includes the form used to specify the details of the draft and the draft itself.

On letter of credit transactions, there are at least four documents:

- The application for a letter of credit, which the importer must complete and present to the opening bank

CHEW INTERNATIONAL CORPORATION	INVOICE	PAGE:
	ORDER NO.: A039608	DATE: (

EXPORT DEPARTMENT
71 MURRY STREET, 9TH. FLOOR
NEW YORK, N.Y. 10007-2114, U.S.A.
TEL: (212) 619-4300, FAX: (212) 619-4273
TLX: 232715, 427413, 177799, 661570

REFERENCE DATA:
    INVOICE NO.: A039608/01
    DATE: 26JUN86
    YOUR REF.:
    ORDER DATE: 08MAY86

BUYER:
_____

ATTN: MR. _____
P.O. BOX _____
ALKHOBAR, SAUDI ARABIA

CONSIGN TO: _____

NOTIFY: _____

ULTIMATE CONSIGNEE: _____

MARKS:
_____ /DAMMAM
SAUDI ARABIA   A039608

TERMS:
    SALES: NET C&F DAMMAM
    DELIVERY: NET C&F DAMMAM|
    PAYMENT: TELEX TRANSFER

SHIPMENT DATA:
    SHIP VIA: OCEAN FREIGHT
    ARRIVES AT: DAMMAM

THIS IS A COMPLETE SHIPMEI

IT	DESCRIPTION	NO. OF UNITS	UN TP	UNIT PRICE	AM(US
1	6/10 Whole Kernel Corn	375	ctn	11.75	4,
2	24/16 Oz. Whole Kernel Corn	375	ctn	8.25	3,
3	24/16 Oz. Sliced Beets	350	ctn	9.50	3,
	Above 3 Items—Super Fresh Brand: English/Arabic Labels with m/e date (shelf life—2 years)				
4	24/16 Oz. Kingsway Cut Wax Beans English/Arabic Labels with m/e date (shelf life—2 years)	215	ctn	9.30	1,

NET C&F DAMMAM $12,

THESE COMMODITIES LICENSED BY U.S. FOR ULTIMATE DESTINATION SAUDI ARABI/
SION CONTRARY TO US LAW PROHIBITED.

WE CERTIFY THAT THIS PRODUCT DOES NOT CONTAIN PORK, ALCOHOL, GELATINE, §
RINE OR CYCLAMATE
    PER _____ , TRAFFIC M

BUYER INSURES

1-20° CONT.NO.IEAU-20845, SEAL.NO.10382
TOTAL CARTONS: 1315 CTNS
TOTAL GR.WT.: 45,728 LBS./20,742KILOS

CERTIFIED TRUE & CORRECT
_____
FOR CHEW INTERNATIONAL CORPOR

Figure 4. Commercial Invoice. (Reprinted with permission of Chew Interr
Corporation.)

- The letter of credit which the opening bank prepares and sends through banking channels to the exporter
- The *advice* of the letter of credit, which is sent by a bank in the exporter's country to the exporter
- One or more *drafts*, which are drawn for collection by the exporter.

Figure 5 is a sample application for a commercial letter of credit. Each bank has a slightly different form but the information required is largely standard.

TRANSPORTATION DOCUMENTS

There are many kinds of transportation documents including all of the following, and more:

Packing list

Delivery instructions to domestic carrier

Inland bill of lading

Dock receipt

Insurance request, insurance certificate

Shipper's letter of instructions (to freight forwarder)

Ocean bill of lading or airwaybill

Booking request (freight forwarder to carrier)

Freight bill (carrier to freight forwarder)

Brokerage payment (carrier to freight forwarder)

Forwarder's invoice (to exporter)

Arrival notice (carrier to importer or broker)

Carrier's certificate and release order (to customs)

Delivery order (consignee to broker or carrier)

Freight release (carrier to consignee)

SCB-293

Please indicate your instructions by placing X in the respective box

Standard ✕ Chartered

To: Standard Chartered Bank
160 Water Street
New York
New York 10038-4995

Application for ☐ Irrevocable ☐ Revocable   Documentary Credit

Bank's Credit Number

Subject to Uniform Customs and Practice for Documentary Credits (1983 Revision) International Chamber of Commerce Publication No. 400.

Credit to be advised by: Airmail ☐
Airmail with brief preliminary advice ☐
Full text cable ☐

Date of expiry:
Place of expiry:
In the country of the beneficiary ☐
At your counters ☐

Documents to be presented within _____ days after the date of issuance of the shipping document(s) but within the validity of the credit.

Applicant (name and address)

Beneficiary (name and address)

Advising bank
(only to be quoted if specifically requested by beneficiary)

Amount (in words and figures)

Partial shipments
Allowed ☐   Not Allowed ☐

Transhipments
Allowed ☐   Not Allowed ☐

Shipment/Despatch/Taking in charge from/at:

Not later than:

To:

Credit available with: Advising bank ☐   Freely available ☐
by: Payment ☐   Acceptance ☐   Negotiation ☐
against presentation of the documents detailed herein, and of drafts at _____ days sight
drawn on Applicant ☐   Yourselves ☐   Advising Bank ☐

Goods ☒
(brief description)

Documents Required

Invoices ☐   Signed Commercial Invoices   in _____ showing the
value of the goods and quoting order/indent no. _____
☐   U.S. Special Customs Invoices   in _____

C.I.F. ☐
C & F ☐
F.O.B. ☐

Bills of Lading ☐   Complete set of not less than 3 original/1 non-negotiable clean On Board Bills of Lading to order and blank
endorsed marked "Freight _____ "
Notify _____

Air Waybill ☐   Air Waybill required showing flight number, endorsed by the carrier with despatch date marked freight
_____ and evidencing goods consigned to _____

Insurance ☐   (a)   Marine and War Risks Insurance Policies or Insurance Certificates in duplicate endorsed in blank not less
than the full C.I.F. invoice value plus _____ % of the shipment in the currency of the the credit.
Transhipment risks to be covered if transhipment effected.
☐   (b)   Insurance on similar terms to (a) will be attended to by ourselves. Policies, certificates or cover notes will
be held at your disposal.

**Other Documents/
Special Instructions**

Charges   All charges outside the United States of America are for ☐ our account   ☐ account of the beneficiary
Acceptance charges for ☐ our account   ☐ account of the beneficiary
Discount charges for ☐ our account   ☐ account of the beneficiary

In consideration of your issuing a letter of Credit substantially conforming with the above request, we hereby
agree to all the terms on the reverse side of this application which are to be considered an integral part hereof
and, when requested by you, to sign and deliver to you an Indemnity Agreement in a form satisfactory to you,
and we further agree that each and all of the provisions of any general Indemnity Agreement heretofore signed
and delivered to you by us, or any of us, relating to Letters of Credit issuable in the absence of written agreement to the contrary, shall be deemed to be incorporated as a part of the above request.

Very truly yours,

*By _____

Please print or type
name and title of signatory _____

Mailing Address _____

*In the event that the applicant is an individual, do not fill in the line marked with an *.

Signature(s) Verified   Application Approved

Figure 5.   Application for Letter of Credit. (Reprinted with permission of William A. Laraque of the Standard Chartered Bank.)

164

Following is a discussion of the items in this list that are likely to concern small-scale importers and exporters.

The purpose of most of these documents is to keep track of merchandise as it passes from one hand to another. If a shipper delivers goods to a trucking company, the shipper gets a receipt to show it has been delivered (the inland bill of lading). The truck driver needs proof of delivery when the goods are delivered to, say, the dock (dock receipt), and so on. If a shipment disappears, there should be a trail of documents that will tell investigators who had custody of the shipment at the time it was lost.

There's another important aspect to these receipts. No one wants to be held accountable for damage to merchandise that was caused by someone else. Therefore each party who receives goods is supposed to examine the boxes. If a steamship company receives a box with no apparent loss or damage, it will simply accept the box and issue a bill of lading (actually will sign the bill of lading previously prepared by the freight forwarder). If the box is wet or badly dented, however, the steamship company will note this as an *exception* on the bill of lading. The document will then be known as a *foul* bill of lading. Letters of credit often stipulate that an exporter must present to the bank a *clean* bill of lading in order to be paid for the shipment. If a box is damaged before being loaded on the ship, and the bill of lading is foul, the exporter's payment will be held up until the situation is resolved.

Packing List

The packing list is a simple document showing how many boxes there are in a shipment, how to identify each, and what is in each. If a box is missing, one can determine from the packing list which one it is and what it contained. If you need to find a specific part of a shipment, the packing list should tell you which box it is in. The simple packing list in Figure 6 is from the book, *A Basic Guide to Exporting,* prepared by the U.S. Department of Commerce and available from the Superintendent of Documents. Note that there are five cases of the same product, from one to five.

Insurance Certificate

Most small importers and exporters use *special* rather than *open* insurance policies, which means they buy insurance on each shipment. The evidence that insurance has been purchased is an *insurance certificate.* This document is normally issued to the party who buys the insurance and is negotiable. For example, if you ship CIF to a foreign importer, he is the one who will have to make a claim if there is loss or damage. When you *present* your documents (take them to the bank in order to be paid), you endorse the insurance certificate giving the importer authority to file a claim and collect on a settlement.

Shipper's Letter of Instructions

An exporter making a shipment usually sends the goods to a port or airport in the custody of a freight forwarder. The freight forwarder needs to know what to do with the goods, and the shipper conveys this information by means of a *letter of instructions.*

There is nothing complicated about this document, and the forwarder will phone the shipper if he has any questions. The example in Figure 7 from an export information manual published in Texas tells the forwarder to ship to La Paz, Bolivia, to prepay the freight, to insure the shipment, and to present the documents to the bank. Note that the shipment is consigned to a bank in Bolivia and probably is being sent with a "To Order" bill of lading.

PACKING LIST

................DEC. 15.......................**19.** 80....
Place and Date of Shipment

To X Y Z COMPANY
LONDON ENGLAND

Gentlemen:

Under your Order No... 123 ....the material listed below
was shipped 12/15/81 **via** TRUCK AND VESSEL
To LONDON

Shipment consists of:	Marks
......5.....Cases..............Packages	X Y Z CO.
............Crates.............Cartons	LONDON ENGLAND
............Bbls.................Drums	MADE IN USA
............Reels....................	#1/5

*LEGAL WEIGHT IS WEIGHT OF ARTICLE PLUS PAPER, BOX, BOTTLE, ETC., CONTAINING THE ARTICLE AS USUALLY CARRIED IN STOCK.

PACKAGE NUMBER	WEIGHTS IN LBS. or KILOS			DIMENSIONS			QUANTITY	CLEARLY STATE CONTENTS OF EACH PACKAGE
	GROSS WEIGHT EACH	*LEGAL WEIGHT EACH	NET WEIGHT EACH	HEIGHT	WIDTH	LENGTH		
1/5	300		250	25	25	25		SPARK PLUGS (AUTO PARTS)

Figure 6.   Packing List. (Reprinted with permission of U.S. Foreign Commercial Service, U.S. Department of Commerce.)

Bill of Lading/Airwaybill

The bill of lading/airwaybill (discussed in detail in Chapter 8) serves as a receipt for the goods, a contract of carriage, and a temporary title document. There are various types: road, rail, ocean or air; "received for shipment" and

EXPORT SHIPPING INSTRUCTIONS

DATE __FEB. 9, 1978__

Shipper's Ref. No. __78-456__

Ship in name of __ABC MANUFACTURING COMPANY, ANY STREET, DALLAS, TEXAS__

Consign to __BANCO DE AMERICA, APTDO. 666, LA PAZ, BOLIVIA__

Notify __XYZ DISTRIBUTING COMPANY, APTDO. 792, LA PAZ, BOLIVIA__

Port of Discharge __LA PAZ__   Final Destination __LA PAZ__

MARKS AND NUMBERS	NO. OF PKGS.	DESCRIPTION OF COMMODITIES	VALUE	GROSS WEIGHT (POUNDS)	MEASURE-MENT
XYZ COMPANY LA PAZ P.O. 78-456 MADE IN U.S.A. CTN. #1	1 CTN.	CONTAINING: OIL WELL DRILLING PARTS Partes para uso en la industria petrolera. 6 #2489 O RINGS @ 2.89 10 #6723 GASKETS @ 1.59 4 #8932 SEALS @ 8.79 18 #8056 BUSHINGS @ 9.30 1 #5741 SHIM TOTAL F.O.B. DALLAS	 $ 17.34 15.90 35.16 167.40 12.68 $250.04		83 LBS.

Letter of Credit Expires _____

Value for Customs Clearance _____

Inland Freight to be Charged to _____

Port Charges to be Charged to _____

Air/Ocean Freight: Prepaid or Collect? __PREPAID__

Insurance Requirements __INSURE SHIPMENT__

Send Documents to __BANK__

Bank Documents Through __BANCO DE AMERICA__

License No. _____

Export Carrier _____

Point of Origin __DALLAS, TEXAS__

Name of Supplier _____

Inland Routing _____

Car No./Truck Line _____

OTHER INSTRUCTIONS

Consular Declaration or Other. _____

_____

_____

_____

_____

_____

_____

Figure 7. Shipper's Letter of Instructions.

"on board;" "short form" and "long form;" "straight" and "to order," and more. Long form bills of lading have a lot of fine print on the back specifying the terms and conditions under which the carrier is transporting the goods. Many of these conditions are determined, not by the carrier but by national regulations and international conventions.

Figure 8 is an example of one kind of bill of lading, "short form," "intermodal." The goods are being sent by air from Dallas to Miami and by sea from Miami to La Paz, and the bill of lading is issued by a freight forwarder. It is called a *forwarder's bill of lading,* and would not be accepted for payment if the importer's letter of credit called for an *on board ocean bill of lading.*

GOVERNMENT CONTROL DOCUMENTS

Both the United States and foreign governments want to know which goods enter and leave their countries. They need to know about imports and exports for statistical purposes, and to facilitate control. A country can't limit imports to 10 million TV sets a year unless it has a good record of the number of sets that are coming in. There exists, therefore, a set of documents to give governments this information.

Import License, Foreign Exchange Authorization

The United States government does not use these documents, but in many countries they're an important way of restricting imports. Importers have to present pro-forma invoices to their licensing authorities (usually the government agency responsible for foreign trade), or to their central banks, or sometimes to both. If the planned importation is legal and meets current requirements for a license or for hard currency, a certificate of approval will be issued. As you can imagine, this kind of system invites both favoritism and corruption.

U.S. exporters have to be sure they don't ship to importers who need licenses until the licenses are actually in hand. Unless payment is received in advance or guaranteed

A. FREIGHT FORWARDER, INC.	SHORT-FORM INTERMODAL BILL OF LADING
DALLAS, TEXAS	NOT NEGOTIABLE UNLESS CONSIGNED "TO ORDER"

SHIPPER / EXPORTER	DOCUMENT NO.
ABC MANUFACTURING COMPANY ANY STREET DALLAS, TEXAS	EXPORT REFERENCES D-74896 P.O. NO. 78-456

CONSIGNEE	FORWARDING AGENT (NAME AND ADDRESS - REFERENCES)
BANCO DE AMERICA APARTADO 666 LA PAZ, BOLIVIA	A. FREIGHT FORWARDER, INC. DALLAS, TEXAS
	(+) GOODS ACCEPTED FOR CARRIAGE AT DALLAS/FORT WORTH, TEXAS

NOTIFY PARTY	DOMESTIC ROUTING / EXPORT INSTRUCTIONS
XYZ DISTRIBUTING COMPANY APARTADO 792 LA PAZ, BOLIVIA	ALSO NOTIFY: HERMANOS SOLARES APARTADO 456 LA PAZ BOLIVIA

PIER	

EXPORT CARRIER (VESSEL) A.N.Y. AIRLINES	PORT OF LOADING MIAMI	(+) GOODS ENGAGED FOR DELIVERY AT
PORT OF DISCHARGE LA PAZ, BOLIVIA	FOR TRANSSHIPMENT TO	

PARTICULARS FURNISHED BY SHIPPER

MARKS AND NUMBERS	NO. OF PKGS.	DESCRIPTION OF PACKAGES AND GOODS	GROSS WEIGHT	MEASUREMENT
XYZ COMPANY LA PAZ P.O. 78-456 MADE IN U.S.A. CTN. #1	1 CTN.	CONTAINING: OIL WELL DRILLING PARTS Partes para uso en la industria petrolera. 6 #2489 O RINGS -Anillos @ 2.89 10 #6723 GASKETS -Empaques @ 1.59 4 #8932 SEALS -Sellos @ 8.79 18 #8056 BUSHINGS -Bujes @ 9.30 1 #5741 SHIM -Planchas TOTAL F.O.B. DALLAS, TEXAS	83 LBS. $ 17.34 15.90 35.16 167.40 12.68 $ 250.04	

(*) TO BE COMPLETED ONLY WHEN GOODS
ACCEPTED ON THROUGH TRANSPORTATION BASIS

FREIGHT/CHARGES	PREPAID	COLLECT	
			Received by _____ for shipment by ocean vessel, between port of loading and port of discharge, and from place of acceptance and/or oncarriage to place of delivery as indicated above; the goods as specified above in apparent good order and condition unless otherwise stated. The goods to be delivered at the above mentioned port of discharge or place of delivery, whichever applies, subject to terms contained on the reverse side hereof, to which the shipper agrees by accepting this Bill of Lading. In witness whereof three (3) original Bills of Lading have been signed, if not otherwise stated above, one of which being accomplished the other(s) to be void.
INLAND FREIGHT (DALLAS/MIAMI)	XXX.XX		
OCEAN FREIGHT (MIAMI/LA PAZ)	XXX.XX		
			A. FREIGHT FORWARDER, INC.
TOTAL	XXX.XX		MO. DAY YEAR B/L NO.

Figure 8.   Intermodal Bill of Lading.

by an irrevocable letter of credit. Just promised isn't good enough.

Sometimes a country that wants to restrict imports requires a *prior import deposit* from firms that seek approval to import. Argentina and Brazil have both used this technique with great effectiveness. When importers apply for a foreign exchange authorization, they must deposit with a government-owned bank a sum of local currency equal to a percentage of the value of what they want to import. In some cases, importers have had to deposit the full value of their shipments and wait several months before they could complete the process of ordering, receiving, selling, and collecting for the goods.

Export License

Many foreign countries require all their exporters to be licensed and/or to apply for a license to make each shipment. In this way, governments have control over what leaves their countries. In Somalia, East Africa, the government once banned export shipments of wood when the wood was needed in the country to make charcoal for cooking. Importers in countries across the Red Sea were left waiting, while the Somali exporters applied for export licenses that had little chance of being granted, but the Somalis had wood for their charcoal.

In the United States, a *validated* license is not required for most shipments to most countries, but if you are exporting and need a validated license you must obtain it. Otherwise your shipment will probably be stopped at the port, and you'll be held in violation of U.S. export control regulations.

You can obtain more information about export licensing regulations and procedures from your local office of the Department of Commerce or by calling the Office of Export

Administration's Exporter Service Staff in Washington D.C. at 202-377-4811. Libya and Nicaragua have joined Cuba, Kampuchea, North Korea, and Vietnam as countries to which American firms cannot export except for strictly humanitarian purposes. The licensing authorities' definition of humanitarian is extremely limited.

Certificate of Origin

Every national government wants to know the country of origin for imported goods, and often an exporter must provide this information by means of a formal document called a "certificate of origin." The purpose is to make it harder for importers to falsify the country of origin in order to pay lower duties or to bring in merchandise from prohibited countries.

A U.S. exporter who needs a certificate of origin can usually get it from the nearest large chamber of commerce by sending three copies of his commercial invoices, a letter stating that the goods are of U.S. origin, and a check (usually around $15) for the organization's fee. The chamber will certify on the invoice that the goods were made in the United States and the certified copies then become certificates of origin. Chambers of commerce vary in their policy toward certificates of origin, but most accept the declarations of exporters that their products were made in the United States, at least until something happens to show that the exporter is not honest. Chambers usually provide better service and lower fees to companies who are members, but most of them issue certificates to nonmembers as well.

U.S. import shipments must be accompanied by certificates of origin if they are intended to be duty-free under the *Generalized System of Preferences* or the *Caribbean Basis Initiative*. Both of these are discussed in the next chapter. The form used is a GATT (Generalized Agreement on Tariffs and Trade) document called a *Form A,* which is available only in developing countries. You must get after your exporter if one isn't sent to you; you can't get it in the United States. The document in Figure 9 is a sample of a Form A. The important part is at the bottom right, where the exporter declares in which country the goods were produced.

Country of origin declarations are complicated by the fact that relatively few goods are produced entirely in one country. A shirt can be made with Egyptian cotton, spun and woven in England, cut in the United States, and sewn and finished in the Dominican Republic. What is the country of origin? In general, the country of origin is that country from which the product is shipped to the United States, provided at least 35 percent of the value of the product was added in that country (or in a combination of eligible countries). Of the 35 percent, up to 15 percent can be American-made materials or components.

Suppose, for example, the Egyptian cotton that goes into the shirt is valued at $0.20. When the finished cloth reaches the United States for cutting, the value has increased to $0.80. After the cloth is cut into parts of a shirt, and delivered to the Dominican Republic, the value has reached $1.20. The FOB Country of Origin value of the finished shirt is $1.80. That makes the value added in the Dominican Republic $1.80 − 1.20 ÷ 1.80, or about 33 percent. By including the value of the processing in the United States, the 35 percent rule is satisfied, and the shirt can be considered a product of the Dominican Republic.

Shippers Export Declaration

This is the document on which American exporters report their shipments to the U.S. government, both for statistical purposes and to help with enforcement of export control regulations. An "Export Dec," as it's known in the trade,

1. Goods consigned from (exporter's business name, address, country)	Reference No. 393557
(SELLER) CO., LTD., 5-8/F., KWUN TONG, KOWLOON, HONG KONG.	GENERALISED SYSTEM OF PREFERENCES **CERTIFICATE OF ORIGIN** (Combined declaration and certificate) **FORM A**
2. Goods consigned to (consignee's name, address, country) (BUYER) NEW YORK 10475, U.S.A.	Issued in HONG KONG (country) See notes overleaf
3. Means of transport and route (as far as known) "SHIPPED AS PER S.S. 'PRES. WASHINGTON' SAILING ON OR ABOUT 20 JULY 1986, FROM HONG KONG TO NEW YORK, NEW YORK, USA."	4. For official use

5. Item number	6. Marks and numbers of packages	7. Number and kind of packages; description of goods	8. Origin criterion (see notes overleaf)	9. Gross weight or other quantity	10. Number and date of invoices
21-1213	O. K. NEW YORK P.O. 29288 MODEL : BC-3-115 C/NO. 1-12 MADE IN HONG KONG	TWELVE (12) CARTONS BATTERY CHARGER	'Y' 45.79%	SIX HUNDRED (600) PIECES	E86-736/S 17 JULY 1986
		I DECLARE THAT THE COST OF DOMESTIC MATERIALS PLUS THE DIRECT COST OF PROCESSING IN HONG KONG EQUALS TO 45.79% OF THE EX-FACTORY PRICE OF THE ARTICLE.			

| 11. Certification It is hereby certified, on the basis of control carried out, that the declaration by the exporter is correct. COUNTERSIGNED FOR DIRECTOR OF TRADE HONG KONG 21 JUL 1986 Place and date, signature and stamp of certifying authority | 12. Declaration by the exporter The undersigned hereby declares that the above details and statements are correct; that all the goods were produced in HONG KONG (country) and that they comply with the origin requirements specified for those goods in the generalised system of preferences for goods exported to For and on behalf of U. S. A. (SELLER) Company Limited (importing country) HONG KONG 17 JULY 1986 Place and date, signature of authorised signatory Authorized Signature |

Figure 9. Form A Certificate of Origin.

174

U.S. DEPARTMENT OF COMMERCE — BUREAU OF THE CENSUS — INTERNATIONAL TRADE ADMINISTRATION

FORM **7525-V-ALT.(Intermodal)** (3-19-85)

SHIPPER'S EXPORT DECLARATION

CONFIDENTIAL — For use solely for official purposes authorized by the Secretary of Commerce (13 U.S.C. 301(g)).

OMB No. 0607-0152

DO NOT USE THIS AREA

2. EXPORTER *(Principal or seller-licensee and address including ZIP Code)*

ZIP CODE

5. DOCUMENT NUMBER

5a. B/L OR AWB NUMBER

6. EXPORT REFERENCES

AUTHENTICATION *(When required)*

3. CONSIGNED TO

7. FORWARDING AGENT *(Name and address — references)*

29. THE UNDERSIGNED HEREBY AUTHORIZES ____

TO ACT AS FORWARDING AGENT FOR EXPORT CONTROL AND CUSTOMS PURPOSES.

EXPORTER ____

(BY DULY AUTHORIZED OFFICER OR EMPLOYEE) ____

8. POINT (STATE) OF ORIGIN OR FTZ NUMBER

30. METHOD OF TRANSPORTATION *(Mark one)*

☐ Vessel ☐ Other — *Specify* ____

☐ Air

4. NOTIFY PARTY/INTERMEDIATE CONSIGNEE *(Name and address)*

9. DOMESTIC ROUTING/EXPORT INSTRUCTIONS

31. ULTIMATE CONSIGNEE *(Give name and address if this party is not shown in item 3.)*

32. DATE OF EXPORTATION *(Not required for vessel shipments)*

33. COUNTRY OF ULTIMATE DESTINATION

12. PRE-CARRIAGE BY

13. PLACE OF RECEIPT BY PRE-CARRIER

34. EXPORTER EIN NUMBER

14. EXPORTING CARRIER

15. PORT OF LOADING/EXPORT

10. LOADING PIER/TERMINAL

35. PARTIES TO TRANSACTION

☐ Related ☐ Non-related

16. FOREIGN PORT OF UNLOADING *(Vessel and air only)*

17. PLACE OF DELIVERY BY ON-CARRIER

11. TYPE OF MOVE

11a. CONTAINERIZED *(Vessel only)*

☐ Yes ☐ No

Export shipments are subject to inspection by U.S. Customs Service and/or the Office of Export Enforcement.

MARKS AND NUMBERS (18)	NUMBER OF PACKAGES (19)	DESCRIPTION OF COMMODITIES *in Schedule B detail* (20)	GROSS WEIGHT *(Pounds)* (21)	MEASUREMENT (22)	D OR F (23)	**Value** — Selling price or cost if not sold (U.S. dollars, omit cents) **Quantity** — Schedule B unit(s) (Nearest whole unit)	
						24. SCHEDULE B NO.	25. QUANTITY
						26. VALUE	
						24. SCHEDULE B NO.	25. QUANTITY
						26. VALUE	

27. VALIDATED LICENSE NO./GENERAL LICENSE SYMBOL

28. ECCN *(When required)*

36. I certify that all statements made and all information contained herein are true and correct and that I have read and understand the instructions for preparation of this document, set forth in the **"Correct Way to Fill Out the Shipper's Export Declaration."** I understand that civil and criminal penalties, including forfeiture and sale, may be imposed for making false or fraudulent statements herein, failing to provide the requested information, or for violation of U.S. laws on exportation (13 U.S.C. Sec. 305; 22 U.S.C. Sec. 401; 18 U.S.C. Sec. 1001; and 50 U.S.C. App. 2410).

(Signature) (Title) (Date)

This form must be privately printed. Sample copies may be obtained from the Bureau of the Census, Washington, D.C. 20233, and local Customs District Directors. The **"Correct Way to Fill Out the Shipper's Export Declaration"** is available from the Bureau of the Census, Washington, D.C. 20233.

Figure 10. Shipper's Export Declaration.

is required for every shipment with value over $1,000, whether it is made with or without a validated license. For mail shipments, the Export Dec is required except for non-commercial shipments valued under $500.

There are three versions of the form, a 7525-V for most shipments, a 7525-V-Alternate for intermodal shipments, and a 7513 for in-transit goods. They can be purchased from the Superintendent of Documents, from UNZ & Co., or from a good commercial stationer. The document in Figure 10 is a blank copy of a 7525-V-Alternate.

10

Know How to Handle Customs and Other Regulatory Agencies

The task of importing products into a country can be simple or difficult, depending on the product, the country's laws (and how they're enforced), and whether the documentation is accurate and correct. In some developing countries, customs duties are actually negotiated between the importer or his agent and the customs inspector.

Since foreign import regulations vary enormously, and most U.S. exporters are able to avoid getting involved with foreign customs clearance, this chapter concentrates mainly on importing to the United States.

U.S. CUSTOMS ·

The U.S. Customs Service is a part of the Department of the Treasury. Its main task is to enforce the laws of the United States at the country's borders with respect to nearly everything entering or leaving except living human beings. The Immigration and Naturalization Service (INS) takes care of them.

Customs is in charge of enforcing laws with respect to both incoming and outgoing cargo. It has a right to inspect all shipments, and can detain or seize cargo for a variety of reasons.

The Customs Service is headquartered in Washington D.C., and is organized into seven regions, which are further divided into about 45 districts. Each has a district director and is responsible for customs activities at the ports of entry in its territory. The number of ports of entry varies widely. In Kansas the only one is Wichita, whereas Washington state and Texas are leaders with 25 and 24 ports respectively.

It also has officers stationed in eleven foreign countries. They advise foreign exporters on U.S. customs procedures and may help facilitate trade with the United States. These officers also assist in investigations of foreign exporters' shipments to the United States.

Under a 1986 ruling, importers pay for customs services by means of a tax (0.22%) on formal merchandise entries.

Relevant Government Regulations

International trade is considered an ease-of-entry business. In many countries, all importers and exporters must have special licenses or approvals, but in the United States the red tape is kept to a minimum.

Anyone can import to or export from the United States. It is possible to conduct foreign trade in this country without being either a citizen or a permanent resident. If one operates on a small scale under his or her own name, it isn't even necessary to register as a business.

Importers must, however, take care to meet the requirements of all relevant federal, state, and local organizations. There are some special requirements for a few products, such as alcoholic beverages, that will be discussed later in this chapter.

Technically, every export shipment valued at more than $1000 must be licensed. Most products to most countries, however, are exported under what is known as *Open General License*. When the exporter or freight forwarder completes the Shipper's Export Declaration, he or she merely writes "G-DEST" in the box reserved for the license symbol. This is tantamount to giving oneself a license to export. It is a crime to falsify information on the Export Dec.

There are a number of products, especially those with military applications or that include new technologies, for which *validated* export licenses are required. In general, the less friendly to the United States the importing country is perceived to be by the government, the more restrictive the licensing requirement. There is a Commodity Control List that shows the products that require validated licenses for various destinations by *Schedule B* numbers. Schedule B is a coding and classification system used by the U.S. Department of Commerce. It is available at USDC field offices (see Appendix B), in many libraries, and from foreign freight forwarders. The country destinations are classified by letter, with the more restricted countries assigned letters near the end of the alphabet.

Applications for validated export licenses are available from field offices of the U.S. Department of Commerce. Applications are supposed to be approved or rejected in about two weeks, unless the product is such that approval by the Department of Defense is also required. If this is the case, delay may be considerable.

Presented here are only the basics of export licensing, which is a very important and complicated subject. Before you export, check with the U.S. Department of Commerce to find out whether you need a validated license and, if so, how to apply for it.

You should contact Customs before you try to import merchandise. To help you, the locations of the customs regions and districts are listed at the end of the chapter. Each customs district employs various kinds of personnel, including inspectors at ports, law enforcement specialists, and the ones most directly concerning you—Classification and Value (C&V) officers. These are the people whose determination is final, unless you lodge a formal protest of, what a product *is* in customs terms, how much it's worth, and how much duty should be charged. The duty you pay when a shipment is entered is only the estimated duty although in most cases the estimated duty turns out to be correct and there is no refund or extra charge.

When you have samples of a product that you're seriously considering importing, you should call your nearest customs district office and ask to speak with a C&V specialist who handles that kind of product. Make sure you get the person's name and direct phone number in case you have to call again.

You should describe your product to the customs officer and ask a number of questions. First, ask what the "TSUS" number is for your product. The TSUS is the Tariff Schedule of the United States, a listing of virtually all imported products with code numbers and descriptions. The TSUS category your product falls under is the main factor in determining its rate of duty. You can buy a TSUS book for about $65, but major libraries usually have either the *Tariff Schedules of the United States Annotated* or the *Custom House Guide,* which also contains the Tariff Schedules (Figure 1).

The next question to ask is the rate of duty for your product from its country of origin. Duties are charged in the United States in one of three ways:

- Ad valorem
- Specific
- Mixed, or compound

TARIFF SCHEDULES OF THE UNITED STATES ANNOTATED (1986)

SCHEDULE 4. - CHEMICALS AND RELATED PRODUCTS
Part 1. - Benzenoid Chemicals and Products

Page 4-25

4 - 1 - B
406.44 - 406.72

Item	Stat. Suf- fix	Articles	Units of Quantity	Rates of Duty 1	Rates of Duty Special	Rates of Duty 2
		Cyclic organic chemical products in any physical form having a benzenoid, quinoid, or modified benzenoid structure, not provided for in subpart A or C of this part (con.): Other (con.): Sulfonamides, sultones, sultams, and other organic compounds: Copper phthalocyanine				
406.44	00	([Phthalocyanato(2-)]copper)	Lb......	18.1% ad val.	17.5% ad val.(D,I) Free (E)	7c per lb. + 67% ad val.
406.47	00	Sulfonamides: 4-Amino-6-chloro-m-benzenedisulfonamide	Lb......	7.6% ad val.	6.8% ad val.(D) Free (A,E,I)	7c per lb. + 41% ad val.
406.49	00	2-Amino-N-ethylbenzene-sulfonanilide; 5-Amino-α,α,α-tri-fluorotoluene-2,4-disulfonamide; Benzenesulfonamide; Benzenesulfonyl hydrazide; 2-Chloro-4-amino-5-hydroxybenzenesulfonamide; 2,5-Dimethoxysulfanilide; and Metanilamide	Lb......	7.6% ad val.	6.8% ad val.(D) Free (E,I)	7c per lb. + 41% ad val.
406.52	00	o-Toluenesulfonamide	Lb......	8.4% ad val.	7.4% ad val.(D,I) Free (E)	7c per lb. + 57.5% ad val.
406.56	00	Other: Products provided for in the Chemical Appendix to the Tariff Schedules	Lb......	1.7c per lb. + 18% ad val. 1/	Free (E) 1.7c per lb. + 18% ad val.(I(s))1/	7c per lb. + 57.5% ad val.
406.58	00	Other...	Lb......	13.5% ad val.	Free (E,I)	7c per lb. + 57.5% ad val.
406.61	00	Other: Products provided for in the Chemical Appendix to the Tariff Schedules	Lb......	1.7c per lb. + 14.5% ad val.	Free (E,I)	7c per lb. + 46.5% ad val.
406.63	00	Other	Lb......	13.5% ad val.	Free (E,I)	7c per lb. + 46.5% ad val.
		All other products, by whatever name known, not provided for in subpart A or C of this part, including acyclic organic chemical products, which are obtained, derived, or manufactured in whole or in part from any of the cyclic products having a benzenoid, quinoid, or modified benzenoid structure provided for in the foregoing provisions of this subpart or in subpart A of this part:				
406.64	00	Acetone	Lb......	0.3c per lb. + 18.7% ad val.	0.1c per lb. + 18.7% ad val.(D,I) Free (E)	7c per lb. + 60% ad val.
406.68	00	Adipic acid	Lb......	0.3c per lb. + 19.8% ad val.	0.1c per lb. + 19.8% ad val.(D,I) Free (E)	7c per lb. + 63% ad val.
406.72	00	Caprolactam monomer	Lb......	1.5c per lb. + 10% ad val.	Free (A,E) 1.5c per lb. + 10% ad val.(I(s))	7c per lb. + 40% ad val.

(s) = Suspended. See general headnote 3(e)(iv).

1/ Duty on Acetylsulfaguanidine temporarily suspended. See item 907.33 in part 1B, Appendix to the Tariff Schedules.

Figure 1. Tariff Schedule of the United States Annotated.

There are political-economic reasons, which we will *not* address, for some duties being one type and some another. Historically, duties are set by Congress largely to protect domestic producers. There are several instances of duties that were set in the past to protect domestic producers of goods that are no longer being grown or manufactured in this country.

Ad valorem means a percentage of value. There are various ways of determining the value of a product, but the most common is *transaction* value—what you pay for the product in the country of origin. If you buy, for example, FOB/Vessel, you will probably pay duty on that amount. If you purchase the same goods on an Ex Factory basis and arrange for the foreign inland freight, the dutiable value should be the Ex Factory price. You'll be saving money on duty.

The law has many intricacies, and knowledgable importers can reduce their duties by ensuring that their transactions are set up to avoid pitfalls and take advantage of benefits. For example, importers who buy through agents overseas may be better off if the agents work for them rather than for their suppliers. This is because buying commissions are not dutiable; selling commissions are.

Specific duties are per unit, such as 10¢ per pound or 15¢ per gallon. A specific duty set by Congress remains the same as prices go up, and the *incidence* (percent) of the duty on the cost of an import is reduced by inflation. Specific duties tend to raise the quality of a product being imported, because high quality items come in at a high price but pay the same duty in *absolute* (not percentage) terms as lower quality items.

Sometimes a product has a *mixed or compound* duty, both ad valorem and specific—"10% + 15¢ a gallon." This usually means that Congress couldn't agree on whether to apply an ad valorem or a specific duty and compromised by using a little of each.

Also the Customs office about the country-of-origin *marking requirements* for your product. Almost all products must be marked with the name of the country of origin, in English, but the type and location of the marking vary. Your product may have to have the country of origin mark on a label and sewn in, or die-stamped in a certain place, or printed on paper and glued to the bottom, or applied in some other way. The intent of the labeling requirement is to permit the final consumer of an item to see where it was produced, and the labels should be in conspicuous places and not come off or be taken off until the final consumer buys the item.

Customs recognizes that certain items cannot be marked, such as individual nails. In such cases, normally, the *package* containing the items must be marked. If an item is *transformed* in the United States, but not *substantially* transformed, the final consumer must still be able to see the country of origin. For example, crude pistachio nuts from Iran, that are roasted and bagged in the United States must still be identified as products of Iran.

Labeling is no laughing matter. If you import 100,000 candy bars, and the Swiss exporter doesn't put his country's name on them, you won't be able to sell them until they are properly marked. You may be able to get them released from Customs by posting a bond, but you can't sell them until you have marked them, redelivered a sample to Customs, and received approval. Sometimes Customs will even clear and release goods that are properly marked, and then (within 30 days) request redelivery. If you can't take the shipment back to Customs you'll be assessed a 10 percent marking duty plus a penalty.

In your conversation with Customs, ask about *other information* that should be on your product. Clothing needs laundering instructions, cigarettes need warnings about the user's health, etc. The officer may be able to tell you information that is required by federal (but not state or local) laws.

Also ask if there are any *other regulatory agencies* you should consult about your product. The customs officer may suggest one of the agencies mentioned in the next section of this chapter, and probably will be able to give you a a telephone number and a name.

Finally, ask if there have been any recent problems with the importation of your product. The office might tell you that a shipment was stopped (the technical term is *detained*) the previous week because of improper labeling or salmonella contamination or for some other reason, and you will know to be careful of that problem.

Going to See Customs

In some cases, especially with apparel, the customs officer won't be able to tell you with certainty over the phone the classification of your product. You will have to show it. Don't mail it or send it some other way; make an appointment to visit a C&V specialist. You need an appointment now because of staff cutbacks under the Reagan Administration. By looking at your product, a customs official can usually tell you the exact classification and the correct rate of duty, although in a few cases even they make mistakes. The officer may also be able to help you by suggesting ways of modifying the product to reduce the duty.

For example, most imported shirts and blouses have just a single row of stitching around the pockets. A single row is necessary to hold the pocket on. If the foreign producer has used a double-stitch for greater strength, the extra row may be considered ornamentation, and the rate of duty will be higher. In a recent bizarre case, the trademark on a shipment of blue jeans was held to be ornamental because the "e" in the trademark was slanted instead of straight!

Another reason for visiting a customs specialist is that some products are really several different products. I once helped start the importation of battery-operated clocks from Taiwan. The clocks were assembled in Taiwan, but used works (motors) and batteries made in Japan. It turned out that the clock, the works, and the battery were all considered separate products, each with its own TSUS number, rate of duty, and marking requirements. To prevent problems with customs clearance, the importer had to instruct the Taiwanese exporter to list the values of these three components separately on the invoice.

Written Rulings

In the United States, you're supposed to pay the same rate of customs duty no matter which port of entry you use. If you want to be sure there's no problem, you can request a written ruling and provide a copy to each broker who is going to clear a shipment for you. These classifications are issued by the National Import Specialists at New York Seaport Customs, 6 World Trade Center, New York, NY 10048. You have to send a product sample, and you shouldn't bother these specialists unless your product is such that different inspectors might classify it differently. Rulings on other aspects of the customs laws, such as which country is the country of origin of an item that is partly manufactured in more than one country, are issued at Customs Headquarters in Washington D.C.

Duty and the Country of Origin

U.S. import duties range from free to about 120 percent, with an average of about 6 percent. Figure 1 reproduces a page from the TSUSA. The TSUS numbers are those under the column headed *Item*. Note that TSUS 406.72 is a chemical product, caprolactam monomer. That product is measured in pounds and is charged a mixed duty. The duty in Column 2 is 7¢ per pound plus 40 percent of the value. This very high duty is charged on products from most Communist countries, such as the Soviet Union. It's one reason you don't see many products here from the Soviet and her closest allies.

Column 1 duty is for non-Communist countries and a few Communist countries that have met specific criteria— China, Yugoslavia, Rumania, and Hungary. Thus most of the world can send us caprolactam monomer for a duty of 1.5¢ per pound plus 10 percent of the value.

The *Special* column is for reduced rates of duty that apply to selected products from specified countries. These special cases are the least developed developing countries, the Generalized System of Preferences, the Caribbean Basin Initiative, and the U.S.-Israel Free Trade Agreement.

There are about 29 of the "least developed developing countries," such as Haiti, Bhutan, Papau New Guinea, and the Central Africa Republic. A *D* in the *Special* column indicates a reduced rate of duty for that product from the LDDC countries.

Nearly all developing countries are beneficiaries of the Generalized System of Preferences, which is a concession made by the GATT (Generalized Agreement on Tariffs and Trade) to permit developed countries to discriminate, in their tariffs, in favor of developing countries. An *A* in the *Special* column indicates that the product is free of duty from GSP countries. There are often movements in Washington to graduate certain advanced developing countries from the GSP. That has not happened yet, but some products formerly under GSP are no longer included.

The Caribbean Basin Initiative (CBI) is a U.S. program that, among other things, gives duty-free entry for nearly all products of most Caribbean and Central American nations. A few countries are excluded (Cuba and Nicaragua) and a few products, that is, apparel (unless sewn from pieces cut in the United States), footwear, and alcoholic beverages are also excluded. Some American, European, and Asian companies are beginning to manufacture in the Caribbean in order to ship to the United States without paying duty. The CBI designation is an *E* in the *Special* column.

The *I* in the *Special* column means that the product is included under the recently concluded free trade agreement between the United States and Israel. This agreement is being phased in gradually, and in a few years all products traded between the two countries will be free of duty.

Shipments must be accompanied by a *Form A* (see Chapter 9) in order to be admitted under the GSP or the CBI, although in some cases, Customs can waive a missing Form A and you will not have to obtain it.

Customs Procedures

When your goods arrive at a port of entry, the air or steamship line should advise the *notify party.* Ideally this won't be necessary because you'll already know which ship or plane your goods are on. You'll want to act fast because you have only five working days to pick up your merchandise. Otherwise it will be taken to customs storage and you'll have to pay cartage in, cartage out, storage charges, and an extra broker's fee. If Customs didn't have this requirement, the ports would be jammed, and the import system would break down.

If your shipment is valued at less than $1000, except (under a recent ruling) for textiles and apparel, it can be cleared from Customs with an *Informal Entry.* You or your broker complete this simple form, pay the duty, if any, and take the goods.

For shipments worth over $1000 that are to enter the United States for consumption in this country, it used to be

CONSUMPTION ENTRY
U. S. CUSTOMS SERVICE

INTERNAL REVENUE COPY

This Space For Census Use Only			Form approved. O.M.B. No. 48-R0217.	This Space For Customs Use Only	
BLOCK AND FILE NO.	M.O.T.			ENTRY NO. AND DATE	
	MANIFEST NO				

FOREIGN PORT OF LADING	U.S. PORT OF UNLADING	Dist. and Port Code	Port of Entry Name	Term Bond No

Importer of Record (Name and Address)

For Account of (Name and Address)

Importing Vessel (Name) or Carrier	B/L or AWB No.	Port of Lading	I.T. No. and Date

Country of Exportation	Date of Exportation	Type and Date of Invoice	I.T. From (Port)

U.S. Port of Unlading	Date of Importation	Location of Goods—G.O. No.	I.T. Carrier (Delivering)

MARKS & NUMBERS OF PACKAGES COUNTRY OF ORIGIN OF MERCHANDISE (1)	DESCRIPTION OF MERCHANDISE IN TERMS OF T.S.U.S. ANNO. NUMBER AND KIND OF PACKAGES (2)		ENTERED VALUE IN U.S. DOLLARS (3)	T.S.U.S. ANNO REPORTING NO (4)	TARIFF OR I.R.C. RATE (5)	DUTY AND I.R. TAX (6)	
	GROSS WEIGHT IN POUNDS (2a)	NET QUANTITY IN T.S.U.S. ANNO. UNITS (2b)				Dollars	Cents

MISSING DOCUMENTS	THIS SPACE FOR CUSTOMS USE ONLY

I declare that I am the ☐ nominal consignee and that the actual owner for customs purposes is as shown above, or ☐ consignee or agent of the consignee. I further declare that the merchandise ☐ was or ☐ was not obtained in pur-

suance of a purchase or agreement to purchase. I also include in my declaration all the statements in the declaration on the back of this entry.

.... DATE

.... (Signature)

.... (Address)

{ ☐ Principal
☐ Member of the firm
☐ .... of the corporation
(Title)
☐ Authorized agent }

CUSTOMS FORM 9-12-73 7501

Figure 2. Consumption Entry. (Reprinted with permission of the U.S. Customs Service, U.S. Department of Treasury.)

188

the practice for the broker to file a *Consumption Entry* (Figure 2). Use this form if you clear your own shipments.

It has become common, however, for the broker to file an *Application for Immediate Delivery.* Customs inspects the goods and either releases or detains them. Customs doesn't open every box; they check some at random and any of which they are suspicious. In this country, the enforcement of customs laws is not by stringent inspection, but by sizable penalties if you get caught doing something illegal, such as importing a product that is dutiable and calling it something that is free of duty.

After filing the Application for Immediate Delivery, the broker has ten working days to file an *Entry Summary* with the commercial invoice and other documents, and pay the duty (see Figure 3). In other words, you'll have your merchandise before the duty is paid. How does Customs know you'll pay the duty? That's another purpose of the bond that was discussed in Chapter 9.

In some cases, especially when goods are highly perishable, your broker may be able to get them pre-cleared so they will be released from Customs as soon as they arrive in the United States. Customs is working on an *Accept* system that will lead to the pre-clearance of a high percentage of shipments.

The final step in the process is called *liquidation:* a commodity specialist reviews the entry and decides whether the proper duty was paid. You should receive, within one year of the date of entry, a notice that liquidation has taken place (in some cases Customs has more than a year to do this). If you aren't happy with the result, you have 90 days to file a protest with Customs. If your protest is denied, you have 180 days from the date of the denial in which to file a summons with the U.S. Court of International Trade. At this point, you need the services of a good customs attorney, and it wouldn't hurt to consult one earlier.

DEPARTMENT OF THE TREASURY
UNITED STATES CUSTOMS SERVICE

ENTRY SUMMARY

Form Approved OMB No. 1515-0065

(1) Entry No.	(2) Entry Type Code	3. Entry Summary Date
4. Entry Date	(5) Port Code	
6. Bond No.	7. Bond Type Code	8. Broker/Importer File No.

9. Ultimate Consignee Name and Address	10. Consignee No.	(11) Importer of Record Name and Address	(12) Importer No.
		(13) Exporting Country	14. Export Date
		(15) Country of Origin	16. Missing Documents
	State	(17) I.T. No.	(18) I.T. Date
(19) B/L or AWB No.	20. Mode of Transportation	21. Manufacturer I.D.	22. Reference No.
(23) Importing Carrier	24. Foreign Port of Lading	25. Location of Goods/G.O. No.	
26. U.S. Port of Unlading	(27) Import Date		

(28) Line No.	(29) Description of Merchandise			33. (A) Entered Value B. CHGS C. Relationship	34. (A) T.S.U.S.A. Rate B. ADA/CVD Rate (C) I.R.C. Rate D. Visa No.	(35) Duty and I.R. Tax	
	30. (A) T.S.U.S.A. No. B. ADA/CVD Case No.	31. (A) Gross Weight B. Manifest Qty.	(32) Net Quantity in T.S.U.S.A. Units			Dollars	Cents

(36) Declaration of Importer of Record (Owner or Purchaser) or Authorized Agent

I declare that I am the

☐ importer of record and that the actual owner, purchaser, or consignee for customs purposes is as shown above. OR ☐ owner or purchaser or agent thereof.

I further declare that the merchandise

☐ was obtained pursuant to a purchase or agreement to purchase and that the prices set forth in the invoice are true. OR ☐ was not obtained pursuant to a purchase or agreement to purchase and the statements in the invoice as to value or price are true to the best of my knowledge and belief.

I also declare that the statements in the documents herein filed fully disclose to the best of my knowledge and belief the true prices, values, quantities, rebates, drawbacks, fees, commissions, and royalties and are true and correct, and that all goods or services provided to the seller of the merchandise either free or at reduced cost are fully disclosed. I will immediately furnish to the appropriate customs officer any information showing a different state of facts.

Notice required by Paperwork Reduction Act of 1980: This information is needed to ensure that importers/exporters are complying with U.S. customs laws, to allow us to compute and collect the right amount of money, to enforce other agency requirements, and to collect accurate statistical information on imports. Your response is mandatory.

U.S. CUSTOMS USE		TOTALS	
A. Liq. Code	B. Ascertained Duty	(37) Duty	
	C. Ascertained Tax	(38) Tax	
	D. Ascertained Other	(39) Other	
	E. Ascertained Total	(40) Total	

(41) Signature of Declarant, Title, and Date

PART 1 — RECORD COPY

Customs Form 7501 (030884)

Figure 3. Entry Summary. (Reprinted with permission of the U.S. Customs Service, U.S. Department of Treasury.)

Quotas and Extra Duties

Some kinds of merchandise (many types of apparel) are under quota, usually a fixed annual ceiling on the amount that can be imported. In some cases, quota goods cannot be cleared through Customs unless you can prove that the exporting country's government has authorized the inclusion of these particular items in its quota for the product. For example, you can't bring in men's shirts from Malaysia unless they're accompanied by a *visa* from the proper authority in Kuala Lumpur. Commodity (C&V) specialists should know the details of quotas on the products they handle, but you may need to get more information from quota specialists at the U.S. Customs Service or the U.S. Department of Commerce. The phone number of the textile group is 202-377-4212. The Customs Service has recorded phone messages on the status of quota fulfillment for eleven countries. To get these numbers call 202-566-5810.

Sometimes a product is being "watched," but is not under quota. You will need a visa to import a watched product from certain countries.

In a few cases, U.S. importers have been charged extra duties for a variety of reasons. If the foreign exporter is benefiting from subsidies that the U.S. government considers illegal under GATT rules, Customs can charge a *countervailing duty* to raise your cost. If your products are being sold in this country at less than their fair market value in the producing country, the International Trade Commission can recommend that the President impose an *antidumping* duty. There have been other systems in the past, such as *American Selling Price* and *trigger price.*

Temporary Entries

In some cases, you may want to reexport the goods you bring to the United States, either in their original form or with alterations, and not pay duty on them, or you may

want to avoid paying customs duty until the goods are actually sold in the United States. There are four systems
that can help in such cases: temporary importation under
bond, duty drawback, bonded warehousing, and foreign
trade zones. Look into these if you become involved in
large transactions of the type just discussed.

There are also other types of customs entries to cover
certain special situations. A source of more detailed information about the material discussed in this chapter is
the book *Importing into the United States*, prepared by the
United States Customs Service. Every U.S. importer will
benefit from buying it.

OTHER FEDERAL REGULATIONS

There are many federal laws that must be enforced on imported as well as on domestic products. Although Customs
is the main enforcement agency at the ports, you may, and
sometimes must, be in contact with the federal agency that
is responsible for administering a law pertaining to your
product.

Much of the information included here is from *Importing into the United States*. The list is not exhaustive; be
sure to check with customs before you order goods from a
foreign country.

Food Products

The Federal Food, Drug and Cosmetic Act is the basic legislation governing imports of products that go in or on the
body, and the responsible agency is the Department of
Health and Human Services of the Food and Drug Administration, Rockville, Maryland 20857. Each FDA district,
however, is the final authority for products entering
through ports in that area. You can't get a written ruling in

Florida that says your beans can be imported in Oregon. Many food products must adhere to standards published in the *Code of Federal Regulations,* which anyone can read but only a food technologist with a law degree can understand.

FDA will not analyze your product before you import it or tell you whether it will pass inspection, but they will comment on the label. You can have the product tested by a private laboratory, which will issue a written report (I've used Werby Labs in Chelsea, Massachusetts). One value of having a food product tested is that the results might warn you not to import it, thus saving you a lot of money.

In one instance, I had a product tested and it met FDA standards, but barely. I knew that if the test were shown to FDA, this agency was likely to run its own test. My goods would gather dust until they were approved for sale, and there was a chance they would be rejected rather than released.

Food products processed at high temperatures are more likely to meet FDA standards than other food products, provided they are properly handled and packed.

Meat and Poultry.   Fresh and frozen meat, poultry and related products are allowed only from foreign factories that have been approved to export to the United States. Spain, which has excellent meat at low prices, cannot supply the United States because the government has not requested approval of any factory. The principal agencies involved are the Food Safety and Quality Service and the Animal and Plant Health Inspection Service, both of the U.S. Department of Agriculture. For some kinds of poultry, such as quail, you should also consult the Fish and Wildlife Service of the Department of the Interior.

Fruits and Vegetables.   These products are subject to approval by the Animal and Plant Health Inspection Service, U.S. Department of Agriculture, Washington D.C. 20782.

Many kinds of fruits and vegetables must also meet grading or other quality standards. You can learn about those from the Agriculture Marketing Service, U.S. Department of Agriculture, Washington D.C. 20250. There are some interesting difficulties. For example, there's a destructive worm that inhabits the seeds of Mexican mangos. Until the recent development of irradiation to kill the worms, the only way to bring in the mangos was by removing the seeds. These regulations may seem a nuisance to U.S. importers, but without them American agriculture would be devastated by imported insects.

Dairy Products.   Many types of cheese are under quota and require import licenses. Contact the Foreign Agricultural Service, U.S. Department of Agriculture, Washington D.C. 20250. Milk and cream are regulated by both the Food and Drug Administration and the Department of Agriculture. Milk is under a *tariff rate quota*, which means the duty goes up after a specific quantity is imported each year. Condensed and evaporated milk, cream, and ice cream are under "absolute" quotas.

Other Food Products.   There are quotas also on various food products including several species of fish, potatoes, chocolate, sugar, and peanuts. Candy containing more than 1/2 percent alcohol is prohibited entirely. Unexpected things can happen; several months ago American companies found it was profitable to import food products containing large amounts of sugar, extract the sugar, and sell it. This was possible because the price of sugar in the United States is maintained at from three to six times the world price (to protect U.S. beet growers and cane growers in Hawaii). The government responded by temporarily banning imports of a category of miscellaneous food items, some of which did not contain any sugar at all. The measure was announced suddenly and caught several importers with newly illegal shipments on their way to the United States.

Textiles and Apparel

Virtually all textile products are subject to extra requirements. They must be labeled with the country of origin, fiber content, laundering instructions, and the name or trademark of the producer, importer, or marketing organization (An RN or registration number can be substituted for some of this information). The Federal Trade Commission, Washington D.C. 20580, can give you information about requirements of the Textile Fiber Identification Act and the Wool Products Labeling Act.

There can be interesting complications. For example, a Pakistani exporter told me recently that U.S. duty on some apparel products varied depending on the chief fiber content by weight. If he exported a blouse that was 51 percent cotton and 49 percent silk, he would come out ahead by reversing the percentages and making the chief fiber silk, which comes in at a lower rate of duty. The problem was that, in Pakistan, exporters have to report the fiber content of exported garments by value. He had much difficulty getting the information required by U.S. Customs.

Also check on regulations enforced by the Consumer Products Safety Commission, Washington D.C. 20207, especially with regard to flammability of fabrics. There are several countries in which flame-resistant cloth is not produced and cannot be imported. I suggest not ordering children's pajamas from one of these countries.

Alcoholic Beverages

Imports of beer, wine, and liquor are well regulated. First you need an Importer's Basic Permit from the Bureau of Alcohol, Tobacco and Firearms, Department of the Treasury,

Washington D.C. 20226. You'll have to fill out forms and pay a fee of around $200. You'll need a similar permit from the state into which you plan to import. Most state permits are more expensive and harder to get than the federal permit.

For wine and liquor, the bottles must be in metric sizes, and the labels must be approved in advance by the Bureau of Alcohol, Tobacco and Firearms. There are several label requirements, one of which is that the alcoholic content should be printed on the label only if your particular state requires it. In some states, beer labels also need prior approval.

For liquor, you'll need to buy the federal *red strip* stamps and send them to your foreign exporter to place on the bottles. These are evidence that the excise tax has been paid. If you import liquor without the strips, you'll have to buy them and paste them on before making any deliveries. Alcoholic beverages are also subject to inspection by the Food and Drug Administration.

Motor Vehicles

Two kinds of laws apply to cars, trucks, and motorcycles— safety and environmental cleanliness. Imported vehicles manufactured after December 31, 1967 must conform to safety regulations. For information contact the Office of Enforcement, Motor Vehicle Program, National Highway Traffic Safety Administration, U.S. Department of Transportation, Washington D.C. 20590. All imported vehicles must meet the requirements of the Clean Air Act. Information about this is available from the Public Information Center (PM-215), Environmental Protection Agency, Washington, D.C. 20460.

It's less expensive to have cars adapted to American standards overseas than to have the work done on arrival in the United States, but I've heard of foreign adaptations that were considered inadequate by the American authorities. Part of the work had to be redone. You can import an automobile under bond and take up to 180 days to bring it into conformity with U.S. standards; this time limit can sometimes be extended. You can not drive the car until it has been appropriately modified and approved.

Other Products

Household Appliances. Household appliances are subject to consumer products safety, energy efficiency, and energy labeling laws. Contact the Consumer Products Effectiveness Branch, U.S. Department of Energy, Washington D.C. 20585 and the division of Energy and Product Information, Federal Trade Commission, Washington D.C.

Electronic Products. Electronic products that emit radiation must meet standards enforced by the Bureau of Radiological Health, Food and Drug Administration, Rockville, Maryland 20857. For electronic products that broadcast on the airwaves, contact the Federal Communications Commission, Washington D.C. 20554.

Plants and Plant Products. Items such as these must always be inspected at the border, by the Department of Agriculture, for potentially destructive insect pests.

Drugs and Cosmetics. These must be safe for human use and are subject to inspection by the Food and Drug Administration. Many foreign drug products are not for sale in the United States because they require formal FDA approval. The testing period here is long, and the standards are strict.

Pesticides and Toxic Substances. For regulations on products of this type, check with the Office of Pesticides and Toxic Substances, Environmental Protection Agency, Washington D.C. 20460.

Hazardous Substances. Dangerous chemicals and similar items must meet regulations enforced by the Food and Drug Administration and the Consumer Products Safety Commission. Their transportation is regulated by the Materials Transportation Bureau, U.S. Department of Transportation, Washington D.C. 20590.

STATE AND LOCAL REGULATIONS

In some cases, U.S. Customs may approve your product for entry into the United States, but state or local regulations prohibit its sale. Here are two examples.

The lovely rag dolls from Columbia mentioned earlier in this book may be high-quality gift items, but some states classify them as toys for which state approval is required. In the Northeast, there were five states in which these dolls could not be sold without being licensed. The licensing process in these states were not hard, but each required the expenditure of time and money.

I once did a small amount of work for a company in Chile that manufactures simple electrical apparatus such as light switches. The firm was planning to export to the United States. Federal regulations on this kind of product were no problem, but no city or county would buy unless the products met local standards. We had to begin by contacting Underwriters Laboratories and having both the products and the factory in Chile inspected by UL personnel. Although the switches were of high quality, the approval process could not be short-circuited.

How do you find out about these kinds of regulations? First, look carefully at products like yours in stores to see if there's any mark or label on them that you don't understand. If there is, find out what it is and why it's there. Second, ask people in the trade as well as local government authorities.

A FEW WORDS FOR EXPORTERS

Export control laws and export licensing have already been discussed. There are at least two other laws that are important to exporters.

Exporters should be aware of the Business Practices and Records Act, formerly the Anti-Corrupt Practices Act. This makes it illegal for U.S. exporters to bribe foreign officials. The definitions of bribe and of foreign official are both important. It's legal to give a small "grease payment" to a foreign customs inspector to get your shipment cleared expeditiously. The small payment would not be considered a bribe, and the customs inspector would not be considered a foreign official. It is not legal to give the brother of the Minister of Health a few thousand dollars to bring about the purchase of your line of antibiotics. If your foreign sales agent makes the bribe, and you didn't know about it, you can still be held accountable if the Justice Department believes that you *should* have known about it. The Reagan Administration has not gone out of its way to find, and fine, violators of this law, but future administrations may be stricter.

Exporters should also know that it is illegal for you to cooperate with boycotts sponsored by foreign governments, especially the Arab boycott of Israel. A buyer in an Arab country might ask you to certify that your goods are not of Israeli origin, were not made by an Israeli-owned company, and will not be shipped on Israeli vessels. If you make such a statement you'll be violating U.S. law. You can usually make a positive statement such as certifying that the goods are the product of the United States. If you

Headquarters
U.S. Customs Service
1301 Constitution Ave., N.W.
Washington, D.C. 20229

**Northeast Region—
Boston, Mass. 02110**
Districts:
Portland, Maine 04111
St. Albans, Vt. 05478
Boston, Mass. 02109
Providence, R.I. 02903
Buffalo, N.Y. 14202
Ogdensburg, N.Y. 13669
Bridgeport, Conn. 06609
Philadelphia, Pa. 19106
Baltimore, Md. 21202
Norfolk, Va. 23510
Washington, D.C. 20041

**New York Region—
New York, N.Y. 10048**
New York Seaport Area
New York, N.Y. 10048
Kennedy Airport Area
Jamaica, N.Y. 11430
Newark Area
Newark, N.J. 07114

**Southeast Region—
Miami, Fla. 33131**
Districts:
Wilmington, N.C. 28401
San Juan, P.R. 00903
Charleston, S.C. 29402
Savannah, Ga. 31401
Tampa, Fla. 33602
Miami, Fla 33131
St. Thomas, V.I. 00801

**South Central Region—
New Orleans, La. 70130**
Districts:
Mobile, Ala. 36652
New Orleans, La. 70130

**Southwest Region—
Houston, Tex. 77057**
Districts:
Port Arthur, Tex. 77640
Galveston, Tex. 77550
Houston, Tex. 77052
Laredo, Tex. 78041
El Paso, Tex. 79985
Dallas/Fort Worth, Tex. 75261

**Pacific Region—
Los Angeles, Calif. 90053**
Districts:
Nogales, Ariz. 85621
San Diego, Calif. 92188
Los Angeles, Calif.,
San Pedro, Calif. 90731
San Francisco, Calif. 94126
Honolulu, Hawaii 96806
Portland, Oreg. 97209
Seattle, Wash. 98174
Anchorage, Alaska 99501
Great Falls, Mont. 59401

**North Central Region—
Chicago, Ill. 60607**
Districts:
Chicago, Ill. 60607
Pembina, N. Dak. 58271
Minneapolis-St. Paul, Minn. 55401
Duluth Minn. 55802
Milwaukee, Wis. 53202
Cleveland, Ohio 44114
St. Louis, Mo. 63105
Detroit, Mich. 48226-2568

Source: United States Customs Service, *Importing Into the United States,* May, 1984, page 3.

Figure 10–4. Customs Districts and Regions.

receive a boycott request, check with the Department of Commerce and perhaps a lawyer to make sure you're on safe legal ground. If you receive a letter of credit that contains boycott provisions, your bank will probably refuse to handle it. All boycott requests should be reported to the Department of Commerce in Washington D.C.

For information about legal requirements of the countries you're exporting to, try those countries' consulates, the U.S. Department of Commerce country specialists in Washington, the Dun and Bradstreet *Exporters' Encyclopedia, Croner's Reference Book for World Traders,* your freight forwarder, and your foreign importer. Your importer should be very cooperative because, if something goes wrong, both you and he will probably suffer for it.

11

Sources of Information And Assistance

This book includes a great deal of information about importing and exporting, but it's only a fraction of what there is to be learned. If you enter the business, and your company grows, you'll need information and assistance on many occasions. You can never know too much.

There are at least five kinds of information sources—government organizations, world trade clubs and associations, printed materials, import and export service organizations, and consulting firms.

GOVERNMENT ORGANIZATIONS

U.S. Department of Commerce

The U.S. Department of Commerce is one of your most important sources of information. The department's International Trade Administration is the organization primarily responsible for promoting U.S. exports. Appendix B contains the addresses and telephone numbers of the ITA field offices, one of which is assigned to cover *your* part of the country.

Some of the services available are foreign trade statistics, World Trader Data Reports (credit information), an excellent magazine (*Business America*), Export Mailing Lists, the Agent/Distributor Service, Trade Opportunities Bulletins, and a new products bulletin that is circulated to American commercial officers abroad. American exporters who travel abroad often visit these commercial offices for advice and assistance. Most American embassies have at least one commercial officer and a small library of business information.

There's a charge for most of the Commerce Department's services, but the charges are reasonable.

Other Federal Organizations

For exporters of agricultural products, the U.S. Department of Agriculture can provide information, some counseling, and in some cases financing.

The U.S. Small Business Administration has a few SCORE (Service Corps or Retired Executives) counselors who understand international trade, and a small loan guarantee facility for exporting firms.

The U.S. Export Import Bank and its Foreign Credit Association can help medium and large exporters with export financing and credit insurance.

The Agency for International Development finances foreign projects that absorb U.S. exports, and the Overseas Private Investment Corporation helps finance projects that involve American investment abroad.

For importers, the U.S. Customs Service is willing to provide information because they know they'll have fewer headaches at ports of entry if importers are better informed. Personnel of the other regulatory agencies often will explain their procedures and the rules they enforce, but usually are not eager to take the time to do so.

State Governments

Most or all U.S. states are involved in export promotion, at least on a small scale. They provide informational publications, sponsor seminars, organize selling missions to foreign countries, and engage in a variety of other helpful activities. If you're exporting, you should look into the services of your state department of commerce. There usually is no assistance available to importers from state governments.

Local Governments

A few counties and cities are involved in international trade on the export side. On Long Island, New York, for example, Nassau and Suffolk Counties have jointly formed a Long Island Regional Export Association. Its most important activity to date has been to rent exhibit space at the airport in Frankfurt, Germany and to make that a showpiece of Long Island products available to European importers.

New York City is an example of a city that is involved in export promotion. It has a one-man office, the main job of which is to connect potential exporters with the people and organizations that can help them. On a cost-benefit basis, this tiny program probably scores very high.

If you plan to work on the export side of international trade, you should find out whether your local governments have any help available

WORLD TRADE CLUBS AND ASSOCIATIONS

Attendance at meetings of clubs and associations can help you stay up to date in the field of international trade and give you a chance to ask questions and get free information. Appendix B lists most of the major organizations throughout the country.

Most clubs and associations are primarily for executives of medium and large exporting organizations. There are, however, a few groups that include importers, exporters, and trade service personnel and that are especially interested in foreign trade procedures. One of these is national, the American Association of Importers and Exporters, 11 West 42nd Street, New York, NY 10036, telephone 212-944-2230. The membership fee is too high for very small companies, but there are excellent services for members. Perhaps in the future there will be more organizations of small scale importers and exporters.

PRINTED MATERIALS

There are literally hundreds of books, magazines, and newspapers that can help you in international trade. A number of them are mentioned in this book, and following is a discussion of a few that are especially important.

The monthly newspaper, *Trade Channel* is the number one choice. (It is described in Chapter 4.) You can get a sea mail subscription for about $50 a year (or an air mail subscription for $70) from American Business Communications, 11 Independence Street, Tarrytown, NY 10591.

Another good choice is the magazine, *Global Trade Executive*, from North American Publishing Co., 401 North Broad Street, Philadelphia, PA 19108. The current price is $45 per year, but it is free to qualified importers and exporters. This monthly journal focuses on trade procedures but is expanding to include information on international procurement and marketing. It also contains information on specific import and export opportunities.

Importers should buy the book, *Importing into the United States.* You can but it for $3.50 at customs houses and government bookstores, and from the Superintendent of Documents, U.S. Government Printing Office, Washington D.C. 20402.

Exporters should also buy the *Philadelphia Export Directory*. This little book, published in 1984, has a wealth of information including names and addresses of both public and private organizations that can give you assistance. It's available from the Philadelphia Export Network, Wharton Applied Research Center, University of Pennsylvania, 3508 Market Street, Philadelphia, PA 19104.

To really understand FOB, CIF, etc., buy a copy of the *Guide to Incoterms*. It's available from the ICC Publishing Corporation, 1212 Avenue of the Americas, New York, NY 10036.

To learn more about paperwork, purchase *A Guide to Export Documentation* from Educational Development for International Trade, Inc., 5508 North Main Street, Dayton, Ohio 45415. Although this book has "export" in the title, importers also can benefit from it.

Exporters should purchase a small book entitled *Foreign Business Practices*, from the U.S. Government printing office. It covers legal aspects of doing business in almost all foreign countries, including patent and trademark laws, regulations pertaining to agency agreements, and much more.

Exporters should subscribe to *Business America*, an expensive but excellent semi-weekly publication of the U.S. Department of Commerce. It gives information on USDC services, foreign trade fairs, market potential in nearly all countries, and other aspects of the exporting business. USDC field offices publish much smaller versions, such as *Business America Illinois*, that are free to executives of exporting companies.

Most international banks publish books on trade finance that are free to their clients. As soon as you open your bank account, ask for one of these books. If you're not yet ready to open a business account, find a friend who has one and can obtain a book for you.

Finally, there are introductory booklets on exporting published by the U.S. Department of Commerce, the U.S. Small Business Administration, some state governments, and private companies, including the investment firm of Price Waterhouse.

EXPORT SERVICE ORGANIZATIONS

The import/export service sector includes several possible sources of assistance. With some types of organizations, the help is free but limited, and other types you'll have to pay from almost the first minute.

Both importers and exporters can get advice on methods of payment from international bankers, on transportation from airlines and steamship lines, and on packing and insurance from insurance brokers and underwriters. Importers can get free ideas about purchasing from foreign countries' trade promotion officials, on documentation from customs brokers, and on marketing from advertising and public relations firms. Exporters can, without paying, speak with American trade associations about sources of supply and with foreign freight forwarders about export procedures. The best source of help with export marketing is the U.S. Department of Commerce.

There are numerous attorneys who specialize in international trade. Their assistance can be invaluable in matters of supply agreements, copyright protection, taxation, etc. Their fees are high, but you have to compare the cost with the expected benefit. A legal agreement for which your lawyer charges a thousand dollars may prevent your losing commissions worth many times that amount.

There are also many educational and training institutions that organize useful courses and seminars, and a number of colleges and universities have day and evening courses on international trade. Most of them are designed for people who plan to begin exporting, but much of the material is useful to importers as well.

There are also numerous training institutes; some of these are listed in the Appendix. The World Trade Institute in New York operates an evening school of world trade and organizes more than 100 seminars every year. The World Trade Education Center of Cleveland State University, Cleveland, Ohio, has become a leader in training in that part of the country. UNZ and Company has seminars on foreign trade procedures, and the Academy of Advanced Traffic in Philadelphia runs excellent evening courses on international cargo transportation.

Around the country there are meetings and seminars held by world trade clubs, international banks, and other organizations. You should be able to find out about these from your local business newspaper or from your nearest office of the U.S. Department of Commerce.

Port authorities can also be useful. American ports compete with each other to get import and export traffic, and often can provide information and advice to shippers who use their facilities. Some, such as Massport in Boston, organize trade missions and exhibits in foreign countries. The Port Authority of New York and New Jersey has, among other things, hosted foreign trade exhibits in the World Trade Center and used its overseas promotion officers to seek customers for American exporters.

Many of the programs sponsored by educational institutions, port authorities, and other organizations are funded at least in part, by the U.S. Department of Commerce. In its efforts to bring about increased exports from the United States, this government organization has provided innumerable grants of "seed" money over the past 15 years.

CONSULTING FIRMS

There are two kinds of consulting firms that may be helpful—marketing consultants and specialized import-export consultants. Firms listed in directories as marketing consultants are usually not qualified to help with exporting or with import procedures, but many of them can assist you once your products are available for sale in the United States. Most marketing consultants work strictly on a fee basis (no percentage of your sales) and shy away from very small projects. It's a good idea to look for a consulting firm with recent experience handling products of the type you plan to deal in, and that will tell you exactly which people will be doing the work for you. Since the quality of marketing consultants varies greatly, you should normally speak with former clients before hiring one.

There are a few firms that specialize in assisting small-scale importers and exporters. The following annotated list is not an endorsement, nor is it complete; in addition, the prices given may have changed.

Kitco International, Inc.
P.O. Drawer 6266
Kansas City, Kansas 66106
(913)268-9466 and (913) 631-7850
H. Keith Kittrell

Membership in the *Kitco Import/Export Club* gets you a subscription to the monthly "Import/Export Newsletter," a detailed listing in the roster of club members, information about the other members, and a membership card and certificate. You will also receive a monthly "Health Letter" and a "Travel Newsletter," and discounts on some travel expenses and print media advertising. You are promised ". . . all the essential 'How-to' Information," although what this consists of is not entirely clear.

For joining you receive two gifts—a publication on selling by phone and a subscription to an export promotion publication from Taiwan.

Kitco is a U.S. representative for a number of foreign publishers, especially from Taiwan, and club members receive 10 percent discounts on subscriptions to these publications. The cost of this service is $25 to join and $10 a month to remain a member.

As far as I can see the primary benefit of joining this club is the 10 percent discount on advertising, which is useful only if you plan to place ads in newspapers and magazines. The newsletter contains little useful information, and the health and travel magazines do not help much in the import/export business. The discounts (actually rebates) on travel can be obtained from other sources, and the card, certificate, and roster of members have little practical value.

Some publications on which club members receive discounts are very good, however, especially *Made in Europe* and *Taiwan Gifts*, and the $25 membership fee is low. You may want to join and find out for yourself if this one is worthwhile.

U.S. International Marketing Co., Inc.
17057 Bellflower Boulevard, Suite 205
Bellflower, CA 90706
(213) 925-2918,
R. Mervyn Heaton

Known as USIMCO, this company sells a package of publications and a consultation service. The package includes several books: *How to Make a Fortune in Import-Export, Exporting—A Step-by-Step Guide for Beginners, Trade Promotion Guide,* and *Business Letters.* There are also sample copies of a few magazines and newsletters: *Taiwan Products, Trade Channel* (editions for both developing and developed countries), and *International New Products Newsletter.* Finally there are some nonserial publications: *American Drop-shippers Directory, Buying and Selling in Overseas Markets,* and 16 lists of trade promotion and business contacts. Any of the publications in the standard package, and others as well, can be purchased separately.

The advisory service allows you to call or write USIMCO with specific questions. The cost as of this writing is $69.95 for the publications (worth $89.80 at regular retail) and one year of the advisory service.

The book, *How to Make a Fortune in Import/Export* is a useful introduction to international trade. The other books also contain useful information, and the serial publications will give you initial ideas of products to import and export (mostly import). The contact lists may be useful to help you get started.

The advisory service may be limited because the advisor won't have in-depth knowledge of you or your situation, but it's actually free because you're getting your money's worth from the publications. If the advice helps at all, you're ahead of the game.

Overall, I think this service is a good bargain for someone who is going into the import/export business and knows little about it.

The Mellinger Co.
6100 Variel Avenue
Woodland Hills, CA 91376
(818) 884-4400
Brainard L. Mellinger, Jr.

When someone joins the Mellinger Club, "International Traders," he or she receives a five-volume publication entitled *World Trade Plan.* The new member also receives a directory of foreign exporters who will drop ship to American clients, a three-year subscription to the monthly magazine, samples of forms used in international business, written information on how to sell by mail, sample agreements (really offers) from foreign exporters, and a membership card and certificate. In addition, eight sample imports, mostly inexpensive novelties, and a consultation service for one year come with joining.

If you join International Traders you'll find there are additional "services" to members, the price of which is not included in the basic package.

As of this writing, the package sells for $198 on the installment plan, or $178 if you pay all at once. If you ask for information about the club but don't respond to their subsequent invitation to join, you'll receive a $20 coupon, which can be used to lower either the installment or the cash price. If you take the second offer, on the installment plan, you'll pay a $9.00 "inspection deposit" and $18.90 a month for nine months.

This is a highly professional marketing company that has been in business for many years. They have helped many individuals to get started in the business of importing and selling by mail order. Unfortunately, they make the business sound as if virtually anyone can import a product, place a few ads, and start counting the profits. It's just not that easy, and I suspect that most of the people who lay out their $178 never make back even that amount.

Still, you may be one of the success stories. Why not invest the $9.00 to inspect the materials, which contain a great deal of useful information and decide whether to put the package back in the mail or to keep it and make your monthly payments.

Anthony Wade (Consultants) Ltd. (A British firm represented in the United States by MultiNational Marketing Associates.)
6715 Seegers Trail Drive
Houston, TX 77066
(713) 527-0422
Irwin D. Nathanson

Anthony Wade's "forte" is helping people become import and export agents. The heart of its service is a set of manuals entitled *Postal Course Export/Import, Theory and Practice of Selling by Post,* and *International Trade.* They were written in Britain, but appendices have been added to the first manual to apply specifically to the United States. You can buy just the first manual, the first two, or all three. The package also includes an advisory service and a monthly magazine.

The basic manual, plus six months of the advisory service and the magazine, costs $125 but an "introductory price reduction" brings it down to $110. The first two manuals with nine months of the service and the magazine are $157, with the introductory discount. All three manuals with 12 months of the service and the magazine are $198, again with the discount.

Anthony Wade is a serious company with a good track record. The manuals are good. The magazine is also good except that it seems sophisticated for a beginner in the United States (in general people abroad know more about the world than the average American does).

MultiNational Marketing Associates reports having a staff of three persons in Houston and two in Washington D.C., and back-up support from the Wade organization in the United Kingdom.

The promotional material makes the agency business sound easier than it is, but by now you have been sufficiently warned. If you are starting an international agency (or perhaps even merchant) business, and think you can benefit from long distance consultation, Wade may be a good choice for you.

TREICO
93 Willets Drive
Syosset, New York, NY 11791
(516) 496-8740
    TREICO gives frequent seminars entitled, "Going Into the Import/Export Business," on which this book has been based. Most are in the New York area, but some are presented in other states under the sponsorship of local organizations. TREICO sometimes offers more advanced seminars on import procurement, export marketing, and import/export procedures, and publishes a monthly newsletter.
    It offers new clients extended (60-90 minutes) consultations, in person or by phone, to help them make the initial decisions about how to begin their import and/or export operations. It can provide ongoing assistance, on a project, open account, or retainer basis, in product selection, procurement, marketing, international transportation and payment, and other aspects of the business.
    The one-day seminars are priced from $25 to $190 per person, depending on the subject and the sponsoring organization. The current price for an initial consultation is $50, and work on open account and retainer are billed per hour of staff time plus out-of-pocket expenses such as telex charges and postage. Fees charged to project clients are predetermined by mutual agreement.
    If you have read and understood this book you don't need the introductory seminar. If you're serious about the business, though, you may want to use the personalized individual consultation. You hope, and I hope, that most of the cost will be paid out of profits.

IN SUMMARY

In Building an Import/Export Business, I have tried to explain the basics of international trade for small businesspersons. There is much more to be said, and there is some possibility of information being misleading because complexities or advanced concepts have been omitted. Also, the ways of trade change rapidly. A shirt sewn in Haiti from American parts was dutiable yesterday, is duty-free today, and tomorrow who knows?

International trade is a worthwhile, exciting, and potentially profitable business. I hope I do not frighten you away by pointing out the dangers and difficulties, but you should know both the good and the bad before you start a business. I hope many readers go into international trade, rise to the challenge, enjoy the adventure, and earn substantial profit.

And, last, we all love to hear success (and sometimes failure) stories. If you have a good story, write me a letter. Let me know what you did, how it turned out, and what plans you have for the future of your business.

Appendix A

Sample Supply Agreements*

AGENCY AGREEMENT
(between foreign exporter and U.S. selling agent)

THIS AGREEMENT is made this ⎯⎯⎯⎯ day of ⎯⎯⎯⎯⎯⎯⎯⎯⎯⎯⎯⎯, 19⎯⎯.

BETWEEN ⎯⎯⎯⎯__A CORP__⎯⎯⎯⎯ incorporated in ⎯⎯⎯⎯⎯⎯⎯⎯⎯⎯⎯
with its registered office at:

⎯⎯⎯⎯⎯⎯⎯⎯⎯⎯⎯⎯⎯⎯⎯⎯⎯⎯⎯⎯⎯⎯⎯⎯⎯⎯⎯⎯⎯⎯⎯⎯⎯⎯⎯⎯⎯⎯⎯

⎯⎯⎯⎯⎯⎯⎯⎯⎯⎯⎯⎯⎯⎯⎯⎯⎯⎯⎯⎯⎯⎯⎯⎯⎯⎯⎯⎯⎯⎯⎯⎯⎯⎯⎯⎯⎯⎯⎯

⎯⎯⎯⎯⎯⎯⎯⎯⎯⎯⎯⎯⎯⎯⎯⎯⎯⎯⎯⎯⎯⎯⎯⎯⎯⎯⎯⎯⎯⎯⎯⎯⎯⎯⎯⎯⎯⎯⎯

(hereinafter called "A Corp") of the one part

AND: ⎯⎯⎯⎯⎯__B CORP__⎯⎯⎯⎯ incorporated in ⎯⎯⎯⎯⎯⎯⎯⎯⎯
with its principal office at:

⎯⎯⎯⎯⎯⎯⎯⎯⎯⎯⎯⎯⎯⎯⎯⎯⎯⎯⎯⎯⎯⎯⎯⎯⎯⎯⎯⎯⎯⎯⎯⎯⎯⎯⎯⎯⎯⎯⎯

⎯⎯⎯⎯⎯⎯⎯⎯⎯⎯⎯⎯⎯⎯⎯⎯⎯⎯⎯⎯⎯⎯⎯⎯⎯⎯⎯⎯⎯⎯⎯⎯⎯⎯⎯⎯⎯⎯⎯

(hereinafter called "B Corp") on the other part

WHEREAS

(A) A Corp designs, develops, manufactures and sells widgets and ancillary equipment for use in the widget industry.

(B) In view of its previous experience in marketing widgets and
ancillary equipment for the widget industry in the United States,
its valuable contacts in that industry and its general marketing
expertise and organization, B Corp wishes to undertake, and A
Corp is willing to support, the marketing of widgets and ancillary

*Provided by Kaplan Russin Vecchi & Kirkwood, New York, N.Y.

217

equipment manufactured by A Corp in the United States under an agency from A Corp.

(C) The parties now wish formally to record the terms and conditions which shall govern their association for the purposes outlined in Recital (b) above.

NOW, THEREFORE, IT IS AGREED AND DECLARED AS FOLLOWS:

Clause 1. SCOPE

The parties agree that the terms and conditions set forth in this Agreement represent the entire agreement between the parties relating to the Agency of B Corp for A Corp and shall supersede any and all prior representations, agreements, statements and understandings relating thereto. The parties further agree that neither party places any reliance whatsoever on any such prior representations, agreements, statements and understandings except to the extent expressly set forth in this Agreement.

Clause 2. APPOINTMENT OF AGENT

A Corp hereby appoints B Corp to be its exclusive Agent in the United States during the currency of this Agreement for the sale of all widgets and ancillary equipment listed in Schedule 1. All such widgets and ancillary equipment are hereinafter collectively referred to as "The Products." A list of The Products which are standard as at the date of this Agreement is set forth in Schedule 1 to this Agreement and A Corp undertakes to give B Corp prompt written notice of any additions to or deletions from such list.

Clause 3. DUTIES OF THE AGENT

3.1 B Corp shall during the currency of this Agreement:

    3.1.1 Use its best endeavors to promote the sale of The Products to customers and potential customers throughout the United States and solicit orders for The Products to be placed with A Corp as per Clause 9 hereof. Without prejudice to the generality of the foregoing B Corp shall:

        3.1.1.1 maintain close marketing relationships with customers and potential customers so that their relevant equipment needs and future plans are ascertained.

        3.1.1.2 draw the attention of customers and potential customers to The Products suitable to their needs and ascertain the equipment and technical commercial proposals being offered by A Corp's competitors.

  3.1.1.3 B Corp shall not, during the currency of this Agreement act as agent or distributor for any products directly competitive in price and specification to the products.

 3.1.2 Establish and maintain a product support service having the capacity of:

  3.1.2.1 dealing with routine service enquiries from customers either by telephone or telex advice or in the field.

  3.1.2.2 maintaining liaison with customers.

  3.1.2.3 asissting customers in the implementation of the A Corp Warranty for The Products.

 3.1.3 Promptly draw to the attention of A Corp any new or revised legislation, regulation or orders affecting the use or sale of The Products in the United States of America as and when such legislation, etc. come to its attention.

 3.1.4 Employ such technically competent sales, commercial and service staff as may be reasonably necessary.

 3.1.5 Receive within its B Corp's offices temporary visiting staff or A Corp and afford to such staff reasonable office, secretarial and communications services.

3.2 Recognizing its obligations to protect the reputation of A Corp, B Corp undertakes that it shall not undertake any obligations in respect of the performance of The Products in excess of the limits specified by A Corp in respect of The Products concerned and shall not offer any time for delivery earlier than that given by A Corp pursuant to the inquiry and order procedure provisions of this Agreement.

Clause 4. SUPPORT OBLIGATIONS OF A CORP

During the term of the Agreement, A Corp shall:

4.1 Continue to develop the Products to meet the requirements of the United States market.

4.2 Supply at its own cost B Corp with all reasonable requirements for technical data in reproducible form for us in catalogues, sales literature, instruction books, technical pamphlets and advertising material relating to The Products including developments of The Products as envisaged under Clause 4.1 above, and will pay the equivalent of _____% of the prior 12 months' gross billing, in every year, for the preparation of such material.

4.3 Make potential customers within the United States aware of the support available from B Corp as agent of A Corp and of A Corp's support of such agency.

Clause 5. DELIVERIES BY A CORP

5.1 Throughout the term of this Agreement A Corp shall assist the sales efforts of B Corp by holding a stock of certain of the Products in an authorized warehouse within 50 miles of B Corp's headquarters at a level not lower than that set forth in Schedule 2 annexed hereto, which schedule may be changed from time to time by the signature of both parties on the revised version thereof.

5.2 A Corp shall provide adequate and suitable storage accommodations for such stock at its authorized warehouse and all deliveries will be dealt with through that warehouse. The costs and charges of the warehouse company shall be billed directly to and settled by A Corp.

5.3 All stock belonging to and warehoused by A Corp as set forth is and shall at all times remain the exclusive property of A Corp, and neither title nor possession thereof or in part thereof, shall pass to B Corp or to any third party customer of B Corp save or until the precise terms and conditions of Clause 5.4 herein below have been completely and exclusively complied with.

5.4 B Corp shall have the authority to instruct A Corp's warehouse to release not more than 5 widgets on any given day. As to widgets released and shipped in accordance with the above authority, B Corp must receive payment in one of the following alternative ways: (a) By cash payment for the widget within 48 hours of such shipment; or (b) by delivery to Barclays Bank, N.Y., Jericho branch, within 48 hours of such shipment, of an irrevocable 45 day Letter of Credit, in the amount of the payment due.

Clause 6. PRICE

6.1 Customers solicited by B Corp shall pay the prices agreed or to be agreed from time to time and annexed as an Exhibit A hereto. Payment shall be made in accordance with paragraph 5.4 hereinabove. The parties hereto further agree that the said prices shall be reviewed every six months beginning on the date of this Agreement.

6.2 A Corp undertakes that it will give not less than three months' notice of any changes to its United States Dollar prices for the sale of The

Products. A Corp further undertakes that any non-standard Products and agreed modifications to The Products shall be priced on a basis consistent with its normal pricing arrangements under this Agreement.

Clause 7. COMMISSIONS EARNED

Upon delivery of, and payment for, each Product pursuant Clause 5 and 6, B Corp shall be entitled to a commission in the amount of _____ percent (_____%) of the list price of each of The Products as set forth in Exhibit _____ hereto less any discounts or other allowances made by B Corp in these prices to achieve the sale and any freight, packing, insurance, or other charges. Commissions shall be calculated at the end of each calendar month based upon deliveries during the preceding month. Payment shall be made within 10 days of the end of the calendar month to B Corp.

Clause 8. DIRECT SALES AND FOREIGN ORDERS

A Corp agrees not to solicit sales for use within the United States during the currency of this Agreement. However, nothing in this Agreement is intended to operate nor shall it be construed as operating to prevent A Corp from selling, should it receive direct orders from and to any customer within the United States or to any customer outside the United States which customer whether within the knowledge of A Corp or not, intends to resell or actually resells to a customer within the United States. In the event of a direct sale by A Corp to a customer within the United States then A Corp shall grant B Corp a commission upon such sale in an amount of _____ percent (_____%) of the sale price charged by A Corp to such customer provided always that thereafter The Product support obligations of B Corp pursuant to this Agreement shall apply in respect of the sale of The Product so made by A Corp to the said customer. A Corp shall notify B Corp of each and every such sale. Further and in addition, if B Corp obtains any order for A Corp's products for shipment outside the United States, A Corp shall grant B Corp the same said commission on such sale.

Clause 9. PROPRIETARY RIGHTS

9.1 The due and proper performance of its obligations and the exercise of its rights hereunder by B Corp shall not be deemed to be a breach of copyright or infringement of patent trademark or other proprietary right owned by A Corp.

9.2 B Corp shall not under any circumstances acquire any rights whatsoever in any copyright, patent, trademark or other proprietary right of A Corp nor shall B Corp acquire any rights whatsoever in relation to the design of The Products.

Clause 10. DELIVERY

10.1 A Corp reserves the right to specify and change delivery dates and shall not be responsible for any delay in delivery or failure to meet delivery schedules where such delay or failure arises due to any cause outside the reasonable control of A Corp.

10.2 The parties hereto agree that, in the event that delivery of Products is delayed by an act or omission of a customer, B Corp shall invoice such customers for the reasonable storage charges incurred by A Corp as a result thereof, and will use reasonable efforts to effect collection. Upon receipt of payment against such invoice, B Corp shall remit such payment to A Corp after deduction of B Corp's commission and costs of such collection.

Clause 11. WARRANTY

11.1 A Corp's warranty on all of The Products is limited to the following: A Corp will repair or replace at its option any Product at its own expense, save as to freight as to which it shall pay 50% of the round-trip cost for all validated warranty claims, as to which Product any defect in design, material or workmanship arises within a period of one year from commencement of operation of such Product or eighteen (18) months from the date of delivery of such Product, whichever shall first occur.

11.2 The warranty contained in Clause 11.1 above is subject to:

11.2.1 The Product not being used for any purpose other than the normal purpose for its specifications.

11.2.2 the observance by the user of all operating instructions and recommendations issued by A Corp in relation thereto.

11.2.3 prompt written notice being given to A Corp within 30 days following discovery of such defect.

11.3 B Corp shall promptly issue a report to A Corp in respect of each warranty claim brought to its attention.

Clause 12. PATENT INDEMNITY

12.1 In the event that any claim should be brought against B Corp that The Products infringe letters patent or other protected proprietary right, valid at the date of acceptance by A Corp of B Corp's order for such Product, owned by any third party, not being an employee or officer or shareholder of B Corp and not being a subsidiary or associated company of B Corp, then A Corp shall indemnify B Corp against and hold B Corp harmless from any and all damages which may be awarded against B Corp by any Court of competent jurisdiction provided that:

12.1.1 B Corp notifies A Corp in writing within 30 days of learning of any such claim as aforesaid.

12.1.2 B Corp permits A Corp to conduct the defense to any such claim as aforesaid and the negotiation of any settlement thereof.

12.1.3 B Corp provides at the expense of A Corp such assistance as A Corp may require in the defense or settlement of such claim as aforesaid.

12.1.4 such indemnity and undertaking as aforesaid shall not apply if the infringement relates to any use other than a use authorized by A Corp.

12.1.5 such indemnity and undertaking as aforesaid shall not apply where the infringement relates to the combination of The Products with equipment not designed, manufactured or sold by A Corp, unless A Corp specifically was aware of and approved such combination in advance thereof.

12.2 A Corp reserves the right to settle any such claim as aforesaid on the basis of substituting non-infringing Products for the alleged infringing Products providing that such substituted Products are capable of performing substantially the same functions as The Products so replaced.

12.3 Such indemnity and undertaking as aforesaid shall not apply in the event the designs, the subject of such claim as aforesaid, were supplied by B Corp's customers. In that event B Corp shall request such customers to indemnify A Corp against any claims made against A Corp alleging the infringement of letters paten tor other protected proprietary rights arising out of the use of such designs or the manufacture or sale of Products utilizing such designs.

Clause 13. LIMITATION OF WARRANTY

13.1 The parties hereto agree that the express undertakings of A Corp pursuant to the provisions of the Warranty contained in Clause 11 constitute the only warranties of A Corp and the said undertakings of Clause 11 are in lieu of and in substitution for all other conditions and warranties express or implied INCLUDING WITHOUT

LIMITATION ANY WARRANTIES AS TO MERCHANTABILITY
OR FITNESS FOR PURPOSE and all other obligations and liabili-
ties whatsoever of A Corp whether in contract or in tort or otherwise, and B Corp shall so inform customers and potential customers. B Corp shall not offer or assume nor authorize anyone to
offer or assume for or on behalf of A Corp any other Warranty or
similar obligation in connection with The Products other than as
authorized by Clause 11 and this Clause 13.

Clause 14. CAPACITY OF THE PARTIES

14.1 B Corp undertakes that it will at all times material to this Agreement make clear to customers and potential customers that it acts
in the capacity of agent of A Corp. Except as specifically authorized under the terms of this Agreement, B Corp is not authorized
to bind or commit or make representations on behalf of A Corp for
any purpose whatsoever, and B Corp shall make this clear to customers and potential customers.

14.2 This Agreement is not intended nor shall it be construed as establishing any form of partnership between the parties.

Clause 15. ASSIGNMENT

The obligations and duties of B Corp hereunder are personal to B Corp
and shall not be subcontracted to any third party without the prior
written consent of A Corp nor shall B Corp assign this Agreement or
any part thereof to any third party without the prior written consent of
A Corp.

Clause 16. CONFIDENTIALITY

Any information which may during the currency of this Agreement be
divulged by either party to the other on the express written basis that
such information is confidential shall be so regarded and be protected
whether in storage or in use. Furthermore, any such information shall
not be used by the party receiving same otherwise than for the express
purpose for which it is divulged and shall not further be divulged except to such of the said party's own servants and agents as may have a
"need to know" for the purposes of this Agreement.

Clause 17. DURATION AND TERMINATION

17.1 This Agreement shall commence on the date of signature hereof
and shall continue unless and until terminated by either party giving to the other not less than 30 days written notice to such effect.

17.2 Any termination in accordance with the provisions of Clause 17.1 above shall not affect the obligations of the parties to fulfill the terms of orders placed and accepted prior to the effective date of such termination.

17.3 If either party should enter into any liquidation, bankruptcy or receivership whether compulsorily or voluntarily or should enter into any Agreement with creditors compounding debts or should suffer the imposition of a receiver in respect of the whole or a material part of its assets or should otherwise become insolvent, then the other party may by notice in writing, forthwith terminate this Agreement.

17.4 Upon termination of this Agreement:

17.4.1 B Corp shall return at its own expense to A Corp any catalogues, sales literature, instruction books, technical pamphlets and advertising material relating to The Products which may have been supplied by A Corp.

17.4.2 B Corp shall immediately cease to trade as an agent of A Corp and shall cease to represent itself in such capacity.

17.4.3 Recognizing that the financial and other commitments to be made by the parties in order to operate this Agreement will be put at risk by a termination pursuant to Clause 17.1 above at any time, the parties agree that any termination by A Corp pursuant to the terms of Clause 17.1, other than a termination pursuant to the terms of Clause 17.3, and other than a termination for cause (which shall include but specifically not be limited to fraud, negligence, breach of the terms of this Agreement), shall entitle B Corp to receive, in addition to sums actually due pursuant to the terms of Clause 17.2 and 17.4.4 herein, an amount equal to the net commissions received by B Corp under this Agreement, during the twelve months immediately preceding the date of notification of such termination, such sum to be paid at the expiration of the 30 day notice period. In the event that termination is by reason of Clause 17.3 herein, or for cause as defined hereinabove, or if termination is at the request or by the notice of B Corp, B Corp shall be entitled only to the amount due to it pursuant to the terms of Clause 17.2 and 17.4.4 hereinabove. Since the exercise of such right to terminate would not constitute any breach of this Agreement such amount as shall be payable as aforesaid shall not be deemed a penalty.

17.4.4 A Corp shall continue to pay commissions on those orders obtained prior to the date of termination as invoices are paid and widgets delivered.

17.4.5 Subsequent to termination of this Agreement by either party in any manner and for any reason whatsoever, neither party shall be prevented or restricted from doing business with any person, corporation, partnership or other business entity within the United States or elsewhere, specifically including but not limited to persons, corporations, partnerships and business entities who have previously purchased A Corp's products, whether through B Corp or otherwise; except that if A Corp terminates this Agreement under circumstances which entitle B Corp to the payment of compensation pursuant to the terms of paragraph 17.4.3 hereinabove, then A Corp agrees that it will not solicit orders from any customers who received the products, or who requested a quotation therefor from B Corp during the currency of this Agreement, for a period of two years from the date of such termination.

Clause 18. NOTICES

Any notice required to be given hereunder shall be sufficiently given if forwarded by any of the following methods: registered mail, cable, telegraph or telex to the registered office of A Corp or the principal office of B Corp as the case may be and shall be deemed to have been received and given at the time when it is ordinary course of transmission it should have been delivered or received at the address to which it was sent.

Clause 19. WAIVER

Failure by either party at any time to enforce any of the provisions of this Agreement shall not constitute a waiver by such party of such provision nor in any way affect the validity of this Agreement.

Clause 20. AMENDMENT

This Agreement may not be amended except by an instrument in writing signed by both parties and made subsequent to the date of this Agreement and which is expressly stated to amend this Agreement.

Clause 21. HEADINGS

The clause headings of this Agreement are for reference purposes only and shall not be deemed to affect the interpretation of any of the provisions of this Agreement.

Clause 22. LAW

This Agreement shall be subject to and interpreted in accordance with the Laws of _____.

IN WITNESS WHEREOF, the parties have caused this Agreement to be signed on their behalf by the hand of a duly authorized officer.

FOR A CORP

_____ (Title)

FOR B CORP

_____ (Title)

DISTRIBUTORSHIP AGREEMENT
(between foreign exporter and U.S. importer/distributor)

AGREEMENT made this _____ day of _____, 1986, by and between A Corp, a company organized under the laws of C Country with its principal place of business located at _____ _____ (hereinafter called the "PRODUCER") and B Corp, located at S State (hereinafter called the "DISTRIBUTOR");

WITNESSETH:

WHEREAS, the PRODUCER is engaged in the design, manufacture and marketing of, among other things, widgets (the "Product"); under the brand name "Widgets."

WHEREAS, the DISTRIBUTOR maintains a marketing organization and markets widgets in the United States; and

WHEREAS, the PRODUCER and DISTRIBUTOR desire to cooperate for the purpose of marketing the product in the United States to civilians under the terms hereinafter set forth;

NOW THEREFORE, in consideration of the foregoing premises, the mutual covenants and agreements contained herein and other good and valuable consideration, the receipt, sufficiency and adequacy of which is hereby acknowledged, the parties hereto agree as follows:

SECTION I. APPOINTMENT

The PRODUCER hereby appoints the DISTRIBUTOR to be its exclusive Distributor of the Product to civilians in the Territories as defined below, and the DISTRIBUTOR hereby accepts that appointment and agrees to act as the exclusive Distributor for the PRODUCER. PRODUCER specifically reserves to itself the right to market the Product to all Local, State and Federal organizations and entities, and the term "civilian" shall not include any such organizations or entities.

A. As used herein, Territories shall mean the States of _____ _____.

B. In addition to paragraph A, Section 1 above, Territories shall also mean all other states east of the Mississippi River at such time as the DISTRIBUTOR delivers to the PRODUCER a marketing plan acceptable to the PRODUCER. DISTRIBUTOR shall have _____ months from the date of this Agreement to deliver such plan.

C. In addition to paragraphs A and B of Section 1 above, the DISTRIBUTOR shall be given the first option to include all States west of the Mississipi River in the above defined Territories, at such time as the DISTRIBUTOR delivers to the PRODUCER a business and marketing plan acceptable to the PRODUCER for all States west of the Mississippi River. The option shall expire if such a plan is not delivered within _____ months from the date of this Agreement.

SECTION II. SALES AND PROMOTION

DISTRIBUTOR during the term of this Agreement shall:

A. Energetically and faithfully use its best efforts to promote the sale of the Product to civilian customers and potential civilian customers throughout the Territories;

B. Carry continuously and have readily available sufficient quantities of the Product to enable it to promptly meet current demands of all customers;

C. Agree to price the Product at competitive levels, at wholesale and at retail, to sell the Product in accordance with the customs in the trade and will abstain from using selling methods or practices which, in the PRODUCER'S opinion, are harmful to the reputation of the Product or the PRODUCER;

D. Employ such technically competent sales, commercial and service staff as may be reasonably necessary;

E. Vigorously advertise and promote the Product within the Territories and bear all expense therefrom, which shall not be less than US$_____ per year;

F. Attend and participate annually in all significant trade shows and exhibitions, which includes, at the minimum, having a booth for demonstrations, promotions and advertising to all attendees of such shows or exhibitions. The booths should be staffed with technically qualified people. Such trade shows and exhibitions shall include, but is not limited to the following shows: _____.

G. Not undertake any obligations or promote/advertise the performance of the Product in excess of the limits specified by the PRODUCER.

H. Be expressly permitted to make public announcements in the press of its appointment as the exclusive Distributor of the PRODUCER in the appropriate Territories.

I. Pay for and send the appropriate personnel of the DISTRIBUTOR to the PRODUCER's manufacturing plant for necessary technical update or general orientation should the PRODUCER find it necessary.

J. Not sell outside of the authorized Territories and if the Product is destined for outside the authorized Territories, the DISTRIBUTOR shall take all necessary and appropriate steps to stop such sales.

SECTION III. TERM

This Agreement shall be for a term of three years from the date first written above and shall continue from year to year thereafter until either of the parties shall give _____ months written notice to the other prior that this Agreement shall terminate. Should the DISTRIBUTOR not purchase the minimum quantities set forth below, the PRODUCER may, at anytime, terminate this Agreement upon _____ days written notice.

SECTION IV. MINIMUM QUANTITIES

Throughout the term of this Agreement, the PRODUCER shall sell and the DISTRIBUTOR shall purchase from the PRODUCER (and from no other source) such minimum quantities of the Product at the minimum prices hereafter set out:

A. In the first year of this Agreement, DISTRIBUTOR shall pruchase at least US$_____ of the Product from the PRODUCER;

B. In the first year of this Agreement, the DISTRIBUTOR shall purchase from the PRODUCER at least _____ pieces of the Product kits;

C. In the second year of this Agreement and every year thereafter, the PRODUCER shall have the option of increasing the above minimum requirements for price and quantities; however, in no event shall any increase by over US$_____ per year, or _____ pieces per year.

SECTION V. PAYMENT AND TERMS

A. Payment shall be made by the DISTRIBUTOR to the PRODUCER (unless otherwise directed by PRODUCER) by irrevocable Letter of Credit in US dollars.

B. The PRODUCER shall sell and the DISTRIBUTOR shall purchase the Products F.O.B. the manufacturing plant at the following prices for the first year:

After _____ months from the date of this Agreement, the PRODUCER shall have the option to raise or lower these prices by giving _____ days notice. However, in no event shall any price be raised by more than _____ percent (_____%) per year of the above prices.

C. Any duty, tax or other charge the PRODUCER may be required by any Federal, State, County, Municipal or other law, now in effect or hereafter enacted, to collect or pay with respect to the sale, delivery or use of the Product shall be added to the prices provided herein exclusive of Paragraph B above and be paid by the Distributor.

Distributor shall also maintain and pay for Product Liability Insurance of US_____ million dollars.

SECTION VI. LEGAL COMPLIANCE

A. The DISTRIBUTOR shall comply with all Local, State and Federal laws concerning the Product.

B. The DISTRIBUTOR shall promptly inform the PRODUCER of all aspects of any new or revised legislation, regulation or orders affecting the use, sale or promotion of the Product in the United States of America.

SECTION VII. TRADEMARKS, PATENTS, COPYRIGHT AND BRAND-NAMES

A. Any and all trademarks, patents, copyrights and brand-names now in effect, created, applied for or received in the future, of the Product shall always be and remain the property of the PRODUCER.

B. The DISTRIBUTOR shall not under any circumstances acquire any rights whatsoever in any trademark, patent, copyright, brand-name or other proprietary right of the PRODUCER.

SECTION VIII. NON-COMPETITION

A. The PRODUCER shall, at its discretion, repair or replace any Product at its own expense found by the DISTRIBUTOR to be defective, provided that:

(1) In the case of visible and apparent defects, immediate written notice is given by the DISTRIBUTOR to the PRODUCER of such defects and the defective Products are returned to the PRODUCER within _____ weeks of the date of their shipment by the PRODUCER;

(2) In the case of functioned or non-apparent defects, written notice is given by the DISTRIBUTOR to the PRODUCER of such defects and the defective Products are returned to the PRODUCER within _____ months of the date of their shipment by the PRODUCER;

B. The PRODUCER shall pay fifty percent (50%) of the round-trip cost for all validated warranty claims.

C. The above limited warranty is subject to:

(1) The Product not being used for any purpose other than the normal purpose that it was manufactured for;

(2) The observance by the user of all operating instructions and recommendations provided by the PRODUCER; and

(3) The DISTRIBUTOR'S cooperation in and with any investigation by the PRODUCER or its representative with respect to said defects, including but not limited to any reports of the circumstances surrounding the defect.

SECTION IX. CONFIDENTIALITY

A. The DISTRIBUTOR shall not, either directly or indirectly, in whole or in part, except as required in the marketing of the Product or by written consent of an authorized representative of the PRODUCER, use or disclose to any person, firm, corporation or other entity, any information of a proprietary nature ("trade secrets") owned by the

PRODUCER or any of its affiliated companies, including, but not limited to, records, customer lists, data, formulae, documents, drawings, specifications, inventions, processes, methods and intangible rights.

B. Any information regarding the Product which, during the term of this Agreement is divulged by either party to the other is confidential and shall be protected from disclosure.

C. The prohibited use or disclosure, as used herein, shall be for the term of the Agreement and at any time within five (5) years after the termination of this Agreement.

SECTION X. ASSIGNMENT

The obligations and duties of the DISTRIBUTOR hereunder are personal and shall not be subcontracted or assigned to any third party without the prior written consent of the PRODUCER.

SECTION XI. TERMINATION AND GOODWILL

A. In the event that the DISTRIBUTOR shall default in the performance of any of its obligations hereunder, or shall fail to comply with any provision of this Agreement on its part to be performed, and if such default or failure shall continue for _____ days after written notice hereof from the PRODUCER, the PRODUCER may terminate this Agreement and the rights granted to the DISTRIBUTOR hereunder upon written notice to the DISTRIBUTOR, and neither waivers by the PRODUCER nor limitations of time may be asserted as a defense by the DISTRIBUTOR for any such failure or default. Such right of termination shall be in addition to any other rights and remedies of the PRODUCER at law or in equity.

B. Upon expiration, termination or cancellation of this Agreement pursuant to the provisions of Section III, Section XI, or for any other reason, with or without cause, the PRODUCER will not be liable for, and the DISTRIBUTOR will not be entitled to, any compensation of any kind for goodwill or any other tangible or intangible elements of damages or costs, nor shall the PRODUCER be liable to the DISTRIBUTOR for any special or consequential damages of any kind or nature whatsoever.

C. Upon the expiration of the term of this Agreement or any renewal thereof, the Products in the DISTRIBUTOR'S inventory may be sold, with the PRODUCER'S trademarks or brandnames thereon, only for one year after such expiration, subject to all the terms covenants and conditions of this Agreement (other than the right of renewal), as though this Agreement had not expired. Any of the Products in the DISTRIBUTOR'S inventory upon the termination or cancellation of this Agreement for any reason other than the natural expiration of its term, as set forth in Section III hereof, shall remain the property of the DISTRIBUTOR and may be sold only upon the removal of the PRODUCER'S owned trademarks and brandnames from the Products.

SECTION XII. RELATIONSHIP OF PARTIES

Nothing in this Agreement shall constitute or be deemed to constitute a partnership between the parties hereto. It is understood and agreed that the DISTRIBUTOR is an independent contractor and is not, nor ever will be, an agent or an employee of the PRODUCER. The DISTRIBUTOR shall not have the right, power or authority, express or implied, to bind, assume or create any obligation or liability on behalf of the PRODUCER.

SECTION XIII. CAPTIONS

The captions in this Agreement are inserted solely for ease of reference and are not deemed to form a part of, or in any way to modify, the text or meaning hereof.

SECTION XIV. NOTICE

Any notice required to be given shall be deemed to be validly served if sent by prepaid registered or certified airmail to the address(es) stated below or to such other address as may be designated by either party in writing. Said notice shall be effective when posted by either party to said address(es), postage prepaid.

A. PRODUCER: (address).

B. DISTRIBUTOR: (address).

SECTION XV. DIVISIBILITY

The provisions of this Agreement contain a number of separate and divisible covenants. Each such covenant shall be construed as a separate covenant and shall be separately enforceable. If a court of competent jurisdiction shall determine that any part of any paragraph or any part of any separate covenant herein contained, is so restrictive as to be deemed void, the remaining part or parts, or the other such separate covenants, shall be considered valid and enforceable, notwithstanding the voidance of such covenant or part of a separate covenant. If certain covenants of this Agreement hereof are so broad as to be unenforceable, it is the desire of the parties hereto that such provisions be read as narrowly as necessary in order to make such provisions enforceable.

SECTION XVI. GOVERNING LAW

This Agreement shall be deemed to have been made in, and the relationship between the parties hereto shall be governed by, the laws of the State of New York, United States of America.

SECTION XVII. PRIOR AGREEMENTS

This Agreement contains a complete statement of arrangements among and between the parties hereto with respect ot its subject matter, supersedes all existing agreements among them concerning the subject matter hereof and cannot be changed or terminated except in writing signed by all parties to this Agreement.

IN WITNESS WHEREOF, the parties hereto have executed this Agreement in duplicate by their duly authorized representatives and affixed their corporate seals (if any) the day and year first above written.

SEAL   PRODUCER:

                                By: _____
                                Title:

SEAL   DISTRIBUTOR:

                                By: _____
                                Title:

Appendix B

Trade Contacts*

Alabama

Alabama Development Office
Jamie Etheredge, Director
State Capitol
Montgomery, Ala. 36130
(205) 263-0048

Alabama State Docks
Bob Hope, Director
P.O. Box 1588
Mobile, Ala. 36633
(205) 690-6113

Alabama World Trade
Association
Peter Kenyon, President
P.O. Box 1508
Mobile, Ala. 36633
(205) 431-9271

Center for International Trade
and Commerce
Dr. Robert Lager, Director
Suite 131, 250 N. Water St.
Mobile, Ala. 36633
(205) 433-1151

Governor's Office of
International Trade
Billy Joe Camp, Director
P.O. Box 2939
Montgomery, Ala.
36105-0930
(205) 284-8722

International Trade Center,
University of Alabama
Nisa Bacon, Director
P.O. Box 6186
University, Ala. 35486
(205) 348-7621

North Alabama International
Trade Association
Colin E. Hammond, President
P.O. Box 927
Huntsville, Ala. 35804
(205) 532-3570

U.S. Department of Commerce
Tad Lidikay, Acting
Department Director
2015 2nd Ave. N.
Birmingham, Ala. 35203
(205) 254-1331

Alaska

Alaska Department of
Commerce and Economic
Development
Loren Lounsbury,
Commissioner
Pouch D
Juneau, Alaska 99811
(907) 465-2500

Alaska State Chamber of
Commerce
George Krusz, President
310 Second St.
Juneau, Alaska 99801
(907) 586-2323

Anchorage Chamber of
Commerce
Wayne Beckwith, Executive
Vice President
415 F St.
Anchorage, Alaska 99501
(907) 272-2401

Fairbanks Chamber of
Commerce

Buki Wright, President
First National Center
100 Cushman St.
Fairbanks, Alaska 99707
(907) 452-1105

U.S. Department of
Commerce (ITA)
Richard M. Lenahan, Director
701 C St., Box 32
Anchorage, Alaska 99513
(907) 271-5041

Arizona

American Graduate School of
International Management
Director of Intercom
Thunderbird Campus
Glendale, Ariz. 85306
(602) 978-7115

Arizona District Export
Council
John E. Carlson, Chairman
Box 26685
Tucson, Ariz. 85726
(602) 748-7555

Arizona-Mexico Commission
Tony Certosimo, Executive
Director
P.O. Box 13564
Phoenix, Ariz. 85002
(602) 255-1345

Arizona Office of Economic
Planning and Development
Beth Jarman, Executive Director
1700 W. Washington, 4th Floor
Phoenix, Ariz. 85007
(602) 255-5371

*Adapted from lists appearing in *Business America,* a publication of the U.S.
Department of Commerce.

Arizona World Trade
Association
Dan Danilewicz, President
c/o Phoenix Chamber of
Commerce
34 W. Monroe, Suite 900
Phoenix, Ariz. 85003
(602) 254-5521

Consular Corps of Arizona
Skipper Ross, Liaison Attache
8331 E. Rose Lane
Scottsdale, Ariz. 85253
(602) 947-6011

Sunbelt World Trade
Association
John Barfield, President
7119 Sabino Vista Circle
Tucson, Ariz. 85715
(602) 866-0364

U.S. Department of
Commerce (ITA)
Donald W. Fry, Director
2750 Valley Bank Center
Phoenix, Ariz. 85073
(602) 261-3285

Arkansas

Arkansas Association of
Planning and Development
Districts
Willeen Hough, Economic
Development Representative
Federal Building
Little Rock, Ark. 72201
(501) 378-5637

Arkansas Exporters Round
Table
Al Pollard
1660 Union National Plaza
Little Rock, Ark. 72201
(501) 375-5377

Arkansas Industrial
Development Commission
Maria Haley
One State Capital Mall
Little Rock, Ark. 72201
(501) 371-7678

District Export Council
Bruce Neimeth, Chairman
Savers Bldg., Suite 635
Capital at Spring St.
Little Rock, Ark. 72201
(501) 378-5794

International Trade Center
Armand Delaurell
University of Arkansas at
Little Rock
33rd and University
Little Rock, Ark. 72204
(501) 371-2992

U.S. Department of
Commerce (ITA)
Lon Hardin, Director
Savers Bldg., Suite 635
Capital at Spring St.
Little Rock, Ark. 72201
(501) 378-5794

World Trade Club of
Northeast Arkansas
Harry Herget
P.O. Box 2566
Jonesboro, Ark. 72401
(501) 932-7550

California

California Association of Port
Authorities
Diane Kelly, Executive
Secretary
1510 14th St.
Sacramento, Calif. 95816
(916) 446-6339

California Chamber of
Commerce
Susanne Hutchinson, Director
of International Trade
Department
1027 10th St.
P.O. Box 1736
Sacramento, Calif. 95808
(916) 444-6670

California Council for
International Trade
Steve Potash, Executive
Director
77 Jack London Sq., Suite L
Oakland, Calif. 94607
(415) 452-0770

California Department of
Commerce
(Formerly Department of
Economic and Business
Development)
Jim Vaughan, Director
Office of Business
Development
1121 L St., Suite 600
Sacramento, Calif. 95814

California State World Trade
Commission
Gregory Mignano, Executive
Director
1121 L St., Suite 310
Sacramento, Calif. 95814
(916) 324-5511

Custom Brokers and Freight
Forwarders Association
Bob Langner, Executive
Director
303 World Trade Center

San Francisco, Calif. 94111
(415) 982-7788

Economic Development
Corporation of Los Angeles
County
Theodore B. Howard, President
1052 W. 6th St., Suite 510
Los Angeles, Calif. 90017
(213) 482-5222

Export Managers Association
of California
Norma Persky, Executive
Secretary
10919 Vanowen St.
North Hollywood, Calif.
91605
(818) 985-1158

Foreign Trade Association of
South California
Fran Swanson, Executive
Secretary
350 S. Figueroa St., Rm. 226
Los Angeles, Calif. 90071
(213) 627-0634

Inland International Trade
Association
Bob Watson
World Trade Center
W. Sacramento, Calif. 95691
(916) 371-8000

International Business
Association, Long Beach
Area Chamber of Commerce
Debby Shey, President
100 Oceangate Plaza, Suite 50
Long Beach, Calif. 90802

International Business Council
Century City Chamber of
Commerce
Joel Baker, Executive Vice
President
2020 Ave. of the Stars, Plaza
Level
Century City, Calif. 90067
(213) 553-4062

International Managers'
Association of San Francisco
Fred Chattey, President
Custom House, P.O. Box 2425
San Francisco, Calif. 94126
(415) 981-6690

International Marketing
Association of Orange
County
Irene Lange
California State Fullerton,
Marketing Department
Fullerton, Calif. 92634
(714) 773-2223

Los Angeles Area Chamber of
Commerce
Richard Hoffman, Director
International Commerce
404 S. Bixel St.
Los Angeles, Calif. 90017
(213) 629-0722

North California District
Export Council
J. H. Dethero, Chairman
450 Golden Gate Ave.
Box 36013
San Francisco, Calif. 94102
(415) 556-5868

Oakland World Trade
Association
Robert W. Ross, Executive
Director
1939 Harrison St.
Oakland, Calif. 94612
(415) 388-8829

San Diego Chamber of
Commerce
Bernice Leyton, Vice President
110 West "C" St., Suite 1600
San Diego, Calif. 92101
(619) 232-0124

San Diego District Export
Council
Bill Ivans, Chairman
P.O. Box 81404
San Diego, Calif. 92138
(619) 293-5395

San Francisco International
Trade Council
John C. Givens
P.O. Box 6052
San Francisco, Calif. 94101
(415) 332-9100

San Francisco World Trade
Association
San Francisco Chamber of
Commerce
Harry Orbelian, Manager,
International Division
465 California St., 9th Floor
San Francisco, Calif. 94104
(415) 392-4511

Santa Clara Valley World
Trade Association
Alexander Bozinovich,
President
P.O. Box 6178
San Jose, Calif. 95150
(408) 998-7000

South California District
Export Council
Thomas Collier, Chairman
11777 San Vicente Blvd.

Los Angeles, Calif. 90049
(213) 209-6707

U.S. Department of
Commerce (ITA)
Daniel J. Young, Director
11777 San Vicente Blvd.
Los Angeles, Calif. 90049
(213) 209-6707

U.S. Department of
Commerce (ITA)
Betty D. Neuhart, Director
450 Golden Gate Ave.
San Francisco, Calif. 94102
(415) 556-5860

U.S. Department of
Commerce (ITA)
Richard Powell, International
Trade Specialist
P.O. Box 81404
San Diego, Calif. 92138
(619) 293-5395

U.S. Department of
Commerce (ITA)
Jesse Campos, International
Trade Specialist
116 W. 4th St.
Santa Ana, Calif. 92701
(714) 836-2461

U.S. Small Business
Administration
James M. Lucas, Trade
Specialist
450 Golden Gate Ave.
San Francisco, Calif. 94102
(415) 556-9902

Valley International Trade
Association
(San Fernando Valley)
Harvey Sacks, Export
Regulation Chairman
c/o QUEP Secretarial Service
21133 Victory Blvd., Suite 221
Canoga Park, Calif. 91303
(818) 704-8626

World Trade Association of
Orange County
Stephen Badolato, Director
200 E. Sandpointe Ave., Suite
480
Santa Ana, Calif. 92707
(714) 549-4160

World Trade Center Association
of San Diego
P.O. Box 81404
San Diego, Calif. 92138
(619) 298-6581

World Trade Council of San
Mateo County

Henry Bostwick, General
Manager
4 West 4th Ave., Suite 501
San Mateo, Calif. 94402
(415) 342-7278

Colorado

Colorado Association of
Commerce and Industry
Donald Jansen, President
1390 Logan St.
Denver, Colo. 80202
(303) 831-7411

Colorado Division of
Commerce and Development
Steve Schmitz, Director
1313 Sherman St., Rm. 523
Denver, Colo. 80203
(303) 866-2205

Denver Chamber of Commerce
Rex Jennings, President
1301 Welton St.
Denver, Colo. 80204
(303) 535-3211

International Trade Association
of Colorado
Paul Bergman, Jr., President
c/o U.S. Department of
Commerce
721 19th St., Rm. 113
Denver, Colo. 80202
(303) 844-2900

U.S. Department of
Commerce (ITA)
San Cerrato, Director
Steve Stoffel, Deputy Director
721 19th St., Rm. 113
Denver, Colo. 80202
(303) 844-2900

U.S. Small Business
Administration
Jerry Martinez, Director
1405 Curtis St.
Exec. Tower, 22nd Floor
Denver, Colo. 80202
(303) 844-5441

Connecticut

Bridgeport Foreign Trade Zone
Ed Musante
45 Lyon Terrace, Rm. 212
Bridgeport, Conn. 06604
(203) 576-7221

Connecticut Department of
Economic Development
Gary Miller, International
Director
210 Washington St.
Hartford, Conn. 06106
(203) 566-3842

Connecticut District Export
Council
David Moore, Chairman
450 Main St., Rm. 610B
Hartford, Conn. 06103
(203) 722-3530

Connecticut Foreign Trade
Association
W.J.R. Hargraves, President
c/o Manufacturing Association
of South Connecticut
608 Ferry Blvd.
Stratford, Conn. 06497
(203) 762-1000

Connecticut International
Trade Association
Len Tatko, President
c/o Suisman and Blumenthal
P.O. Box 119
Hartford, Conn. 06141

(Greater) Hartford Foreign
Trade Zone
Joseph Dinelli
c/o Schuyler Corporation
999 Asylum Ave.
Hartford, Conn. 06105
(203) 728-0237

(Greater) Hartford Chamber
of Commerce
Robin Johnson
250 Constitution Plaza
Hartford, Conn. 06103
(203) 525-4451

Legal Assistance, Coordinator
Philip Ettman
111 Pearl St.
Hartford, Conn. 06103
(203) 547-1330

(Greater) New Haven
Chamber of Commerce
Doug Marsh, President
195 Church St.
New Haven, Conn. 06506
(203) 787-6735

Quinnipiac College
Vasant Narkarni
Mt. Carmel Ave.
Hamden, Conn. 06518
(203) 288-5251

Service Corps of Retired
Executives (SCORE)
Leslie Gillette
1 Hartford Sq. W.
Hartford, Conn. 06103
(203) 722-3293

Southwest Area Commerce and
Industry Association
Manuel Abete, Trade Specialist

1 Landmark Sq., 2nd Floor
Stamford, Conn. 06901
(203) 359-3220

U.S. Department of
Commerce (ITA)
Eric B. Outwater, Director
450 Main St., Rm. 610B
Hartford, Conn. 06103
(203) 722-3530

U.S. Small Business
Administration
Ed Jekot, International
1 Hartford Sq. W.
Hartford, Conn. 06103
(203) 722-2544

West Connecticut International
Trade Association
Manual Reiriz, President
P.O. Box 787
Green Farms, Conn. 06436
(914) 478-3131

World Affairs Council
Marjorie Anderson
Hartford, Conn. 06105
(203) 236-5277

Delaware

Delaware Development Office
Louis Papinau, Director
P.O. Box 1401
Dover, Del. 19903
(302) 736-4271

Delaware-East Pennsylvania
Export Council
Philip D. Saxon, Vice Chairman
9448 Fed. Bldg.
600 Arch St.
Philadelphia, Pa. 19106
(215) 597-2850

Delaware State Chamber of
Commerce
William Wyer, President
One Commerce Center, Suite
200
Wilmington, Del. 19801
(302) 655-7221

Governor's International
Trade Council
Senator Andrew G. Knox
State of Delaware
Legislative Hall
Dover, Del. 19901
(302) 736-4136

Port of Wilmington
Robert E. Mescal, Jr., Director
of International Operations
P.O. Box 1191
Wilmington, Del. 19899
(302) 571-4600

U.S. Department of Commerce
Robert E. Kistler, Director
9448 Fed. Bldg.
600 Arch St.
Philadelphia, Pa. 19106
(215) 597-2866

District of Columbia

Greater Washington Board of
Trade
John Tyddings, Vice
President
1129 20th St. NW.
Washington, D.C. 20036
(202) 857-5900

Montgomery County Office of
Economic Development
Moritza Friedman
101 Monroe St., 15th Floor
Rockville, Md. 20580
(301) 251-2345

U.S. Department of
Commerce (ITA)
Branch Office
Stephen B. Hall, Trade
Specialist
101 Monroe St., 15th Floor
Rockville, Md. 20580
(301) 251-2345

Florida

Florida Council of
International Development
Marvin Kaiman, Chairman
2701 Le Jeune Road, Suite 330
Coral Gables, Fla. 33134
(305) 448-4035

Florida Customs Brokers and
Forwarders Association
Incorporated
Susanne Fontana, President
P.O. Box 522022
Miami Springs, Fla. 33166
(305) 871-7177

Florida Department of
Commerce
Gerald F. Wilson, Director
Bureau of International Trade
Collins Bldg.
107 W. Gaines St.
Tallahassee, Fla. 32304
(904) 488-6124

Florida Department of
Commerce
John Macho, Director
Caribbean Basin Development
Center
2701 LeJeune Road, Suite 330
Coral Gables, Fla. 33134
(305) 446-8106

Florida Department of
Commerce
Peter Genero, Chief
Latin American Trade
2701 LeJeune Road, Suite 330
Coral Gables, Fla. 33134
(305) 446-8106

Florida District Export Council
Charles F. McKay, Chairman
c/o Miami Commerce District
Office
Fed. Bldg., Suite 224
51 S.W. 1st Ave.
Miami, Fla. 33140
(305) 350-5267

Florida Exporters and
Importers Association,
Incorporated
Tom Travis, President
P.O. Box 450648
Miami, Fla. 33145
(305) 446-6646

Florida International Bankers
Association
Coleman Travelstead,
Executive Director
800 Douglas Entrance, Suite 21
Coral Gables, Fla. 33134
(305) 446-6646

Florida Small Business
Development Center
Gregory L. Higgins, Jr., State
Coordinator
University of Florida
P.O. Box 32026
Pensacola, Fla. 32514

Fort Lauderdale Area World
Trade Council
Olga Driggs, President
208 SE. 3rd Ave.
Ft. Lauderdale, Fla. 33302

International Center of Florida
Coleman Travelstead,
Executive Director
800 Douglas Entrance, Suite
211
Coral Gables, Fla. 33134
(305) 446-6646

Jacksonville International
Trade Association
Arnie T. Frankel, Executive
Director
P.O. Box 329
Jacksonville, Fla. 32201
(904) 353-0300

(City of) Miami
Charlotte Gallogly, Director
Bureau of International Trade
174 E. Flagler St., 7th Floor

Miami, Fla. 33133
(305) 579-3324

Okaloosa/Walton County
Area World Trade Council
Jerry Melvin, Executive Vice
President
P.O. Drawer 640
Fort Walton Beach, Fla.
32548
(904) 224-5151

Orlando World Trade
Association
Janice Warren, Executive
Director
75 E. Ivanhoe Blvd.
Orlando, Fla. 32804
(305) 425-1234

Pensacola World Trade Council
Michael Pugh, Executive
Director
40 N. Palasox St., Suite 400
Pensacola, Fla. 32501
(904) 438-4081

Space Coast World Trade
Council
W. G. "Doc" Strawbridge,
Executive Director
1005 E. Strawbridge Lane
Melbourne, Fla. 32901
(305) 724-5400

Sun Coast Export Council
Paul L. Getting, Executive
Vice President
St. Petersburg Area Chamber
of Commerce
P.O. Box 1371
St. Petersburg, Fla. 33731
(813) 821-4069

Tampa Bay International
Trade Council
Cliff Topping, Executive
Director
P.O. Box 420
Tampa, Fla. 33601
(813) 228-7777

U.S. Department of
Commerce (ITA)
Ivan Kosimi, Director
Fed. Bldg., Suite 224
51 SW. 1st Ave.
Miami, Fla. 33140
(305) 350-5267

World Trade Council, Palm
Beach County
James Stuber, Chairman
1983 PGA Blvd.
N. Palm Beach, Fla. 33408
(305) 832-5955

World Trade Council, Volusia
County
Lutz I. Perschmann, President
P.O. Box 5702
Daytona Beach, Fla. 32018
(904) 255-8131

Georgia

Georgia Department of
Agriculture
Thomas T. Irvin,
Commissioner
328 Agriculture Bldg.
Atlanta, Ga. 30334
(404) 656-3740

Georgia Ports Authority
George J. Nichols, Executive
Director
P.O. Box 2406
Savannah, Ga. 31412
(912) 964-1721

Georgia Department of
Industry and Trade
George Barry, Commissioner
1400 N. Omni Intl.
P.O. Box 1776
Atlanta, Ga. 30301
(404) 656-3571

Business Council of Georgia
Gene Dyson, Executive Director
575 N. Omni Intl.
Atlanta, Ga. 30335
(404) 223-2263

U.S. Department of
Commerce (ITA)
George Norton, Trade
Specialist in Charge
1365 Peachtree St., N.E.,
Suite 600
Atlanta, Ga. 30309
(404) 881-7000

U.S. Department of
Commerce (ITA)
James W. McIntire, Director
27 E. Bay St.
P.O. Box 9746
Savannah, Ga. 31401
(912) 944-4204

Hawaii

Chamber of Commerce of
Hawaii/World Trade
Association
Robert B. Robinson, President
735 Bishop St.
Honolulu, Hawaii 96813
(808) 531-4111

Hawaii Department of Planning
and Economic Development
Kenneth H. S. Kwak, Director

International Services Branch
P.O. Box 2359
Honolulu, Hawaii 96806
(808) 548-3048

Economic Development
Corporation of Honolulu
Frederick A. Sexton, President
1001 Bishop St.
Pacific Tower, Suite 855
Honolulu, Hawaii 96813
(808) 545-4533

Foreign Trade Zone No. 9
Homer A. Maxey, Jr.,
Administrator
Pier No. 2
Honolulu, Hawaii 96813
(808) 548-5435

U.S. Department of
Commerce (ITA)
Stephen K. Craven, Director
P.O. Box 50026
Honolulu, Hawaii 96850
(808) 546-8694

Idaho

Division of Economic and
Community Affairs
Barbara Swaczy
Statehouse, Rm. 108
Boise, Idaho 83720
(208) 334-3417

International Trade Committee
Greater Boise Chamber of
Commerce
P.O. Box 2368
Boise, Idaho 83701
(208) 344-5515

Idaho World Trade Association
Ken High, President
Box 660
Twin Falls, Idaho 83301
(208) 326-5116

District Export Council
Lieutenant Governor David
Leroy, Chairman
Statehouse, Rm. 225
Boise, Idaho 83720
(208) 334-2200

Idaho International Institute
c/o Helen Huff
1112 S. Owyhee
Boise, Idaho 83705

U.S. Department of
Commerce (ITA)
Janet D. Lenz, International
Trade Specialist
Statehouse, Rm. 113
Boise, Idaho 83720
(208) 334-9254

Illinois

American Association of
Exporters and Importers
David A. Parker, Executive
Secretary
7763 S. Kedzie Ave.
Chicago, Ill. 60652
(312) 471-1958

Automotive Exporters Club of
Chicago
George R. Smith, Vice President
3205 S. Shields Ave.
Chicago, Ill. 60616
(312) 567-6500
Toll Free—(800) 621-1552

Carnets
U.S. Council for International
Business
Pam Shroeder
1900 E. Golf Road, Suite 740
Schaumburg, Ill. 60195
(312) 490-9696

Central Illinois Coordinating
Committee for International
Trade
J. Terry Iversen
205 Arcade Bldg.
725 Wright St.
Champaign, Ill. 61820
(217) 333-1465

Chamber of Commerce of
Upper Rock Island County
John Verona Executive Director
622 19th St.
Moline, Ill. 61265
(309) 762-3661

Chicago Association of
Commerce and Industry
John M. Coulter
World Trade Division
200 N. Lasalle
Chicago, Ill. 60603
(312) 580-6900

Chicago Convention and
Tourism Bureau, Incorporated
Joseph P. Hannon, President
McCormick Place-on-the-Lake
Chicago, Ill. 60616
(312) 225-5000
Visitor Eventline: (312) 225-2323

Chicago Economic
Development Commission
International Business Division
Robert Mier, Commissioner
20 N. Clark St., 28th Floor
Chicago, Ill. 60602
(312) 744-8666

Chicago Midwest Credit
Management Association

Rick Sanders, Credit
Reporting Manager
315 South NW. Hwy.
Park Ridge, Ill. 60068
(312) 696-3000

Chicago Regional Port District
Gilbert J. Cataldo, General
Manager
12800 S. Butler at Lake Calumet
Chicago, Ill. 60633
(312) 646-4400

Customs Brokers and Foreign
Freight Forwarders
Association of Chicago,
Incorporated
Len Lesiak, President
P.O. Box 66365
Chicago, Ill. 60666
(312) 992-4100

Foreign Credit Insurance
Association
David E. Hanas, Senior Sales
Representative
20 N. Clark St., Suite 910
Chicago, Ill. 60602
(312) 641-1915

Illinois Department of
Agriculture
Jim Sevcik
1010 Jorie Blvd.
Oak Brook, Ill. 60521
(312) 920-9256

Illinois Department of
Commerce and Community
Affairs
Dan Rutherford, Manager
International Business Division
310 S. Michigan Ave., Suite 1000
Chicago, Ill. 60604
(312) 793-7164

Illinois District Export Council
Frederick Auch, Chairman
55 E. Monroe, Rm. 1406
Chicago, Ill. 60603
(312) 353-4450

Illinois Manufacturers'
Association
Jack Roadman, Secretary
175 W. Jackson Blvd., Suite 1321
Chicago, Ill. 60604
(312) 922-6575

Illinois State Chamber of
Commerce
International Trade Division
20 N. Wacker Dr., Suite 1960
Chicago, Ill. 60606
(312) 372-7373

International Business Council
MidAmerica (IBCM)

Robert Swaney, Executive
  Director
401 N. Wabash Ave., Suite 538
Chicago, Ill. 60611
(312) 222-1424

Mid-America International
  Agri-Trade Council
  (MIATCO)
Drayton Mayers, Executive
  Director
828 Davis St.
Evanston, Ill. 60201
(312) 368-4448

Northwest International
  Trade Club
Harvey Shoemaker, President
P.O. Box 454
Elk Grove Village, Ill. 60007
(312) 793-2086

Overseas Sales and Marketing
  Association of America,
  Incorporated
Peter Reinhard, President
3500 Devon Ave.
Lake Bluff, Ill. 60044
(312) 679-6070

Peoria Area Chamber of
  Commerce
Philip L. Carlson, President
230 SW. Adams St.
Peoria, Ill. 61602
(309) 676-0755

U.S. Customs Service
District Director
55 E. Monroe, Suite 1501
Chicago, Ill. 60603
(312) 686-2143

U.S. Department of
  Commerce (ITA)
Joseph Christiano, Director
55 E. Monroe, Suite 1406
Chicago, Ill. 60603
(312) 353-4450

U.S. Small Business
  Administration
Nagi Kheir, Specialist
Regional Export Development
219 S. Dearborn St., Suite 838
Chicago, Ill. 60604
(312) 886-0848

U.S. Great Lakes Shipping
  Association
Vera Paktor, Executive Director
3434 E. 95th St.
Chicago, Ill. 60617
(312) 978-0342

World Trade Club of North
  Illinois

Gerry Sibley, President
515 N. Court
Rockford, Ill. 61101
(815) 987-8100

Indiana

Forum for International
  Professional Services,
  Incorporated
Patricia Monter, President
One Merchants Plaza, Suite 770S
Indianapolis, Ind. 46255
(317) 267-7309

Hudson Institute
Thomas D. Bell, Jr., President
620 Union Dr.
P.O. Box 648
Indianapolis, Ind. 46206
(317) 632-1787

International Banking
  Committee
Indiana Bankers Association
Robert J. Schindler, Chairman
1 N. Capitol, Suite 315
Indianapolis, Ind. 46204
(317) 632-9533

International Center of
  Indianapolis
Barbara Coles, Executive
  Director
1050 W. 42nd St.
Indianapolis, Ind. 46208
(317) 923-1468

International Development
  Group
Fort Wayne Chamber of
  Commerce
Don Doxsee, Chairman
826 Ewing St.
Fort Wayne, Ind. 46802
(219) 424-1435

International Law Section
Indiana State Bar Association
Jack C. Dunfee, Jr., Chairman
230 E. Ohio St.
Indianapolis, Ind. 46204
(317) 639-5465

Indiana Association of Credit
  Management
J. David Mohr, Vice President
International Credit
  Management
130 E. New York St.
Indianapolis, Ind. 46204
(317) 632-4444

Indiana Consortium for
  International Programs
Tom Sargent, Executive Director
N. Quad 240

Ball State University
Muncie, Ind. 47306
(317) 285-8780

Indiana Council on World
  Affairs
Institute of Transnational
  Business
Connie V. Faulhaber,
  Executive Director
Ball State University
Muncie, Ind. 47306
(317) 285-5526

Indiana Department of
  Commerce
Agriculture Division
Gary Swaim, Director
One N. Capitol, Suite 700
Indianapolis, Ind. 46204
(317) 232-8770

Indiana Department of
  Commerce
International Trade Division
Phillip M. Grebe, Director
Indiana Commerce Center,
  Suite 700
One N. Capitol
Indianapolis, Ind. 46204-2243
(317) 232-8845

Indiana Export Council
Richard A. Dickinson, Chairman
Mel R. Sherar, Executive
  Secretary
c/o U.S. Department of
  Commerce
Indiana Commerce Center,
  Suite 700
1 N. Capitol
Indianapolis, Ind. 46204
(317) 269-6214

Indiana Manufacturers
  Association
Frederick K. McCarthy, President
115 N. Pennsylvania St.,
  Rm. 950
Indianapolis, Ind. 46204
(317) 632-2474

Indiana Port Commission
  Headquarters
Garth L. Whipple, Executive
  Director
143 W. Market St., Suite 204
Indianapolis, Ind. 46204
(317) 232-7150

Indiana State Chamber of
  Commerce
John Evans, International
  Liaison
1 North Capitol, Suite 200
Indianapolis, Ind. 46204
(317) 634-6407

Indianapolis Airport Authority
Dan Orcutt, Executive Director
Indianapolis International
Airport
P.O. Box 51605
Indianapolis, Ind. 46241
(317) 248-9594

Indianapolis Business
Development Foundation
Henry Taylor, President
One Virginia Ave., 2nd Floor
Indianapolis, Ind. 46204
(317) 639-6131

Indianapolis Chamber of
Commerce
Robert Palmer, International
Liaison
310 N. Meridian
Indianapolis, Ind. 46204
(317) 267-2900

Indianapolis Economic
Development Corporation
Dave Bennett, Director of
International Trade
Services
48 Monument Circle
Indianapolis, Ind. 46204
(317) 236-6262

Indianapolis Foreign Trade
Zone, Incorporated
Dave Bennett (Indianapolis
Economic Development
Corporation)
Park Fletcher Industrial
Research Center
5545 W. Minnesota St.
P.O. Box 51681
Indianapolis, Ind. 46251
(317) 247-1181

Michiana World Trade Club
Steve Queior, Executive
Secretary
401 E. Colfax, Suite 310
P.O. Box 1677
South Bend, Ind. 46634
(219) 234-0051

Southwind-Maritime Center
Chris V. Kinnett, Port Manager
P.O. Box 529
Mount Vernon, Ind. 47620
(812) 838-4382

Tippecanoe World Trade
Council
Greater Lafayette Chamber of
Commerce
Rita Pickering, Chairperson
P.O. Box 348
Lafayette, Ind. 47902
(317) 742-4041

Tri-State World Trade Council
Philip Williams, President
329 Main St.
Evansville, Ind. 47708
(812) 425-8147

U.S. Customs Service
Harry McKay, Port Director
Indianapolis Airport
P.O. Box 51612
Indianapolis, Ind. 46251-0612
(317) 248-4060

U.S. Department of
Commerce (ITA)
Mel R. Sherar, Director
357 U.S. Courthouse
46 E. Ohio St.
Indianapolis, Ind. 46204
(317) 269-6214

U.S. Small Business
Administration
Robert Gastineau
575 N. Pennsylvania, Rm. 578
Indianapolis, Ind. 46204
(317) 269-7272

World Trade Club of Indiana,
Incorporated
Bert Faulhaber, President
P.O. Box 986
Indianapolis, Ind. 46206
(317) 285-5207

Iowa

International Trade Bureau
Richard Petska, Secretary
P.O. Box 4860
Cedar Rapids, Iowa 52407
(319) 398-5310

Iowa Association of Business
and Industry
F.L. Peters, President
706 Employers Mutual Bldg.
Des Moines, Iowa 50309
(505) 281-3138

Iowa Development Commission
Bob Sanner, International
Marketing Manager
600 E. Court Ave., Suite A
Des Moines, Iowa 50309
(515) 281-3581

Iowa-Illinois International
Trade Association
Loyle A. Mueller, Director
Membership and Community
Relations
112 E. 3rd St.
Davenport, Iowa 52801
(319) 322-1706

Siouxland International Trade
Association

Thomas Rubel, Director
Legislative and Agriculture
Affairs
101 Pierce St.
Sioux City, Iowa 51101
(712) 255-7903

U.S. Department of
Commerce (ITA)
Jesse N. Durden, Director
817 Fed. Bldg.
210 Walnut St.
Des Moines, Iowa 50309
(515) 284-4222

Kansas

International Trade Club of
Greater Kansas City
Kate White, Executive Secretary
920 Main St., Suite 600
Kansas City, Mo. 64105
(816) 221-1460

International Trade Institute
Raymond Coleman, Director
1627 Anderson
Manhattan, Kans. 66502
(913) 532-7699

Kansas Board of Agriculture
Eldon Fastrup, Director of
Marketing
109 SW. 9th St.
Topeka, Kans. 66612
(913) 296-3736

Kansas Department of
Economic Development
John J. Watson, Director
International Development
503 Kansas Ave., 6th Floor
Topeka, Kans. 66603
(913) 296-3483

Kansas-Northwest Missouri
District Export Council
William Laas, Chairman
P.O. Box 626
Beliot, Kans. 67420
(913) 738-2261

U.S. Department of
Commerce (ITA)
James D. Cook, Director
601 E. 12th St., Rm. 635
Kansas City, Mo. 64106
(816) 374-3141

U.S. Department of
Commerce (ITA)
George Lavid, Trade
Specialist
River Park Place, Suite 656
727 N. Waco
Wichita, Kans. 67203
(316) 269-6160

World Trade Council of Wichita
Dharma deSilva, Chairman
350 W. Douglas Ave.
Wichita, Kans. 67202
(316) 265-7771

Kentucky

Bluegrass Area Development
District
Susan Anglin, Specialist
3220 Nicholasville Road
Lexington, Ky. 40503
(606) 272-6656

Kentucky Commerce Cabinet
Ted Sauer, Executive Director
Office of International
Marketing
Capital Plaza Tower, 24th Floor
Frankfort, Ky. 40601
(502) 564-2170

Kentucky District Export Council
Stanley J. Byers, President
P.O. Box 33247
Louisville, Ky. 40232
(502) 966-0550

Kentuckiana World Commerce
Council
Marsha J. Adkins, Business
Manager Secretary
P.O. Box 58456
Louisville, Ky. 40258
(502) 583-5551

(City of) Louisville
Bibi Monsky, Economic
Development Cabinet
609 W. Jefferson St.
Louisville, Ky. 40202
(502) 587-3051

North Kentucky Chamber of
Commerce
Walter Dunlevy, President
1717 Dixie Hwy.
Covington, Ky. 41011
(606) 341-9500

TASKIT (Technical Assistance
to Stimulating Kentucky
International Trade)
Bobby L. Hart, Progress
Coordinator
College of Business and
Economics
University of Kentucky
Lexington, Ky. 40506-0205
(606) 257-7663

U.S. Department of
Commerce (ITA)
Don R. Henderson, Director
U.S.P.O. & Courthouse Bldg.
601 W. Broadway, Rm. 636B

Louisville, Ky. 40202
(502) 582-5066

Louisiana

Chamber of Commerce/New
Orleans and River Region
Tom Purdy, President/Chief
Executive Officer
301 Camp St.
New Orleans, La. 70130
(504) 527-6900

International Trade Mart
Eugene Schreiber, Managing
Director
Executive Offices, Suite 2900
2 Canal St.
New Orleans, La. 70130
(504) 529-1601

Louisiana Department of
Commerce
Terry Medicus, Director
Office of International Trade,
Finance and Development
P.O. Box 94185
Baton Rouge, La. 70804-9185
(504) 342-5362

Port of New Orleans
Denis B. Grace, Deputy Port
Director, Trade Development
P.O. Box 60046
New Orleans, La. 70160
(504) 528-3259

U.S. Department of
Commerce (ITA)
Paul Guidry, Director
432 International Trade Mart
2 Canal St.
New Orleans, La. 70130
(504) 589-6546

World Trade Club of Greater
New Orleans
Rose Mary PeDotti, Executive
Secretary
1132 International Trade Mart
2 Canal St.
New Orleans, La. 70130
(504) 525-7201

Maine

Maine State Development
Office
Leslie E. Stevens, Director
State House, Station 59
Augusta, Maine 04333
(207) 289-2656

Maine World Trade Association
Bob W. Ziegelaar, President
1 Memorial Circle
Augusta, Maine 04330
(207) 622-0234

U.S. Department of
Commerce (ITA)
Stephen Nyulaszi, Trade
Specialist
c/o Maine Development
Foundation
1 Memorial Circle
Augusta, Maine 04330
(207) 622-8249

Maryland

Greater Baltimore Committee,
Incorporated
Donald D. Moyer, Director
2 Hopkins Plaza, Suite 900
Baltimore, Md. 21201
(301) 727-2820

Baltimore Economic
Development Corporation
Bernard Berkowitz, President
36 S. Charles St., Suite 2400
Baltimore, Md. 21201
(301) 837-9305

(The) Export Club
William Boucher, III, Chairman
326 N. Charles St.
Baltimore, Md. 21201
(301) 727-8831

Maryland Department of
Economic and Community
Development
Thomas H. Maddux, Secretary
45 Calvert St.
Annapolis, Md. 21401
(301) 269-3176

Maryland/Washington, D.C.,
Export Council
John F. Caffey, Chairman
415 U.S. Customhouse
Gay and Lombard Sts.
Baltimore, Md. 21202
(301) 962-3560

Maryland Port Administration
William G. Halpin, Director
World Trade Center
Baltimore, Md. 21202
(301) 659-4500

U.S. Department of
Commerce (ITA)
LoRee P. Silloway, Director
U.S. Customhouse, Rm. 415
40 S. Gay St.
Baltimore, Md. 21202
(301) 962-3560

U.S. Small Business
Administration
Arnold Feldman, Director
10 N. Calvert St.
Baltimore, Md. 21202
(301) 962-2233

Massachusetts

Associated Industries of
Massachusetts
Walter P. Muther, President
462 Boylston St.
Boston, Mass. 02116
(617) 262-1180

Central Berkshire Chamber of
Commerce
Glenn F. Harvey, President
Berkshire Common
Pittsfield, Mass. 01201
(413) 499-4000

Chamber of Commerce of
Attleboro Area
William N. Ward
42 Union St.
Attleboro, Mass. 02703
(617) 222-0801

Commonwealth of Massachusetts
Evelyn F. Murphy, Secretary
Byron F. Battle
1 Ashburton Place
Boston, Mass. 02108
(617) 727-8380

Fall River Area Chamber of
Commerce
Dennis Orvis, Executive Vice
President
200 Pocasset St.
P.O. Box 1871
Fall River, Mass. 02722
(617) 676-8226

Foreign Trade Zone No. 28
Industrial Development
Commission
Norman A. Bergeron
1213 Purchase St.
New Bedford, Mass. 02740
(617) 997-6501

Greater Boston Chamber of
Commerce
James L. Sullivan, President
125 High St.
Boston, Mass. 02110
(617) 426-1250

Greater Lawrence Chamber of
Commerce
Laurence R. Smith, Executive
Vice President
300 Essex St.
Lawrence, Mass. 01840
(617) 687-9404

Greater Springfield Chamber
of Commerce
Robert J. Schwartz, Executive
Vice President
600 Bay State W. Plaza, Suite 600
1500 Main St.

Springfield, Mass. 01115
(413) 734-5671

International Business Center
of New England, Incorporated
Prescott C. Crafts
22 Batterymarch St.
Boston, Mass. 02109
(617) 542-0426

Massachusetts Commission
on International Trade and
Foreign Investment
Sheldon Fischer
State House, Suite 413F
Boston, Mass. 02133
(617) 722-1673

Massachusetts Department of
Commerce and Development
Ronald M. Ansin
100 Cambridge St.
Boston, Mass. 02202
(517) 727-3218

Massachusetts Department of
Food and Agriculture
Scheiva Gandhi
100 Cambridge St.
Boston, Mass. 02202
(617) 727-3108

Massport
David W. Davis, Executive
Director
99 High St.
Boston, Mass. 02110
(617) 482-2930

National Marine Fisheries
Service
Allen E. Peterson, Jr.
14 Elm St.
Gloucester, Mass. 01930
(617) 281-3600

New Bedford Area Chamber
of Commerce
Frederick A. Rubin, Executive
Vice President
First National Bank Bldg.,
Rm. 407
New Bedford, Mass. 02742
(617) 999-5231

New England Council,
Incorporated
Eric Swider, President
1020 Statler Bldg.
Boston, Mass. 02116
(617) 542-2580

New England Governors'
Conference, Incorporated
William A. Gildea
76 Summer St.
Boston, Mass. 02110
(617) 423-6900

North Suburban Chamber of
Commerce
Bonnie Walsh, Executive Director
25-B Montvale Ave.
Woburn, Mass. 01801
(617) 933-3499

Smaller Business Association of
New England, Incorporated
Lewis A. Shattuck, Executive
Vice President
69 Hickory Drive
Waltham, Mass. 02154
(617) 890-9070

South Middlesex Area
Chamber of Commerce
Michelle Cunha, Executive
Vice President
615 Concord St.
Framingham, Mass. 01701
(617) 879-5600

South Shore Chamber of
Commerce, Incorporated
Ronald E. Zooleck, Executive
Vice President
36 Miller Stile Road
Quincy, Mass. 02169
(617) 479-1111

U.S. Department of
Commerce (ITA)
Francis O'Connor, Director
441 Stuart St.
Boston, Mass. 02116
(617) 223-2312

U.S. Small Business
Administration
Arnold Rosenthal
60 Batterymarch St.
Boston, Mass. 02110
(617) 223-3891

Waltham/West Suburban
Chamber of Commerce
Theodore L. Manning,
Executive Vice President
663 Main St.
Waltham, Mass. 02154
(617) 894-4700

Watertown Chamber of
Commerce
Paul L. Shakespeare, President
75 Main St.
Watertown, Mass. 02172
(617) 926-1017

Worcester Chamber of
Commerce
William J. Short, Jr., Executive
Vice President
Mechanics Tower, Suite 350
100 Front St.
Worcester, Mass. 01608
(617) 753-2924

Michigan

Adcraft Club of Detroit
Lee H. Wilson, Executive
  Secretary
2630 Book Bldg.
Detroit, Mich. 48226
(313) 962-7225

Ann Arbor Chamber of
  Commerce
Rodney F. Benson, Executive
  Director
207 E. Washington
Ann Arbor, Mich. 48104
(313) 665-4433

BC/CAL/KAL Port of Battle
  Creek
Foreign Trade Zone No. 43
Marilyn E. Parks, Director
P.O. Box 1438
Battle Creek, Mich. 49016
(616) 968-8197

City of Detroit
Nancy Allen, Industrial
  Committee Specialist
Community and Economic
  Development Department
150 Michigan Ave. 7th Floor
Detroit, Mich. 48226
(313) 224-6533

Detroit Customhouse Brokers and
  Foreign Freight Forwarders
  Association, Incorporated
Les Jones, President
155 W. Congress, Rm. 420
Detroit, Mich. 48226
(313) 962-4681

Detroit/Wayne County Port
  Authority
James H. Kellow, Executive
  Director
100 Renaissance Center,
  Suite 1370
Detroit, Mich. 48243
(313) 259-8077

Downriver Community
  Conference
Bunny Starrett, Government
  Marketing Manager
15100 Northline
Southgate, Mich. 48195
(313) 283-8933

Flint Area Chamber of
  Commerce
Larry Ford, President
708 Root, Rm. 123
Flint, Mich. 48503
(313) 232-7101

Greater Port Huron-Marysville
  Chamber of Commerce

Miles Benedict, Executive
  Director
920 Pine Grove Ave.
Port Huron, Mich. 48060
(313) 985-7101

Greater Saginaw Chamber of
  Commerce
Michael L. Kiefer, President
901 S. Washington
Saginaw, Mich. 48606
(517) 752-7161

Great Lakes Trade Adjustment
  Assistance Center
Marian Krzyzowski, Progress
  Director
Institute of Science and
  Technology
University of Michigan
2901 Baxter Road
Ann Arbor, Mich. 48109
(313) 763-4085

Greater Detroit Chamber of
  Commerce
Frank E. Smith, President
150 Michigan Ave.
Detroit, Mich. 48226
(313) 964-4000

Greater Grand Rapids
  Chamber of Commerce
Joseph D. Powers, Senior Vice
  President of Economic
  Development
17 Fountain St., NW.
Grand Rapids, Mich. 49502
(616) 459-7221

Kalamazoo Chamber of
  Commerce
Mark V'Soske, Executive Vice
  President
P.O. Box 1169
Kalamazoo, Mich. 49007
(616) 381-4000

Macomb County Chamber of
  Commerce
Rodney Crider, Executive
  Director
10 North Ave.
Mt. Clemens, Mich. 48043
(313) 463-1528

Michigan Bankers Association
Donald A. Booth, Executive
  Vice President
6105 W. St. Joseph Hwy.
Lansing, Mich. 48917
(517) 321-1600

Michigan Department of
  Agriculture
Carol Keyes, International
  Marketing Specialist

P.O. Box 30017
Lansing, Mich. 48909
(517) 373-1054

Michigan Department of
  Commerce
Marc Santucci, Director
Office of International
  Development
P.O. Box 30105
Lansing, Mich. 48909
(517) 373-6390

Michigan District Export Council
David E. Reichard, Chairman
445 Fed. Bldg.
Detroit, Mich. 48226
(313) 226-3650

Michigan Manufacturers
  Association
John G. Thodis, President
124 E. Kalamazoo
Lansing, Mich. 48933
(517) 372-5900

Michigan State Chamber of
  Commerce
Philip G. Guyeskey, Manager
Small Business Programs
200 N. Washington Sq.,
  Suite 400
Lansing, Mich. 48933
(517) 371-2100

Motor Vehicle Manufacturers
  Association of USA
V.J. Adduci, President
300 New Center Bldg.
Detroit, Mich. 48202
(313) 872-4311

Muskegon Area Chamber of
  Commerce
Thomas J. Morris, President
1065 4th St.
Muskegon, Mich. 49441
(616) 722-3751

Technology International
  Council
Charles Gelman, Chairman
207 E. Washington St.
Ann Arbor, Mich. 48104
(313) 665-4433

Twin Cities Area Chamber of
  Commerce
Marie Franz, Executive Vice
  President
P.O. Box 1208
685 W. Main St.
Benton Harbor, Mich. 49022
(616) 925-0044

U.S. Customs Service
William L. Morandini, Director

Patrick V. McNamara Bldg.,
2nd Floor
Detroit, Mich. 48226
(313) 226-3177

U.S. Department of
Commerce (ITA)
George R. Campbell, Director
445 Fed. Bldg.
Detroit, Mich. 48226
(313) 226-3650

U.S. Small Business
Administration
Raymond L. Harshman,
Director
515 Patrick V. McNamara Bldg.
Detroit, Mich. 48226
(313) 226-7240

West Michigan World Trade
Club
Rebecca Heffner, Director
P.O. Box 2242
Grand Rapids, Mich. 49501
(616) 456-9622

World Trade Club of Detroit
George C. Kiba, Director
150 Michigan Ave.
Detroit, Mich. 48226
(313) 964-4000

Minnesota

Minnesota Export Finance
Authority
Duc Lam, Executive Director
90 W. Plato Blvd.
St. Paul, Minn. 55107
(612) 297-4659

Minnesota Trade Office
William Dietrich, Governor's
Special Trade Representative
90 W. Plato Blvd.
St. Paul, Minn. 55107
(612) 297-4655

Minnesota World Trade
Association
George P. Johnson, President
33 E. Wentworth Ave., 101
West St. Paul, Minn. 55118
(612) 457-1038

Minnesota World Trade Center
Richard Brolker, Executive
Director
1300 Conwed Tower
444 Cedar St.
St. Paul, Minn. 55101
(612) 297-1580

Seaway Port Authority of
Duluth
Davis Helberg, Executive
Director

P.O. Box 6877
Duluth, Minn. 55806
(218) 727-8525

U.S. Department of
Commerce (ITA)
Ronald E. Kramer, Director
108 Fed. Bldg.
110 S. 4th St.
Minneapolis, Minn. 55401
(612) 349-3338

Mississippi

Greenville Port Commission
John W. Brennan, Port Director
P.O. Box 446
Greenville, Miss. 38701
(601) 335-2683

International Trade Club of
Mississippi Incorporated
Bob M. Anthony, President
P.O. Box 16353
Jackson, Miss. 39236
(601) 956-1715

Jackson County Port Authority
Paul D. Pella, Executive Director
P.O. Box 70
Pascagoula, Miss. 39567
(601) 762-4041

Mississippi Department of
Economic Development
Marketing Division
William A. McGinnis, Jr.,
Director
P.O. Box 849
Jackson, Miss. 39205
(601) 359-3444

Mississippi State Port Authority
at Gulfport
William T. Duke, Assistant
Port Director for Trade
Development
P.O. Box 40
Gulfport, Miss. 39502
(601) 865-4306

U.S. Department of
Commerce (ITA)
Mark E. Spinney, Director
328 Jackson Mall Office Center
300 Woodrow Wilson Blvd.
Jackson, Miss. 39213
(601) 960-4388

Missouri

International Trade Club of
Greater Kansas City
Kate White, Executive Secretary
920 Main St., Suite 600
Kansas City, Mo. 64105
(816) 221-1460

Greater Ozarks International
Trade Club
P.O. Box 1687
Springfield, Mo. 65805
(417) 862-5567

Missouri Department of
Agriculture
International Marketing
Division
Michel Jajko
P.O. Box 630
Jefferson City, Mo. 65102
(314) 751-5611

Missouri Department of
Commerce
International Business Office
L. Glenn Boos, Director
P.O. Box 118
Jefferson City, Mo. 65102
(314) 751-4855

Missouri District Export
Council
Audrey Marsh King, Chairperson
120 S. Central, Suite 400
St. Louis, Mo. 63105
(314) 425-3302

U.S. Department of
Commerce (ITA)
James Cook, Director
601 E. 12th St.
Kansas City, Mo. 64106
(816) 374-3142

U.S. Department of
Commerce (ITA)
Donald R. Loso, Director
120 S. Central, Suite 400
St. Louis, Mo. 63105
(314) 425-3301

World Trade Club of St. Louis,
Incorporated
Joseph Licata, President
111 N. Taylor Ave.
Kirkwood, Mo. 63122
(314) 965-9940

Montana

49th Parallel Institute
Lauren McKinsey, Director
Department of Political Science
Montana State University
Bozeman, Mont. 59717
(406) 994-6690

Montana Department of
Commerce
Business Assistance Division
Kieth Colbo, Director
1424-9th Ave.
Helena, Mont. 59620
(406) 444-3923

U.S. Department of
Commerce (ITA)
Sam Cerrato, Director
Steve Stoffel, Deputy Director
721 19th St., Rm. 113
Denver, Colo. 80202
(303) 844-2900

Nebraska

Midwest International Trade
Association
Paul Warfield, President
c/o NBC, 13th & O Sts.
Lincoln, Neb. 68108
(402) 472-4321

Nebraska Department of
Economic Development
Robert Y. Valentine, Director
State Development and
International Division
301 Centennial Mall S.
Lincoln, Neb. 68509
(402) 471-4670

Omaha Chamber of Commerce
Vicki Krecek, Director,
Agricultural Council and
International Affairs
1301 Harney St.
Omaha, Neb. 68102
(402) 346-5000

U.S. Department of
Commerce (ITA)
George H. Payne, Director
300 S. 19th St.
Omaha, Neb. 68102
(402) 221-3664

U.S. Small Business
Administration
Jerry Kleber, International
Trade Specialist
300 S. 19th St., 2nd Floor
Omaha, Neb. 68102
(402) 221-3607

Nevada

Commission on Economic
Development
Andrew P. Grose, Executive
Director
600 E. Williams, Suite 203
Carson City, Nev. 89710
(702) 885-4325

Economic Development
Authority of West Nevada
Shelby Dill, Executive Director
P.O. Box 11710
Reno, Nev. 89510
(702) 322-4004

Latin Chamber of Commerce
Otto Merida, Executive Director

P.O. Box 7534
Las Vegas, Nev. 89125-2534
(702) 385-7367

Nevada Development Authority
Al Dague, Acting Executive
Director
P.O. Box 11128
Las Vegas, Nev. 89111
(702) 739-8222

Nevada District Export
Council
Hans R. Wolfe, Chairman
P.O. Box 11007
Reno, Nev. 89520
(702) 784-3401

U.S. Department of
Commerce (ITA)
J. Jerry Jeremy, Director
1755 E. Plumb Lane, Suite 152
Reno, Nev. 89502
(702) 784-5203

New Hampshire

(State of) New Hampshire
J. Michael Hickey, Director of
Economic Development
Department of Resources and
Economic Development
P.O. Box 856
Concord, N.H. 03301
(603) 271-2341

South New Hampshire
Association of Commerce
and Industry
Dolly Bellavance, Director of
Programs
4 Manchester St.
P.O. Box 1123
Nashua, N.H. 03601
(603) 882-8106

U.S. Department of
Commerce (ITA)
Francis J. O'Connor, Director
441 Stuart St.
Boston, Mass. 02116
(617) 223-2312

New Mexico

Economic Development and
Tourism Department
International Division
Bataan Memorial Bldg.
Santa Fe, N.M. 87503
(505) 827-3145

Foreign Trade Zone,
New Mexico
Oscar Barrajas, President
P.O. Box 26928
Albuquerque, N.M. 87125
(505) 842-0088

New Mexico Department of
Agriculture
Bob Toberman, Director,
International Marketing
P.O. Box 5600
Las Cruces, N.M. 88003
(505) 646-4929

New Mexico Foreign Trade
and Investment Council,
Incorporated
Joe Zanetti, Chairman
Mail Stop 150, Alvarado Sq.
Albuquerque, N.M. 87158
(505) 848-4632

New Mexico Industry
Development Corporation
Leland Alhorn, Executive
Director
300 San Mateo NE., Suite 815
Albuquerque, N.M. 87118

U.S. Department of
Commerce (ITA)
Bill Dwyer, Director
517 Gold SW.
Albuquerque, N.M. 87102
(505) 766-2386

New Jersey

Delaware River Port Authority
Ray Heinzelman, Director
World Trade Division
Bridge Plaza
Camden, N.J. 08101
(609) 963-6420, ext. 264

International Business Council
240 W. State St., Suite 1412
Trenton, N.J. 08608

International Round Table
Bergén County Community
College
Lynda Icochea, Professor
400 Paramus Road
Paramus, N.J. 07652
(201) 477-7167

(State of) New Jersey Division
of International Trade
Ming Hsu, Director
744 Broad St., Rm. 1709
Newark, N.J. 07102
(201) 648-3518

New Jersey/New York Port
Authority
Herb Ouida, Project Director
One World Trade Center, 63-S
New York, N.Y. 10048
(212) 466-8499

Rutgers Small Business
Development Center
Daine Burke, Manager

180 University Ave.
Newark, N.J. 07102
(201) 648-5950

Union County Chamber of
Commerce
International Trade
Committee
Thomas K. Spear, Associate
Director
135 Jefferson Ave.
P.O. Box 300
Elizabeth, N.J. 07207
(201) 352-0900

U.S. Association of Credit and
Finance Executives
John B. Gelke, Executive Vice
President
Foreign Credit Division
P.O. Box 130
405 Washington Ave.
Kenilworth, N.J. 07033
(201) 272-9191

U.S. Department of
Commerce (ITA)
Thomas J. Murray, Director
Capital Plaza, 8th Floor
240 W. State St.
Trenton, N.J. 08608
(609) 989-2100

World Trade Association of
New Jersey
Jerry Hall, Director
5 Commerce St.
Newark, N.J. 07102
(201) 623-7070

New York
Albany-Colonie Regional
Chamber of Commerce
Thomas N. Stainback, President
14 Corporate Woods Blvd.
Albany, N.Y. 12211
(518) 434-1214

American Association of
Exporters and Importers
Suzi Evalenko, Director,
Export Activities
11 W. 42nd St.
New York, N.Y. 10036
(212) 944-2230

American Management
Associations
Frances Taniey, International
Division Manager
135 W. 50th St.
New York, N.Y. 10020
(212) 586-8100

Buffalo Area Chamber of
Commerce

Wayne D. Hazard, Vice
President, Economic
Development
107 Delaware Ave.
Buffalo, N.Y. 14202
(716) 849-6682

Buffalo World Trade Association
538 Ellicott Sq. Bldg.
Buffalo, N.Y. 14203
(716) 854-1019

Foreign Credit Insurance
Association
Terry Dolan, Manager
Patricia Ralph, Assistant Vice
President
40 Rector St., 11th Floor
New York, N.Y. 10006

International Business
Council of Rochester Area
Chamber of Commerce
Charles M. Goodwin, Vice
President
International Trade and
Transportation
55 St. Paul St.
Rochester, N.Y. 14604
(716) 454-2220

International Trade Council,
Greater Syracuse Chamber
of Commerce
Joseph W. Lewis, Vice President
for Government Relations
100 E. Onondaga St.
Syracuse, N.Y. 13202
(315) 470-1343

International Executives
Association, Incorporated
Ed Flanagan, Executive Director
114 E. 32nd St., Suite 1301
New York, N.Y. 10016
(212) 683-9755

Long Island Association
Incorporated
James La Rocca, President
80 Hauppage Road
Commack, N.Y. 11725
(516) 499-4400

Mohawk Valley World Trade
Council
Deborah Smith, President
P.O. Box 4126
Utica, N.Y. 13540
(315) 797-1630

National Association of Credit
Managers (NACM)
Foreign Credit Insurance
Bureau (FCIB)
Cook Oneil, Executive Vice
President of NACM

Gerd-Peter Lota, Executive
Vice President of FCIB
475 Park Ave. S.
New York, N.Y. 10016
(212) 578-4710

National Association of Credit
Managers (NACB)—Upstate
New York
Frederick Knight, Executive
Vice President
250 Delaware Ave.
Buffalo, N.Y. 14202
(716) 845-7018

National Association of Export
Companies, Incorporated
Peter S. Greene, Executive
Director
396 Broadway, Suite 603
New York, N.Y. 10013
(212) 966-2271

National Customs Brokers and
Forwarders Association of
America, Incorporated
John Hammon, Executive Vice
President
One World Trade Center,
Rm. 1109
New York, N.Y. 10048
(212) 432-0050

New York Chamber of
Commerce and Industry
Edward S. Cabot, President
200 Madison Ave.
New York, N.Y. 10016
(212) 561-2028

New York State Department
of Commerce
Division of International
Commerce
230 Park Ave.
New York, N.Y. 10169
(212) 309-0500

Overseas Automotive Club,
Incorporated
Secretary
222 Cedar Lane
Teaneck, N.J. 07666
(212) 836-6999

Port Authority of New York
and New Jersey Trade
Development Office
John Savage, General Manager
Rm. 64-E
One World Trade Center
New York, N.Y. 10048
(212) 466-8333

Rochester Area Chamber of
Commerce
World Trade Department

Charles M. Goodwin, Vice
President International
Trade and Transportation
55 St. Paul St.
Rochester, N.Y. 14604
(716) 454-2220

Tappan Zee International
Trade Association
Carol Falis, Job Developer
One Blue Hill Plaza
Pearl River, N.Y. 10965
(914) 735-7040

U.S. Council for International
Business
1212 Ave. of the Americas
New York, N.Y. 10036
(212) 354-4480

U.S. Department of
Commerce (ITA)
R. McGee, Director
1312 Fed. Bldg.
Buffalo, N.Y. 14202
(716) 846-4191

U.S. Department of
Commerce (ITA)
A. Nadler, Acting Director
26 Fed. Plaza, Rm. 3718
New York, N.Y. 10278
(212) 264-0634

U.S. Department of
Commerce (ITA)
William Freirt, Branch Manager
121 E. Ave.
Rochester, N.Y. 14604
(716) 263-6480

U.S. Small Business
Administration
Fred Strauss or Milton Beards,
Counselors on Exports
26 Fed. Plaza, Rm. 3130
New York, N.Y. 10278
(212) 264-4507

U.S. Small Business
Administration
Robert Mergle, Management
Assistance Officer
100 S. Clinton St.
Syracuse, N.Y. 13260
(315) 423-5383

Westchester County
Association, Incorporated
World Trade Club of Westchester
Ted Von Eiff, Secretary-Treasurer
235 Mamaroneck Ave.
White Plains, N.Y. 10605
(914) 948-6444

World Commerce Association
of Central New York

Joseph Lewis, Vice President
for Government Relations
100 E. Onandaga St.
Syracuse, N.Y. 13202
(315) 470-1343

World Trade Club of Long Island
Lawrence S. Wizel, Chairman
c/o LIREX, 1425 Old Country
Road
Plainview, L.I., N.Y. 11803

World Trade Club of New York,
Incorporated
Peter Green, Executive Vice
President
396 Broadway, Suite 603
New York, N.Y. 10013
(212) 966-2271

World Trade Institute
Thomas J. Kearney, Director
One World Trade Center
New York, N. Y. 10048
(212) 466-4044

North Carolina
North Carolina Department of
Agriculture
Britt Cobb, International
Marketing Specialist
P.O. Box 27647
Raleigh, N.C. 27611
(919) 733-7912

North Carolina Department of
Commerce
International Division
James R. Hinkle, Director
430 N. Salisbury St.
Raleigh, N.C. 27611
(919) 733-7193

North Carolina District
Export Council
William F. Troxler, President
Troxler Electronic Labs,
Incorporated
P.O. Box 12057
Research Triangle Park, N.C.
27709
(919) 787-2530

North Carolina State
University
International Trade Center
Charles A. Shields, Director
P.O. Box 5125
Raleigh, N.C. 27650
(919) 737-7912

North Carolina World Trade
Association
Robert J. Mack
P.O. Box 327
Wilmington, N.C. 28402
(919) 763-9841

U.S. Department of
Commerce (ITA)
John F. Whiteley, Deputy
Director
P.O. Box 1950
Greensboro, N.C. 27402
(919) 378-5345

North Dakota
Fargo Chamber of Commerce
John C. Campbell, Executive
Vice President
321 N. 4th St.
Fargo, N.D. 58108
(701) 237-5678

North Dakota Economic
Development Commission
Bruce Bartch, Director
Industrial Development and
International Division
Liberty Memorial Bldg.
State Capital Grounds
Bismarck, N.D. 58505
(701) 224-2810

U.S. Department of
Commerce (ITA)
George H. Payne, Director
300 S. 19th St.
Omaha, Neb. 68102
(402) 221-3664

U.S. Small Business
Administration
James Floyd, International
Trade Specialist
P.O. Fed. Bldg.
Fargo, N.D. 58108
(701) 237-5771, ext. 131

Ohio
Cincinnati Council on World
Affairs
William C. Messner, President
1028 Dixie Terminal Bldg.
Cincinnati, Ohio 45202
(513) 621-2320

Cleveland Council on World
Affairs
Emory C. Swank, President
601 Rockwell Ave.
Cleveland, Ohio 44114
(216) 781-3730

Cleveland World Trade
Association
Richard N. Kirby, Staff Director
690 Huntington Bldg.
Cleveland, Ohio 44115
(216) 621-3300

Columbus Area Chamber of
Commerce
Robert W. Forsblom, Director
World Trade

37 N. High St.
Columbus, Ohio 43216
(614) 221-1321

Columbus Council on World
 Affairs
Virginia Frick, Executive Director
57 Jefferson Ave.
Columbus, Ohio 43215
(614) 461-0632

Commerce and Industry
 Association of Greater Elyria
Jonathan B. Bates, President
P.O. Box 179
Elyria, Ohio 44036
(216) 322-5438

Dayton Council on World Affairs
Pam Pease, Director
300 College Park
Dayton, Ohio 45469
(513) 229-2319

Dayton Development Council
Gary Geisel, International
 Trade Manager
1980 Kettering Tower
Dayton, Ohio 45423-1980
(513) 226-8222

Greater Cincinnati Chamber
 of Commerce
Joseph Kramer, Director
 International Marketing
120 W. 5th St.
Cincinnati, Ohio 45202
(513) 579-3143

Greater Cincinnati World
 Trade Association
Neal Hensley, Business Manager
120 W. 5th St.
Cincinnati, Ohio 45202
(513) 579-3122

International Business and
 Trade Association of Akron
Regional Development Board
James A. Kroeger, Director of
 Economic Development
One Cascade Plaza, Suite 800
Akron, Ohio 44308
(216) 379-3157

International Trade Institute
5055 N. Main St.
Dayton, Ohio 45415
(513) 276-5995

North Central Ohio
 International Trade Club
Mansfield Richland Area
Chamber of Commerce
William J. Hartnett,
 President
55 N. Mulberry St.
Mansfield, Ohio 44902
(419) 522-3211

North Ohio District Export
 Council
Herbert Hubben, Chairman
Plaza Nine Bldg.
55 Erieview Plaza, Suite 700
Cleveland, Ohio 44114
(216) 522-4750

Ohio Department of Agriculture
Dale Locker, Director
Ohio Department Bldg., Rm. 607
65 S. Front St.
Columbus, Ohio 43 15
(614) 466-4104

Ohio Department of
 Development
Phillip Code, Deputy
 Director
International Trade Division
30 E. Broad St.
Columbus, Ohio 43216
(614) 466-5017

Ohio Foreign Commerce
 Association, Incorporated
Lester P. Aurbach, Executive
 Secretary
1111 Chester Ave., Rm. 506A
Cleveland, Ohio 44114
(216) 696-7000

Port of Cleveland
C. Thomas Burke, Director
Cleveland-Cuyahoga County
 Port Authority
101 Erieside Ave.
Cleveland, Ohio 44114-1095
(216) 241-8004

Port of Toledo
Norman A. Fox, Director of
 Trade Development
Toledo-Lucas County Port
 Authority
One Maritime Plaza
Toledo, Ohio 43604-1866
(419) 243-8251

South Ohio District Export
 Council
Charles J. Berthy, Chairman
9504 Fed. Bldg.
550 Main St.
Cincinnati, Ohio 45202
(513) 684-2944

Toledo Area International
 Trade Association
J. Michael Porter, President
218 Huron St.
Toledo, Ohio 43604
(419) 243-8191

U.S. Customs Service
John F. Nelson, Director
55 Erieview Plaza
Cleveland, Ohio 44114
(216) 522-4284

U.S. Department of
 Commerce (ITA)
Gordon B. Thomas, Director
9504 Fed. Bldg.
550 Main St.
Cincinnati, Ohio 45202
(513) 684-2944

U.S. Department of
 Commerce (ITA)
Zelda W. Milner, Director
Plaza Nine Bldg.
55 Erieview Plaza, Suite 700
Cleveland, Ohio 44114
(216) 522-4750

U.S. Small Business
 Administration
S. Charles Hemming, District
 Director
317 AJC Fed. Bldg.
1240 E. 9th St.
Cleveland, Ohio 44199
(216) 522-4194

World Trade Committee of
 Youngstown
Area Chamber of Commerce
Weston O. Johnstone, President
200 Wick Bldg.
Youngstown, Ohio 44503-1474
(216) 744-2131

World Trade Education Center
Cleveland State University
Ivan R. Vernon, Director
University Center Bldg.,
 Rm. 460
Cleveland, Ohio 44115
(216) 687-3733

World Trade and Technology
 Center
Paul D. Griesse, Chairman
10793 State Rte. 37 W.
Sunbury, Ohio 43074
(614) 965-2974

Oklahoma

Foreign Trade Zone No. 53
Bob James
Tulsa Port of Catoosa
5555 Bird Creek Ave.
Catoosa, Okla. 74015
(918) 266-5830

Foreign Trade Zone No. 106
Jesse W. Matheny, Jr.
One Santa Fe Plaza
Oklahoma City, Okla. 73102
(405) 278-8900

Metropolitan Tulsa Chamber
 of Commerce
Rick L. Weddle, Vice President
Economic Development Division
616 S. Boston Ave.
Tulsa, Okla. 74119
(918) 585-1201

Muskogee City-County Port Authority
Diddy Pennington, Executive Secretary
Rte. 6, Port 50
Muskogee, Okla. 74401
(918) 682-7886

Oklahoma City Chamber of Commerce
Richard Clements, Acting Director
Economic and Community Development
One Santa Fe Plaza
Oklahoma City, Okla. 73102
(405) 278-8900

Oklahoma City International Trade Association
P.O. Box 66
Perry, Okla. 73077
(405) 336-4402

Oklahoma Department of Economic Development
William A. Maus, Director
International Division
4024 Lincoln Blvd.
Oklahoma City, Okla. 73105
(405) 521-2401

Oklahoma District Export Council
Warren L. Jensen, Chairman
4024 Lincoln Blvd.
Oklahoma City, Okla. 73105
(405) 231-5302

Oklahoma State Chamber of Commerce
Jack G. Springer, Executive Vice President
4020 Lincoln Blvd.
Oklahoma City, Okla. 73105
(405) 424-4003

Oklahoma State Department of Agriculture
Alan Huston, Director
International Marketing
2800 Lincoln Blvd.
Oklahoma City, Okla. 73105
(405) 521-3864

Tulsa Port of Catoosa
Robert W. Portiss, Port Director
5350 Cimarron Road
Catoosa, Okla. 74015
(918) 266-2291

Tulsa World Trade Association
Brian Edlich, President
Burlington Northern Airfreight
1821 N. 106th E. Ave.
Tulsa, Okla. 74116
(918) 836-0338

U.S. Department of Commerce (ITA)
Ronald L. Wilson, Director
4024 Lincoln Blvd.
Oklahoma City, Okla. 73105
(405) 231-5302

Oregon

Eugene Area Chamber of Commerce
Shary Shahr
1401 Willamette
P.O. Box 1107
Eugene, Ore. 97440
(503) 484-1314

Institute for International Trade and Commerce
Jim Manning
Portland State University
1912 S.W. Sixth Ave., Rm. 260
Portland, Ore. 97207
(503) 229-3246

Oregon District Export Council
Gordon Fromm
1220 SW. 3rd Ave., Rm. 618
Portland, Ore. 97209
(503) 292-9219

Oregon Economic Development Department
Richard H. Carson, Manager
Business Information Division
595 Cottage St., NE.
Salem, Ore. 97310
(503) 373-1231

Pacific Northwest International Trade Association
Gary Conkling
200 SW. Market
Suite 220
Portland, Ore. 97201
(503) 228-4361

U.S. Department of Commerce (ITA)
Lloyd R. Porter, Director
1220 SW. 3rd Ave., Rm. 618
Portland, Ore. 97209
(503) 221-3001

Western Wood Products Association
Bob Hunt
Yeon Bldg.
Portland, Ore. 97204
(503) 224-3930

Pennsylvania

American Society of International Executives, Incorporated
Anthony M. Swartz, President
Dublin Hall, Suite 419
Blue Bell, Pa. 19422
(215) 643-3040

Assessment of International Markets Program
Gerald Zaltman
382 Mervis Hall
University of Pittsburgh
Pittsburgh, Pa. 15260
(412) 624-1777

Delaware River Port Authority
Raymond G. Heinzelmann
Bridge Plaza
Camden, N.J. 08101
(215) 925-8780

Foreign Trade Zone No. 33
Hiram Milton, President
Regional Industrial Development Corporation
Union Trust Bldg.
Pittsburgh, Pa. 15219
(412) 471-3939

International Business Forum
Dolores L. Jordan, Executive Director
42 S. 15th St., Suite 315
Philadelphia, Pa. 19102
(215) 568-2710

International Trade Development Association
Paul A. Caracciolo, President
P.O. Box 279
Chalfont, Pa. 18914
(215) 822-6893

International Trade Executives Club of Erie
John McCartney, Executive Secretary
c/o Manufacturers Association of Erie
33 E. 8th St.
Erie, Pa. 16507
(814) 459-3335

International Trade Executives Club of Pittsburgh
William Bradley, Executive Secretary
2002 Fed. Bldg.
1000 Liberty Ave.
Pittsburgh, Pa. 15222
(412) 644-2850

North Central Pennsylvania Regional Planning and Development Commission
Mark Meinert
651 Montmorenci Ave.
Ridgeway, Pa. 15853
(814) 773-3162

Northwest Pennsylvania Regional Planning and Development Commission
Rich Mahalic, Maureen Sweeney
Biery Bldg., Suite 406

Franklin, Pa. 16323
(814) 437-3024

Pennsylvania Department of
Agriculture
Gretchen E. Anderson
Bureau of Agricultural
Development
2301 N. Cameron St.
Harrisburg, Pa. 17110
(717) 783-8460

Pennsylvania Department of
Commerce
Bureau of Domestic and
International Commerce
Paul Bucher, Acting Director
453 Forum Bldg.
Harrisburg, Pa. 17120
(717) 787-7190

(City of) Philadelphia
David Brenner, Director of
Commerce
Municipal Services Bldg.,
Rm. 1660
Philadelphia, Pa. 19102
(215) 686-3647

(Greater) Philadelphia
Chamber of Commerce
G. Fred Dibona, Jr., President
1346 Chestnut St., Suite 800
Philadelphia, Pa. 19107
(215) 545-1234

Philadelphia Export Network
Hans H.B. Koehler, Director
3508 Market St., Suite 100
Philadelphia, Pa. 19104
(215) 898-4189

Philadelphia Port Corporation
John J. Malone, President
6th & Chestnut St.
Philadelphia, Pa. 19106
(215) 928-9100

Pittsburgh Consular Association
C. Murray Jones, President
Consul de Mexico, Suite 3201
4297 Greensburg Pike
Pittsburgh, Pa. 15221
(412) 271-5900

Pittsburgh Council for
International Visitors
Barbara Platt
139 University Place
Pittsburgh, Pa. 15260
(412) 624-7929

Port Authority of Allegheny
County
Edward Beachler, Director of
Waterways
514 Wood St.
Pittsburgh, Pa. 15222
(412) 237-7460

Port of Erie-West
J.G. Rosenthal
507 Municipal Bldg.
Erie, Pa. 16501
(814) 456-8561

Reading Foreign Trade
Association
Henrick Ersbak, President
35 N. 6th St.
Reading, Pa. 19603
(215) 320-2976

South Alleghenies Regional
Planning and Development
Commission
Stephen Mandes, Lorraine Clark
S. Alleghenies Plaza, Suite 100
1506 11th Ave.
Altoona, Pa. 16601
(814) 946-1641

Southwest Pennsylvania
Economic Development
District
James Eggars, Jang Kim
355 5th Ave., Rm. 141
Pittsburgh, Pa. 15222
(412) 391-1240

Trade Adjustment Assistance
Center
Jim Helm, Director
One E. Penn Sq., Suite 14
Philadelphia, Pa. 19107
(215) 568-7740

Trade Adjustment Assistance
Center
Alex Botkin
Investment Bldg., Rm. 1001
239 4th Ave.
Pittsburgh, Pa. 15222
(412) 566-1732

U.S. Customs Service
William Booth, Port Director
of Customs
822 Fed. Bldg.
1000 Liberty Ave.
Pittsburgh, Pa. 152232
(412) 644-3589

U.S. Department of
Commerce (ITA)
Erie Associate Office
John A. McCartney, Trade
Specialist
c/o Manufacturers Association
of Erie
33 E. 8th St.
Erie, Pa. 16507
(814) 459-3335

U.S. Department of
Commerce (ITA)
Robert Kistler, Director
9448 Fed. Bldg.

600 Arch St.
Philadelphia, Pa. 19106
(215) 597-2866

U.S. Department of
Commerce (ITA)
William Bradley, Director
2002 Fed. Bldg.
1000 Liberty Ave.
Pittsburgh, Pa. 15222
(412) 644-2850

U.S. Small Business
Administration
William T. Gennetti, District
Director
One Bala Plaza, Suite 400
E. Lobby
Bala Cynwyd, Pa. 19004
(215) 596-5801

U.S. Small Business
Administration
Clarence Ritter, Export
Assistance
Convention Tower, 5th
Floor
960 Penn Ave.
Pittsburgh, Pa. 15222
(412) 644-5438

West Pennsylvania District
Export Council
F.J. Sarknas, Chairman
1000 Liberty Ave., Rm. 2002
Pittsburgh, Pa. 15222
(412) 644-2850

Women's International Trade
Association
Rose Blair
P.O. Box 40004, Continental
Station
Philadelphia, Pa. 19106
(215) 923-6900

World Trade Association of
Philadelphia, Incorporated
Victor Federicci, President
820 Land Title Bldg.
Philadelphia, Pa. 19110
(215) 563-8887

Puerto Rico

District Export Council
Walter Fournier, Chairman
252 Tetuan St.
San Juan, P.R. 00901
(809) 721-7600

Puerto Rico Chamber of
Commerce
Rafael Rivera, Executive Director
P.O. Box 3789
San Juan, P.R. 00904
(809) 721-6060

Puerto Rico Department of
Commerce

Jorge Luis Aquino, Secretary
P.O. Box 4275
San Juan, P.R. 00905
(809) 721-3290

Puerto Rico Economic
Development Administration
Antonio Colorado, Administrator
GPO Box 2350
San Juan, P.R. 00936
(809) 758-4747

Puerto Rico Manufacturers
Association
Vicente Dordal, President
P.O. Box 2410
Hato Rey, P.R. 00919
(809) 759-9445

Puerto Rico Products
Association
Oscar Prieto, Executive Director
GPO Box 3631
San Juan, P.R. 00936
(809) 753-8484

U.S. Department of
Commerce (ITA)
Enrique Vilella, Director
Fed. Bldg., Rm. 659
Hato Rey, P.R. 00918
(809) 753-4555

Rhode Island

(Greater) Providence Chamber
of Commerce
Donald H. Fowler, Vice President
10 Dorrance St.
Providence, R.I. 02903
(401) 521-5000

Rhode Island Department of
Economic Development
Louis A. Fazzano, Director
7 Jackson Walkway
Providence, R.I. 02903
(401) 277-2601

U.S. Department of
Commerce (ITA)
Raymond Meerbach, Trade
Specialist
c/o Rhode Island Department
of Economic Development
7 Jackson Walkway
Providence, R.I. 02903
(401) 277-2601

South Carolina

Governor's Export Advisory
Committee
William O. Young, Jr.,
Chairman
Rt. 1, Box 501
Spartanburg, S.C. 29302
(803) 579-3050

Low County International
Trade Club (Charleston)

Diane Westfall, President
P.O. Box 159
Charleston, S.C. 29402
(803) 571-0510

Midlands Trade Club (Columbia)
Johanna Costello, President
Rt. 2, Box 50A
Elgin, S.C. 29045
(803) 254-1237

Pee Dee International Trade
Club (Florence)
Ralph W. Strong, President
P.O. Box 716
Kingstree, S.C. 29556
(803) 382-9393

South Carolina State
Development Board
John Patrick, International
Specialist
P.O. Box 927
Columbia, S.C. 29202
(803) 758-2384

South Carolina District
Export Council
Herman Goldstein, Chairman
Strom Thurmond Fed. Bldg.,
Suite 172
1835 Assembly St.
Columbia, S.C. 29201
(803) 765-5345

South Carolina State Port
Authority
Charles A. Marsh, Director of
Trade Development
P.O. Box 817
Charleston, S.C. 29402
(803) 577-8100

West South Carolina
International Trade Club
(Greenville)
Henry Burwell, President
P.O. Box 8764
Greenville, S.C. 29604-8764
(803) 232-1045

U.S. Department of
Commerce (ITA)
J. E. Brown, Director
Strom Thurmond Fed. Bldg.,
Suite 172
1835 Assembly St.
Columbia, S.C. 29201
(803) 765-5345

South Dakota

Rapid City Area Chamber of
Commerce
Wes Shelton, Director, Economic
Development Division
P.O. Box 747
Rapid City, S.D. 57709
(605) 343-1744

Sioux Falls Chamber of
Commerce
Clifford A. Scott, Director of
Marketing
127 E. 10th St.
Sioux Falls, S.D. 57101
(605) 336-1620

South Dakota Department of
State Development
David Anderson, Analyst
Capitol Lake Plaza
Pierre, S.D. 57501
(605) 773-5032

U.S. Department of
Commerce (ITA)
Harvey Roffman, Trade Specialist
300 S. 19th St.
Omaha, Neb. 68102
(402) 221-3664

U.S. Small Business
Administration
E. Duane Harder, Management
Assistance
101 S. Main Ave.
Sioux Falls, S.D. 57102
(605) 336-2980, ext. 231

Texas

Amarillo Chamber of Commerce
International Trade Specialist
Amarillo Bldg.
301 S. Polk
Amarillo, Tex. 79101
(806) 374-5238

Brownsville Navigation District
of Cameron County
Al Cisneros, Port Director
P.O. Box 3070
Brownsville, Tex. 78520
(512) 831-4592

Center for International
Business
Mark B. Winchester, Executive
Director
World Trade Center, Suite 184
P.O. Box 58428
Dallas, Tex. 75258
(214) 742-7301

Dallas Chamber of Commerce
International Trade Specialist
1507 Pacific
Dallas, Tex. 75201
(214) 954-1111

Dallas Council on World Affairs
Willard Latham, Executive
Director
Fred Lange Center
1310 Annex, Suite 101
Dallas, Tex. 75204
(214) 827-7960

El Paso Chamber of Commerce
International Trade Specialist
10 Civic Center Plaza
El Paso, Tex. 79944
(915) 544-7880

Foreign Credit Insurance
Association
Bohdan Sosiak, Manager
600 Travis, Suite 2860
Houston, Tex. 77002
(713) 227-0987

Fort Worth Chamber of
Commerce
700 Throckmorton
Fort Worth, Tex. 76102
(817) 336-2491

Houston Chamber of Commerce
Miguel San Juan, Director of
International Affairs
1100 Milan Bldg., 25th Floor
Houston, Tex. 77002
(713) 651-1313

Houston District Export Council
Robert C. Kelly, Chairman
6101 W. View Drive
Houston, Tex. 77055
(713) 686-4331

Houston Port Authority
Richard Leach, Port Director
1519 Capitol Ave., Box 2562
Houston, Tex. 77001
(713) 225-0671

Houston World Trade
Association
Robert Handy, Executive
Director
1520 Texas Ave., Suite 239
Houston, Tex. 77002
(713) 225-0967

Lubbock Chamber of Commerce
International Trade Specialist
14th St. & Ave. K
P.O. Box 561
Lubbock, Tex. 79408
(806) 763-4666

North Dallas Chamber of
Commerce
Harold Edwards, International
Committee
10707 Preston Road
Dallas, Tex. 75230
(214) 368-6653

North Texas Commission
Worth M. Blake, President
P.O. Box 61246
DFW Airport, Tex. 75261
(214) 574-4430

North Texas Customs Brokers
and Foreign Freight
Forwarders Association

Darrell J. Sekin, Jr., President
P.O. Box 225464
DFW Airport, Tex. 75261
(214) 456-0730

North Texas District Export
Council
Ray Whitson, Chairman
4448 Willow Lane
Dallas, Tex. 75234
(214) 788-1340

Odessa Chamber of
Commerce
International Trade Specialist
P.O. Box 3626
Odessa, Tex. 79760
(915) 332-9111

Port of Beaumont
Jim Martin, Port Director
P.O. Drawer 2297
Beaumont, Tex. 77704
(713) 835-5367

Port of Corpus Christi
Wayne Page, Director of
Transportation and
Industrial Development
P.O. Box 1541
Corpus Christi, Tex. 78403
(512) 882-5633

Port of Port Arthur
Dow Wynn, Port Director
Box 1428
Port Arthur, Tex. 77640
(713) 983-2011

(Greater) San Antonio
Chamber of Commerce
International Trade Specialist
P.O. Box 1628
San Antonio, Tex. 78296
(512) 227-8181

Texas City Terminal Railway
Company (Port)
J.B. Wimberly, General Manager
P.O. Box 591
Texas City, Tex. 77590
(713) 945-4461

Texas Department of Agriculture
Paul Lewis, Director of
International Affairs
Export Services Division
P.O. Box 12847, Capitol Station
Austin, Tex. 78711
(512) 475-2760

Texas Economic Development
Commission
Larry Lucero, International
Trade Division
P.O. Box 12728, Capitol
Station
Austin, Tex. 78711
(512) 472-5039

Texas Foreign Trade Center of
Dallas
Jerry Small, President
P.O. Box 50007
Dallas, Tex. 75250
(214) 570-1455

Texas Industrial Development
Council Incorporated
Jim Heath, International
Trade Chairman
P.O. Box 1002
College Station, Tex. 77841
(409) 845-2911

Texas International Business
Association
Eugene Flynn, President
P.O. Box 29334
Dallas, Tex. 75229
(214) 692-1214

U.S. Chamber of Commerce
Dick Rush, Manager
4835 LBJ Freeway, Suite 750
Dallas, Tex. 75324
(214) 387-0404

U.S. Customs Service
David Greenleaf, District Director
P.O. Box 61050
DFW Airport, Tex. 75261
(214) 574-2170

U.S. Department of
Commerce (ITA)
C. Carmon Stiles, Director
1100 Commerce St., Rm. 7A5
Dallas, Tex. 75242
(214) 767-0542

U.S. Department of
Commerce (ITA)
Felicito C. Guerrero, Director
515 Rusk Ave., Rm. 2625
Houston, Tex. 77002
(713) 226-4231

U.S. Small Business
Administration
James Reed, District Director
1100 Commerce St., 3rd Floor
Dallas, Tex. 75242
(214) 767-0492

World Trade Association of
Dallas/Fort Worth
Eugene Flynn, President
P.O. Box 29334
Dallas, Tex. 75229
(214) 760-9105

Tennessee

Chattanooga World Trade
Council
Michael K. Uchytil, President
1001 Market St.
Chattanooga, Tenn. 37402

East Tennessee International
Trade Club
Betty Martin, President
P.O. Box 280
Knoxville, Tenn. 37901
(615) 971-2027

Memphis World Trade Club
Dan Williams, President
P.O. Box 3577
Memphis, Tenn. 38103
(901) 320-2210

Mid-South Exporters
Roundtable
Charlotte Helton, President
P.O. Box 3521
Memphis, Tenn. 38173
(901) 320-5811

Middle Tennessee World
Trade Club
Debbie Garcia, President
1101 Kermit Dr., Suite 112
Nashville, Tenn. 37217

Tennessee Department of
Agriculture
Randle Richardson, Deputy
Commissioner
Ellington Agricultural Center
P.O. Box 40627, Melrose Station
Nashville, Tenn. 37204
(615) 360-0103

Tennessee Department of
Economic and Community
Development
Frank Pledger, Assistant
Commissioner
320 6th Ave., 7th Floor
Nashville, Tenn. 37219-5308
(615) 741-4815

Tennessee District Export
Council
John Dwyer, Chairman
3074 Sidco Dr.
Nashville, Tenn. 37210
(615) 259-9300

U.S. Department of
Commerce (ITA)
One Commerce Place, Suite 1427
Nashville, Tenn. 37239
(615) 251-5161

Utah

Salt Lake Area Chamber of
Commerce
S. Floyd Mori, Chairman
Export Development Committee
19 E. 2nd S.
Salt Lake City, Utah 84111
(801) 364-3631

U.S. Department of
Commerce (ITA)
Stephen P. Smoot, Director

U.S.P.O. and Courthouse Bldg.,
Rm. 340
350 Main St.
Salt Lake City, Utah 84101
(801) 524-5116

U.S. Small Business
Administration
Gary Peterson, Trade Specialist
2237 Fed. Bldg.
125 S. State St.
Salt Lake City, Utah 84138
(801) 524-6714

(State of) Utah
International Business
Development Office
Andrew Johnson, Coordinator
6150 State Office Bldg.
Salt Lake City, Utah 84114
(801) 533-5325

World Trade Association of Utah
Joseph C. Rust, President
2000 Beneficial Life Towers
Salt Lake City, Utah 84111
(801) 355-9333

Vermont

(Greater) Burlington Industrial
Corporation, Incorporated
C. Harry Behney, Executive
Director
7 Burlington Sq.
P.O. Box 786
Burlington, Vt. 05402
(802) 862-5726

U.S. Department of
Commerce (ITA)
Francis J. O'Connor, Director
441 Stuart St.
Boston, Mass. 02116
(617) 223-2312

(State of) Vermont Agency of
Development and
Community Affairs
James A. Guest, Secretary
Pavilion Office Bldg.
109 State St.
Montpelier, Vt. 05602

Virginia

Fairfax County Economic
Development Authority
April Young, Executive Director
8330 Old Court House Road
Vienna, Va. 22180
(703) 790-0600

International Trade Association
of North Virginia
Beverly Spottswood, President
P.O. Box 2982
Reston, Va. 22090
(703) 860-8795

Newport News Export
Trading System
Department of Development
Kevin Rowe, Director
Peninsula Export Program
2400 Washington Ave.
Newport News, Va. 23607
(804) 247-8751

Piedmont Foreign Trade Council
Hendrik Schmidt, President
P.O. Box 1374
Lynchburg, Va. 24505
(804) 782-4231

U.S. Department of
Commerce (ITA)
Philip Ouzts, Director
8010 Fed. Bldg.
400 N. 8th St.
Richmond, Va. 23240
(804) 771-2246

VEXTRAC (Export Trading
Company of Virginia Port
Authority)
Barry Owens, Director
600 World Trade Center
Norfolk, Va. 23510
(804) 623-8000

Virginia Chamber of Commerce
Edwin C. Luther, III,
Executive Vice President
611 E. Franklin St.
Richmond, Va. 23219
(804) 644-1607

Virginia Department of
Agriculture and Consumer
Affairs
S. Mason Carbaugh,
Commissioner
1100 Bank St., Rm. 710
Richmond, Va. 23219
(804) 786-3501

Virginia Department of
Economic Development
Scott Eubanks, Director
Washington Ofc. Bldg., 9th
Floor
Richmond, Va. 23219
(804) 786-3791

Virginia District Export
Council
Philip H. Anns, Chairman
P.O. Box 10190
Richmond, Va. 23240
(804) 771-2248

Washington

Economic Development
Partnership of Puget Sound
18000 Pacific Hwy., Suite 400
Seattle, Wash. 98188
(206) 433-1629

Export Assistance
Center of Washington
Robert Sebastian, President
312 First Ave. N.
Seattle, Wash. 98109
(206) 464-7123

Inland Empire World Trade Club
P.O. Box 3727
Spokane, Wash. 99220
(509) 489-0500

National Marine Fisheries
Service
Fisheries Development
Division
Linda Chaves-Michael,
Deputy Chief
7600 San Point Way NE.,
Bin C15700
Seattle, Wash. 98115
(206) 526-6117

Northwest Trade Adjustment
Assistance Center
F.J. McLaughlin, Director
1900 Seattle Tower
1218 3rd Ave.
Seattle, Wash. 98101
(206) 622-2730

Seattle Chamber of Commerce
Trade and Transportation
Division
Jim Schone, Manager
One Union Sq., 12th Floor
Seattle, Wash. 98101
(206) 447-7263

U.S. Department of
Commerce (ITA)
C. Franklin Foster, Director
1700 Westlake Ave., Suite 706
Seattle, Wash. 98109
(206) 442-5615

Tri-Cities Chamber of Commerce
Jane Foreman, Acting
Manager
P.O. Box 2322
Kennewick, Wash. 99302
(509) 735-1000

Washington Council on
International Trade
George Taylor, President
4th and Vine Bldg., Suite 350
Seattle, Wash. 98121
(206) 621-8485

Washington Public Ports
Association
Lewis Holcomb, Executive
Secretary
P.O. Box 1518
Olympia, Wash. 98507
(206) 943-0760

Washington State Department
of Commerce and Economic
Development
International Trade and
Investment Division
G. Stephen Crane, Managing
Director
312 First Ave. N.
Seattle, Wash. 98109
(206) 464-7149

Washington State International
Trade Fair
999 3rd Ave.
3501 First Interstate Center
Seattle, Wash. 98104
(206) 682-6900

World Affairs Council
515 Madison Ave., Suite 526
Seattle, Wash. 98104
(206) 682-6986

World Trade Club of Seattle
1402 3rd Ave., Suite 414
Seattle, Wash. 98101
(206) 621-0344

World Trade Committee of
Bellevue
110 110th NE., Suite 300
Bellevue, Wash. 98004
(206) 454-2464

West Virginia

West Virginia District Export
Council
Sam Silverstein, Chairman
P.O. Box 26
Charleston, W. Va. 25321
(304) 343-8874

West Virginia Manufacturers
Association
Robert Worden, President
405 Capitol St., Suite 414
Charleston, W. Va. 25301
(304) 342-2123

West Virginia Department of
Commerce
Lysander L. Dudley, Director
Economic Development
Rotunda 150, State Capitol
Charleston, W. Va. 25305
(304) 348-0400

West Virginia Chamber of
Commerce
John Hurd, President
P.O. Box 2789
Charleston, W. Va. 25330
(304) 342-1115

U.S. Department of
Commerce (ITA)
Roger L. Fortner, Director

3000 Fed. Office Bldg.
500 Quarrier St.
Charleston, W. Va. 25301
(304) 347-5123

Wisconsin

Foreign Trade Zone of
Wisconsin Limited
Vincent Boever, President
2150 E. College Ave.
Cudahy, Wis. 53110
(414) 764-2111

Milwaukee Association of
Commerce
John Duncan, President
756 N. Milwaukee St.
Milwaukee, Wis. 53202
(414) 273-3000

(Port of) Milwaukee
Roy F. Hoffman, Municipal
Port Director
500 N. Harbor Dr.
Milwaukee, Wis. 53202
(414) 278-3511

Small Business Development
Center
Robert W. Pricer
602 State St.
Madison, Wis. 53703
(608) 263-7766

Wisconsin Department of
Development
Steven Lotharius, Director
123 W. Washington Ave.
Madison, Wis. 53707
(608) 266-1767

U.S. Department of
Commerce (ITA)
Patrick A. Willis, Director
517 E. Wisconsin Ave.
Milwaukee, Wis. 53202
(414) 291-3473

Wyoming

State of Wyoming
Office of Governor
Cynthia Ogburn, International
Business Officer
Herschler Bldg., 2nd Floor E.
Cheyenne, Wyo. 82002
(307) 777-7574

U.S. Department of
Commerce (ITA)
Sam Cerrato, Director
Steve Stoffel, Deputy Director
721 19th St., Rm. 116
Denver, Colo. 80202
(303) 844-2900

Index